To Be Self-Evident

To Be Self-Evident

The Universal History of How Libertas
Has Irreversibly Improved the Human Condition

by R. L. Hogan

Libertas Press
Atlanta, Georgia

To Be Self-Evident
The universal history of how Libertas
has irreversibly improved the human condition

by R.L. Hogan

Published by:
Libertas Press, LLC.
Post Office Box 500399
Atlanta, GA 31150
orders@libertaspress.net

Visit the author's website at http://tobeselfevident.com

ISBN, print ed. 978-0-9786985-2-2

Hogan, R. L. (Robby Lee)
   To be self-evident : the universal history of how
   libertas has irreversibly improved the human condition /
   by R.L. Hogan.
   p. cm.
   Includes bibliographical references and index.
   LCCN 2006908075
   ISBN-13: 978-0-9786985-2-2
   ISBN 10: 0-9786985-2-5

   1. Civilization — History. 2. Liberty. 3. Social
evolution. 4. Progress. I. Title.

CB69.H64 2006   909
                       QBI06-600423

For Kathy, Philip, and Christopher.

Acknowledgments

I wish to thank all my friends and family that have helped in this endeavor, whether by exchanging ideas or by providing encouragement. The most important assistance has been from my wife and sons who have supported and encouraged me continuously in the extended research and writing that resulted in this book.

Contents

Introduction

"...WE hold these truths to be self-evident..."[1]

— Declaration of Independence, 1776

The term *self-evident* is intriguing. It defines itself. The definition is essentially: That which is readily evident to us, presumably without the need to be argued by others. An alternative definition might be: That which is *common sense*. The title *To Be Self-Evident* was chosen because it describes the heart of the conclusions throughout this work. These conclusions were not difficult to arrive at, nor did they necessitate encyclopedic research. The conclusions did not require complex or tortuous logic. These are largely conclusions of common sense and common knowledge, albeit often obscured by a cloudy, modern perspective.

There has been an attempt to add value to the equation by bringing together different components in a way that proves both interesting and illuminating. There also has been an attempt to consolidate the diverse thoughts of scholars across multiple specialties into a broader understanding of our history as humans. This understanding includes the identification of a significant trend in human history, which will be discussed thoroughly.

There is also an intentional double meaning in choosing for the title of this book what might be described as *common sense* (that which is self-evident). Common sense is used as the application method of inquiry and is also the fundamental subject of the book at the same time. In the final analysis, *common* sense

---

1. Quote from *Declaration of Independence* 1776, collaborative authorship.

1

is ultimately more valuable than *uncommon* sense. It is better to let we commoners make our own decisions in life than to assume that decisions should be made for us by strangers who may have official positions or high personal intelligence. All this boils down to one fundamental point: It is common sense that common sense is the best method of human guidance.

That being said, one could reasonably ask why the title *Common Sense* was not chosen. An obvious reason is that Thomas Paine already used that title in his famous book. A less obvious reason is that some of the conclusions herein do not easily reconcile with all of the general philosophy of Thomas Paine, although there are many areas of agreement.[2] Most importantly, the conclusions *do* easily reconcile with the general principles behind the American Revolution of 1776 and the drafting of the United States Constitution of 1787. It was desirable to find a short phrase from the Founding Fathers of the United States that supported the general conclusions in this book. The phrase *To Be Self-Evident* was appropriately selected.

I am a proud American and personally fascinated by the Founding Fathers. I also happen to be a great admirer of that particular sentence in the Declaration of Independence. However, you should not suppose from these facts, or from the title of this book, that the conclusions are partisan to the United States. One need only look to the sentence itself to understand the universality of the point. The Founding Fathers did not limit the statement to residents of the colonial states. They said *all* men are created equal.[3] Their points, as well as the points in this book, are as applicable to a person in Bangalore or Baghdad as

---

2. More specifically, they reconcile best with Paine's *Common Sense* and least with his *The Rights of Man*.

3. Although the use of the term "men" may have meant different things to different collaborators of the original text (probably not applying to natives, slaves, or women), our modern interpretation would substitute the more accurate use of the term "humans," rather that "men." Also, the term "created equal" is obviously meant to represent equality in political rights, not in physical attributes or in general outcomes.

to a person in Boston or Baltimore.

It is questionable whether any better statement concerning liberty was ever put to pen than that one sentence in the Declaration of Independence: "WE hold these Truths to be self-evident, that all Men are created equal, that they are endowed by their Creator with certain unalienable Rights, that among these are Life, Liberty, and the Pursuit of Happiness..."[4] These words have an inspirational character to them. Despite the continual interpretative argument of scholars, Thomas Jefferson created a phrase that has instructed and inspired multitudes for over two hundred years. The remainder of his entire existence, both good and bad, is somewhat overshadowed by his achievement in masterfully crafting this one poetic phrase.[5]

The world has changed substantially since those words, *to be self-evident*, were written in 1776. What is considered today to be self-evident or common sense was somewhat of a leap of faith in 1776 and very presumptuously called self-evident at that time. We now have well over two hundred more years of experience and evidence to prove the validity of their declaration. In particular, the latter half of the twentieth century provided ample historical evidence to now claim similar ideas and concepts are certainly self-evident. This includes the basic concept that all humans should have "unalienable[6] rights to life, liberty, and the pursuit of happiness."

The concept of these inalienable rights was not completely new in 1776. Such rights had been discussed extensively in Europe over the preceding two centuries. They became a focal point in the American drive for independence. Eventually, they began to take root throughout much of the world. The precise definition of those rights and the application of those rights have remained a matter of considerable disagreement. How-

---

4. Quote from *Declaration of Independence* 1776, collaborative authorship.

5. Although the vast majority of the Declaration was penned by Thomas Jefferson, the actual word "self-evident" was apparently suggested by Benjamin Franklin.

6. This term is used interchangeably with the term inalienable.

ever, the general acceptance and application of the inalienable rights of life, liberty, and the pursuit of happiness has caused a fundamental change in the progress of humans. The historical record of human development will be utilized to ask and answer a series of questions regarding this change in the progress of the species.

The historical evidence of the phenomenon of human progress will be documented and discussed throughout this book. The root cause of this transformation of the human experience will be abundantly clear, to the point of becoming common sense or self-evident. The transformation is so fundamental that we have essentially entered into a new age of human development. This new age is one where the *individual* is now the highlight of history, as opposed to traditional *elites* of civilization, such as royalty, dictators, ruling classes, intelligentsia, or even democratic representatives.

This work seeks to answer some key questions. Has the condition of humans improved over time? If so, when and why? What do those answers portend for our future? What is the *Universal History* of our species? These are very broad questions and they require an extensive range of consideration. It will include an analysis of human nature because that is at the core of human development. There will also be extensive discussion of the basic methods of human interaction. The primary inquiry will focus on how a change in those methods of human interaction caused a dramatic break with the previous pattern of historical development. Finally, the analysis will address what this new historical pattern means to us today and in the future.

PART ONE

The March of History

ONE

Historical Perspective

"For the great enemy of truth is very often not the lie — *deliberate, contrived, and dishonest, but the* myth *— persistent, persuasive..."*[1]

—John F. Kennedy, 1962

It covers a little over 3,000 square kilometers in size, with a population of only about 270,000 and was founded as a Greek colony in the eighth century B.C. It was an important and bustling port during the Greek and Roman empires; essentially in the middle of the development of civilization. Now it is an obscure province on an island that is separated from the larger peninsula of the mother country, which itself is only one minor component of the larger European Union. Messina is in the northeast corner of Sicily; the point of the island closest to the Italian peninsula. The port there is still busy, now with tourism, and the local seafood cuisine is renowned. By all accounts it is a pleasant little corner of the world.

Messina has a place in history too. It was where the first Punic War started more than two millennia ago. Later, the Romans used the port at Messina as an important strategic point in their domination of the Mediterranean Sea. It was one of the last Sicilian cities to fall to the Muslims in the ninth century A.D., and it was used by Richard the Lionhearted as a military port during the Crusades.

There is also a tragic history of Messina and that is the purpose of its inclusion here. There were a few obvious calami-

---

1. John F. Kennedy speech at Yale on June 11, 1962

ties in and around the area over the years, such as the large and devastating earthquakes of 1783 and 1908, as well as the nearby eruption of Mt. Etna in 1669. Nevertheless, something much more horrendous occurred within Messina when the community served as the gateway for arguably the greatest human catastrophe of all time. Messina was the unfortunate portal between Asia, Europe, and Africa when all three continents suffered substantially. The following is an eyewitness account from that point in time in Messina:

> *At the beginning of October, in the year of the incarnation of the Son of God 1347, twelve Genoese galleys…entered the harbor of Messina. In their bones they bore so virulent a disease that anyone who only spoke to them was seized by a mortal illness and in no manner could evade death. The infection spread to everyone who had any intercourse with the diseased. Those infected felt themselves penetrated by a pain throughout their whole bodies and, so to say, undermined. Then there developed on the thighs or upper arms a boil about the size of a lentil which the people called 'burn boil.' This infected the whole body, and penetrated it so that the patient violently vomited blood. This vomiting of blood continued without intermission for three days, there being no means of healing it, and then the patient expired.*

> *Not only all those who had intercourse with them died, but also those who had touched or used any of their things. When the inhabitants of Messina discovered that this sudden death emanated from the Genoese ships they hurriedly ordered them out of the harbor and town. But the evil remained and caused a fearful outbreak of death. Soon men hated each other so much that if a son was attacked by the disease his father would not tend him. If, in spite of all, he dared to approach him, he was immediately infected and was bound to die within three days. Nor was this all; all those dwelling in the same house with him, even the cats and other domestic animals,*

followed him in death. As the number of deaths increased in Messina many desired to confess their sins to the priests and to draw up their last will and testament [sic]. But ecclesiastics, lawyers and attorneys refused to enter the houses of the diseased...

Soon the corpses were lying forsaken in the houses. No ecclesiastic, no son, no father and no relation dared to enter, but they hired servants with high wages to bury the dead. The houses of the deceased remained open with all their valuables, gold and jewels...When the catastrophe had reached its climax the Messinians resolved to emigrate. One portion of them settled in the vineyards and fields, but a larger portion sought refuge in the town of Catania... The disease clung to the fugitives and accompanied them everywhere where they turned in search of help. Many of the fleeing fell down by the roadside and dragged themselves into the fields and bushes to expire. Those who reached Catania breathed their last in the hospitals there. The terrified citizens would not permit the burying of fugitives from Messina within the town, and so they were all thrown into deep trenches outside the walls...

Thus the people of Messina dispersed over the whole island of Sicily and with them the disease, so that innumerable people died.[2]

The Genoese galleys were traveling from Crimea back to the Mediterranean. They brought with them a pestilence that initiated what was in Europe eventually called the "Black Death." The most recent scholarship on this epidemic leads to its origin on the steppes of what is now southern Russia, among the Golden Horde of Mongols led by Kipchak Khanate. The forces of the Golden Horde transmitted the pestilence (via rat fleas) to the

---

2. Piazza, Michael de. "The Plague" *The Black Death: A Chronicle of the Plague.* Ed. Johannes Nohl. New York: Ballantine Books, 1960. 15-17.

Italian traders at the port of Kaffa on the Crimean coast of the Black Sea. The Italian galleys proceeded to return to the Mediterranean and made the infamous landing at Messina described above. From Sicily, the pestilence moved northward through the Italian peninsula and onward throughout the remainder of the continent, most of which had received the plague by the end of 1348.

The actual disease or diseases remain under debate. Traditionally, historians have attributed the Black Death to bubonic, pneumonic, and septicemic plagues. Regardless of the exact medical causes, this outbreak of pestilence killed at least one quarter of the inhabitants of Europe, perhaps as many as a third, and a large number of Asians and Africans. It irreversibly altered the social fabric of European life and created conditions for substantial structural changes in society.[3]

Those are the historical aspects. But for the humans involved, it was the ultimate devastation. The Black Death must have seemed to them to be the end of the world. It tore apart the essential composition of society; fathers abandoned sons and friends abandoned friends. The survivors were scarred and the dead were uncountable. It is practically unfathomable for us in the twenty-first century to fully comprehend this frame of reference. In fact, despite the historical evidence of immense human suffering centuries ago, many modern observers tend to romanticize the past and denigrate the present. And it is with this viewpoint — the perspective from one person from one little

---

3. The Black Death of 1348-1350 has been categorized here as "arguably" the greatest human catastrophe of all time. This is especially true when the category refers to a short-term, continuous event. It is less true when the category is widened to include the various plagues that decimated the native population of the post-Columbian Americas over many decades, even centuries. Those plagues began with the first voyage of Columbus and continued with many other explorers. In most cases, they were first received by minimal contact with Europeans and then spread widely by the natives in ways that often obscured the devastation to the eyes of the European conquistadors and settlers. A prime example is found in the exploration of Hernando de Soto, which occurred nearly one hundred years before permanent settlers arrived in most of the southeast of North America.

corner of the world called Messina — that we begin the important discussion about historical outlook.

What is Our Perspective of History and Current Events?

It is prudent to begin the reflection on the history of humans by discussing the perspective we bring to the process. Many observers have noted the obvious cultural and personal biases that any author brings to historical discussion. An ever-increasing amount of attention has been dedicated to the two most prominent aspects of such biases, those being the potential for an author to exhibit cultural superiority and the potential to promote a political agenda. These are legitimate concerns. However, the very attention these potential problems have received is generally the solution itself. The attention causes authors to be more aware of their own bias and it causes readers to be more cautious and discerning.

This success in recognizing the negative aspects of cultural superiority and political agenda is healthy for the proper study of humans. Unfortunately, there is a newer concern affecting historical *perspective*. It is a problem that has received considerably less attention. It is an issue that must be recognized if we are to have fruitful reflection on the history of humans over time. This is our uniquely modern problem of the inaccurate impressions of the past and the present created by the audio/video inventions begun in the days of Thomas Edison.

It is rather common for those of us born after World War II to be so enveloped in our modern lives that we fail to fully appreciate the vast difference between our daily existence and that of our ancestors merely a couple of centuries ago. Some of our modern inventions have in fact caused our lack of appreciation of times past to grow considerably wider. This issue of *perspective* is of crucial importance in analyzing history over all of recorded time.

There is no more powerful tool for shaping human thought than the audio/video images created by film. The vast majority of us have had our perspective of past generations etched in our minds by what we have seen displayed in theatres, on televisions, personal computers, and other devices. The same is true for our perspective of current events and the condition of our world today. Our perspective of the past and the present is constantly distorted by two separate, but related, phenomena.

What Is the "Romantic Image of the Past"?

The first of these phenomena is what could be described as the *romantic image of the past*. This romantic image is created by the multitude of representations we have seen depicting historical characters and events. These images are based mostly on books, especially fictional works. Books, television shows, and movies are produced with the goal of being entertaining and popular.

These works of art are rarely, if ever, designed for the purpose of showing the daily reality of previous generations. They are instead created for the purpose of presenting drama and they emphasize the spectacular and the theatrical. No one would expect otherwise. This is what we pay for and it is the way artists become successful. We witness Elizabethan characters, the court of Louis XIV, American cowboys, Cleopatra, Japanese Shogun, or Roman gladiators as they deal with historic events or universal human emotions. We expect to be entertained and entertainment is what we receive.

The craft of video art continually improves. It is now so developed and elaborate that it becomes ever more difficult to separate our thoughts of reality from those of make-believe. The historical impression we develop is of characters living in different time periods. They act out important historic events or they deal with the human emotions that we ourselves deal with in the world today. These characters are often presented with such incredible skill and realism that we feel a part of the scene and the time period. In the best of the art, the costumes are impeccable and the sets are superb. We cannot help but come away from this experience sensing we understand the historical time and place. Yet, despite the realism of the characters and the costumes, the perspective created is very limited and relatively inaccurate.

We see compelling characters and events, but we do not see everyday existence. We see mostly the very upper strata of previous societies. If we do see commoners, it is usually as they fight heroically in meaningful, but isolated and largely fictional portrayals of events. What we do not see is the everyday struggle for existence by commoner and noble alike.

We do not see the extremely high rate of death at childbirth (both of mother and child). We do not see the characters struggling with dysentery. We do not see the majority of characters spending virtually every waking hour from birth to death striving to obtain enough food to survive starvation. We do not see multitudes exterminated by common diseases mostly absent now in the modern world. We do not see the human depravity of parents selling their children. We do not see the dangerous use of common water supply as both reservoir and toilet. We do not see the pervasive illiteracy and superstition. We do not see the almost absolute exposure to the whims of violent weather. We do not see the complete lack of humane treatment for the weak and disabled. Simply put, we do not see the untold misery of life as experienced by the vast majority of our ancestors.

Instead of these realistic perspectives of what life was like in previous centuries, we see limited and unrealistic characters. These characters on the video screen fascinate us. We become engrossed in their drama. We feel as if we can relate to them as humans. And we may very well be able to relate to their emotions and actions, but it is impossible for us to relate to their everyday existence because we do not see their true daily life.

It is much easier to find meaning in the trends of history once we appreciate this gap in our own perspective. This understanding of perspective is crucial as we continue the discussion of human development throughout this book. It is necessary to wipe away the limited perspective of history ingrained in our minds by video images. It is imperative to imagine a much different reality of what life was actually like in previous times.

What is "News Reporting as the Opposite of Average Existence"?

It is also important to properly understand our perspective of *current* events. The second problematic phenomenon of perspective is what can be termed "news reporting as the opposite of average existence." This is not referencing either inaccurate reporting or political bias on the part of news media. It is rather referencing an inherent, but mostly unobserved, feature of our news culture. It represents the difference between *news* and *common* existence.

We receive daily images from television, radio, and print media concerning news events. These images are designed to present highlights and they focus on the dramatic. Locally, we hear about deadly traffic accidents or isolated murders. Internationally, we hear about the remote conflicts and problems of destitution in the Third World.

We never wake up in the morning to read or hear a story about all the millions of automobile trips that successfully carried multitudes from point to point during the previous day. Nor do we wake up to read or hear about the overwhelming majority of people in the prosperous part of the world who had plenty to eat and did not suffer from plagues and widespread disease. This incredibly positive picture of daily life today simply is not newsworthy.

The events that are newsworthy are mostly negative. This is not caused by some conspiracy of news editors. It is simply a fact of life. People are caught up in their daily routines. They do not have the time or the patience to concentrate on the full stories of our average human condition. The news reporting therefore focuses on anomalies.

Yet, anomalies are in essence the opposite of truth, when truth is defined as attempting to gain an accurate perspective of human existence. Anomalies are a "deviation from the common rule."[4] Therefore, if we gain our perspective of the average human condition from news stories, we are destined to form an incorrect perspective. The perspective of the current human existence based on news stories is a perspective based on the exception, rather than the rule.

It is not easy to come by the *truth* of the average human condition today, just as it is not easy to come by the truth of historical times. The most active consumer of the news media might actually be the least likely to have an accurate perspective concerning the human condition. Similar to the problem of historical viewpoints, it is essential for the objective observer of current events to wipe out the images of the nightly news report when attempting to appreciate the current world in general. The objective observer must instead look at dry statistics and obscure writings to fully understand our world.

The importance of proper perspective simply cannot be overemphasized. There is no way to appropriately discuss how humans have lived throughout history without first gaining an accurate understanding of the *common* and de-emphasizing the *uncommon*. This is no small task in the world today. The video images about historical times and the news reports of today create conditions that make the task extremely arduous, but not impossible.

Overcoming this phenomenon of inappropriately focusing on anomalies is one of the prime factors of intelligence, whether it is overcome by deep thought or by simple common sense. One of the keys to success in all aspects of life is the ability to sort the bigger truth and trends out of the multitude of details, of which the most spectacular and fascinating are often distracting us away from the average truth. In our case of developing an accurate historical perspective, the key is to think broadly with a deliberate attempt to extricate the video images that bombard us at every turn. In this way, we can more clearly see how the

---

4. *Webster's Universal Encyclopedic Dictionary.* Merriam-Webster. New York. 2002. 73.

human condition has changed over time and, especially, how best to compare our world of today to that of the past.

We know definitively that the daily life experience of the average person in our Prosperous World[5] today is infinitely better than those of similar status hundreds of years ago. We can track this improvement in many quantifiable terms, but it can only be fully appreciated by understanding the difference in personal, human terms.

The difference in life experience between today and other centuries goes far beyond the amount of wealth produced per person. Even the greatest wealth in Elizabethan England could not prevent a prince from dying from an infected sore or his princess from dying in childbirth. Even a good job and good wage for a commoner in early American history could not buy indoor plumbing or a forty-hour workweek. In our Prosperous World of today we have almost universal education, inoculations, and suffrage. We have sanitation, health, and peace. All that and plentiful leisure time too.

The commoner of previous centuries had to struggle daily for enough food to survive, while we casually shop at supermarkets with tens of thousands of food choices at comparatively low prices.[6] The commoner of previous centuries had to fear death daily at the hands of the local authorities, invaders,

---

5. The term Prosperous World will be used throughout this book to describe what was once termed the First World. The First World was previously used as the term for the free and relatively prosperous sections of the world in comparison to the Second World that was controlled through totalitarian communism and the Third World that was variously controlled but included thoroughly impoverished countries. This new term (Prosperous World) is necessary to distinguish those countries that are mostly free and relatively prosperous. Such countries can no longer be segregated geographically because they are represented in each hemisphere and on each habitable continent. They can no longer be distinguished by race, ethnicity, religion, or language because they diversely represent so many different people. As of this writing, the Prosperous World would include most of Europe and North America, much of Oceania, some of Asia, and a very small portion of Africa. The two largest nations in the Impoverished World, China and India, are making rapid progress as of this writing in joining the Prosperous World.

6. Prices adjusted for inflation and compared to average income.

or criminals, while we go securely about our daily routine. The commoner of previous centuries was always in danger of contracting deadly diseases or dying of minor accidents without any hope of medical care, while we have sophisticated emergency care at our fingertips via wireless telephones and helicopter ambulances. The commoner of previous centuries had to drink water filled with the excrement of his neighbors, while we have the luxury of sprinkling perfectly sanitized water on our garden flowers. This list of everyday differences (that is so useful for our historical understanding) could continue for pages.

The difference between our existence and the existence of our ancestors is substantial and self-evident. The consistent pessimism of current generations is astounding, given the evidence of progress to the contrary. Despite the clear and monumental improvement in the human condition, we are bombarded with negativism by people who insist that our human condition is dire and that the end of the world is near. They ask: "Oh, but what about this group that is hindered?" Or they lament: "Oh, but what about that impoverished nation?" They say these things out of sincere caring for others and a deep misunderstanding of history. There are still parts of the world sharing the dire circumstances of our ancestors, but those areas are shrinking.

Admitting that the world is tremendously better than generations ago does not absolve us from continuing the effort to improve it. Nor does it deny that there are some laggards. Yet, at the same time, denying our human improvement and the reasons for that improvement condemns us to lesser improvement in the future or, at the very worse, possible degradation. It is for this reason we must be careful to examine our past and appreciate our advancement. The successes and failures of the past can give us wisdom on how best to proceed.

This is a story that will be explored throughout the book. It is a story of immense importance. It is the story of how humans started and how humans advanced. It will include our victories and our failures. It will attempt to produce an objective overall analysis of the growth of our species. Are we changing and, if so, are we improving or are we deteriorating? Most importantly, it will attempt to answer the colossal question of "why?" Why are we changing or not changing and what might it mean for our future? This is the story of human history. It is the story of all of us, not just the story of the famous, such as Cleopatra, Qin Shi Huang, or Alexander. It is the story of far more than just historic icons. It is the story of the common person. It is the story of all of us.

TWO

The Flow of History

"It is quite true what philosophy says: that life must be understood backwards. But then one forgets the other principle: that it must be lived forwards."[1]

—Soren Kirkegaard, 1843

Can We Interpret History?

Interpreting historical patterns and developing a universal theme of history is fraught with difficulty. Many skeptics believe it cannot be done. They are comfortable with the laws of the physical sciences, but uncomfortable with the ambiguity surrounding history. Those skeptics do not appreciate the human ability to rationally review the past and the present. Yet, as so clearly stated by the Marquis de Condorcet during the Enlightenment:

> *If man can, with almost complete assurance, predict phenomena when he knows their laws, and if, even when he does not, he can still, with great expectation of success, forecast the future on the basis of his experience of the past, why, then, should it not be regarded as a fantastic undertaking to sketch, with some pretence to truth, the future destiny of man on the basis of his history?*[2]

---

1. Kierkegaard, Soren. *Papers and Journals: A Selection*. London: Penguin Books, 1996. 161. This quotation from Kierkegaard is often paraphrased as "Life can only be understood backwards, but it must be lived forwards."

2. Condorcet, Marquis de. "The Future Progress of the Human Mind." *The Portable*

The process of analyzing history is indeed *interpretive*. It is not as certain as the laws of physics, nor will it ever be as definitive as the physical sciences. It might even be inappropriate to call such analysis "history." It might be better classified as philosophy. Francois-Marie Arouet Voltaire named it the *philosophy of history*. Such luminaries as Voltaire, Immanuel Kant, Johann Herder, and Friedrich Hegel have all attempted to develop themes of universal history. Despite these early noble attempts, the concept of universal history obtained very negative connotations with the proliferation and eventual repudiation of the theories of Karl Marx. The analysis of universally applicable historical themes has not been particularly popular or successful since Marx.

Voltaire, Kant, Herder, and Hegel were all deeply influenced by the dramatic changes of thought during the Enlightenment and the substantial socio-political changes from the Revolutionary Era of the late 1700s and into the early 1800s. Perhaps it takes such conditions to foster wide consideration of universal history. If this is true, then we have entered into such an age again. Evidence of this fact can be found in the many recent attempts at interpretative universal history, including new insights from other fields of study such as biology, sociology, and statistics.

Since it is still early in the new millennium, our time may not currently appear as revolutionary in thought and action as the late 1700s, but it is a truly historic time nonetheless. The fall of communism in the late twentieth century created a new world order, unique in human history. It is a world order that encompasses most of the globe and has no genuine rivals. Francis Fukuyama was one of the first to take note of this monumental historical shift and to write about the aspects of universal history emanating from this rare point in time.[3] His work entitled

Enlightenment Reader. Ed. Isaac Kramnick. New York: Penguin Books, 1995. 26.

3. Fukuyama, Francis. *The End of History and the Last Man.* New York: The Free Press, 1992.

The End of History and the Last Man was the consummate spring-board for generating discussion about the new world order after the demise of communism.

Before the fall of communism, there had been plenty of valuable works about the dramatic changes of the twentieth century and futuristic possibilities. These primarily concentrated on the impact of technology, but many also dealt with changes in human interaction and patterns of behavior. In most cases, such works either concentrated on futuristic aspects or, if they dealt more substantially with the historical past, they were somewhat overshadowed by the lingering Cold War. Now, since the end of the Cold War, serious academic inquiry has blossomed regarding how humans have changed over time resulting in our current state of existence.

The inquiries cross numerous academic disciplines, some of which are newly emerging fields of study. These differing areas of study help build the evidence of universal history even if they are originally considered works of Anthropology, Archeology, Political Science, Sociology, Biology, Economics, Genetics, Psychology, Game Theory, Sociobiology, Chaos Theory or other varied disciplines. A comprehensive understanding of history must reach broadly into many specialties to attempt to explain how humans have changed over time since the advent of agriculture and civilizations.

Where Should a Search for a Universal History Begin?

The origin of the universe is subject to constant debate among scientists and laypeople. The planet Earth has been host to life forms for millions of years. Yet it is not the goal of this author to explore the history of the universe, the planet, or life forms. This work is designed to be an exploration of the human species.[4] More specifically, the intent is to discuss how the condi-

---

4. The term "human" is usually utilized by the scientific community to refer to all hominid species. Hominid species include *Homo sapiens* (the only surviving homi-

tion of the species has changed over time. This does not require an encyclopedic listing of historical events. Rather, it will include broad interpretation of the most consequential changes in the human condition over time.

There has been a wide range of arduous field research, detailed laboratory testing, and intricate theorization about the early development of the species known as *Homo sapiens*. The exact starting point of the journey of *Homo sapiens* is not relevant to our purpose here, although the modern version of the species probably became distinct about 150,000 years ago. Anthropologists and archeologists — and now geneticists — continue to advance the study of pre-historical life and ancient civilizations with exciting new findings. In general, it is clear that our earliest ancestors were incredibly primitive and lived in a similar way to many of the wild primates we find in the jungles of today. However, humans (hominids) were different than the other animals. No other animals had the combined attributes of opposable thumbs, the ability to walk upright, and impressive vocal capabilities. Most importantly, no other animal rivaled humans in the complexity and capacity of their brains.

These special attributes make humans different and allowed the species to set itself apart from the remainder of life forms. This process did not occur overnight. It proceeded at an almost imperceptible pace. The first humans were simple foragers and scavengers. They slowly became hunters and rudimentary toolmakers. This represented the beginnings of human improvement that continues to this day.

The period of human life prior to the beginning of civilizations, around 3500 B.C., is generally known as *prehistory*. There were numerous developmental events in prehistory that were obviously crucial to the progress of the species. The development of the first tools, the taming of fire, the invention of metal-

---

nid), *Homo helmei* (our most immediate ancestors), as well as less closely related species such as the Neanderthals and others. The majority of the focus of this book concentrates on the later stages of human development which includes only the species of *Homo sapiens*.

lurgy, and the establishment of family structure are some important examples.

The list of substantial developments is quite long and will not all be outlined here. Yet there are three additional examples that are not only pivotal, but also relate more directly to the topics in this work. All three are monumental changes. The last of these three was the turning point to the transition of civilized life.

The first of these was the development of spoken language. Although we do not have much evidence to suggest exactly how this occurred, it is reasonable to assume it began with simple sounds and slowly progressed into more complex representations. This would have developed naturally among the different small groups or tribes, each with unique attributes. The importance of the development of spoken language is obvious. Humans could improve their chances of survival by working together in hunting and gathering. Language improved their ability to do so. The ability of humans to interact effectively is the key ingredient throughout human history.

The second of these key developments was the migration of the species across the globe. From the apparent roots of hominids and *Homo sapiens* in Africa, the species spread around the world, first into Asia about 75,000 years ago, then Australasia about 60,000 years ago, then Europe probably around 45,000 years ago, and eventually into the Americas about 20,000 years ago.[5] The cause of this sweeping expansion is not certain — although climate shift is the most probable explanation — but it clearly illustrates the resourcefulness and adaptability of the species. The details of this migration are becoming more evident to us now through the use of sophisticated DNA technology.[6] The migration path was once considered wild conjecture.

---

5. These dates are still under constant scrutiny and revision based upon the latest estimates. There is wide disagreement among different scholars on the exact migration paths and dates.

6. Excellent summaries of various genetic researches have been accumulated and presented in both book and video forms by Stephen Oppenheimer in *The Real Eve*

It is now becoming more exact and definitive.

The third and final of the key events of prehistory is the reason the prehistorical age ended and civilizations could begin. It is the development of agriculture, based on the domestication of plants and animals. This revolution in human advancement occurred near the conclusion of the last major Ice Age about 12,000 years ago. The origination of agriculture allowed human groups to establish more permanent bases of operation, eventually creating stability by ending much of the nomadic lifestyle of the hunter-gatherer predecessors. The coming of agriculture required new conditions of human interaction and social behavior. The more steady supply of sustenance and the stability of being able to stockpile grains and animal herds allowed humans to support greater specialization of labor. It also allowed for deeper and more consistent human thought, beyond the previous cycle of concentrating on the immediate hunting or gathering of food each day.

Small and unsophisticated agricultural societies formed in numerous locales after about 10,000 B.C. and some of these began crystallizing into the earliest civilizations by 3,500 B.C. The definition of civilization in this respect is subjective. Most scholars deem civilization to have been reached once a discernable degree of culture has been achieved, along with some urbanization, perhaps accompanied by attempts at the codification of conduct, and resulting in greater civic cohesion. In any case, the concept remains subjective.

This transition to agriculture and civilizations did not occur simultaneously or evenly across the globe. There are even some hunter-gatherer tribes remaining in the world today. However, in many varying locations and at many different times, some of the primitive hunter-gatherer bands or tribes began growing and centralizing into chiefdoms and, eventually, into civili-

---

and by Spencer Wells in *The Journey of Man*. Oppenheimer, Stephen. *The Real Eve*. Paperback ed. New York: Carroll & Graf, 2003. Wells, Spencer. *The Journey of Man*. Paperback ed. New York: Random House, 2003.

zations based upon agriculture. Other hunter-gatherer groups were generally annihilated or subsumed by the new civilizations.

Why some of these human societies grew in numbers and in sophistication faster than others is a source of constant study and analysis. In the remarkable work *Guns, Germs, and Steel*,[7] Jared Diamond very plausibly explains that the primary causes were geographic in origin, including weather. This is not a new topic. Many historians from previous eras have emphasized geography. However, Diamond takes the study to a new level. He articulates four specific geographical factors, which then later led to the more proximate causes of some civilizations dominating others, in particular, the modern domination by the Western European civilization.

His four geographic factors can be summarized as follows. First was the difference in availability of wild plants and animals suitable for domestication. The second was the alignment of major land mass axis in ways that are more (east-west) or less (north-south) conducive to migration and trade due mostly to similarity or differences in climate. The third factor was the geographical demarcations *within* continents that are more or less conducive to migration and trade. Finally, the fourth factor was the geographical demarcations *between* continents that are more or less conducive to migration and trade. These geographic differences caused vast disparity in the initial development patterns of civilizations. Then additional geographic variation caused Europe to be the place of fastest growth in the generation of the more proximate causes of European material supremacy around 1500 A.D. These more proximate causes were notably (but not limited to) guns, germs, and steel.

The early developmental history of the world will not be discussed in great detail here. Despite Professor Diamond's well-reasoned conclusions about the influence of geography

---

7. Diamond, Jared. *Guns, Germs, and Steel*. Paperback ed. New York: W. W. Norton & Company, 1999.

in early development, there are many other factors posited by reputable scholars and the topic is highly complex. However, the one theory that has been irrefutably disproved is the theory of racial disparity. Even the mere concept of *race* is of questionable value, especially in our world today, and represents an artificial attempt at classification within the human species. The physical and mental characteristics of humans across all races, however defined, are remarkably similar, differing only in minor details such as skin color. This point is highlighted not for reasons of sensitivity, but only because it will be important in a later discussion about the future of human development.

Whether caused by geography, chaotic accidents, or other factors, civilizations arose in divergent locations and at different times. Describing historical patterns becomes more perplexing once the species matured into the development of substantial civilizations. Numerous contrasting economic, political, and social structures have risen and fallen during the more than 5,000 years that humans have produced civilized developments. Each of these represent attempts, whether intentional or not, to improve the methods of human interaction and advance the life of humans — at least for those in power. History has been told largely as the rise and fall of these civilizations, including the Mesopotamian, Egyptian, Minoan, Indian, Chinese, Phoenician, Persian, Greek, Roman, Byzantine, Islamic, Incan, Aztec, Mayan and other recognized civilizations.

The question of universal history can be answered by seeking to determine if there has been a discernible advancement of humans since civilizations began to develop. Of course, the definition of *advancement* must first be clarified. Advancement would constitute the betterment of methods of human interaction to such a degree that positive and sustained improvement occurred in the average *well-being* of humans. The definition of *"well-being"* is next in need of scrutiny, but it will be discussed at much greater length later.

The key for now is to focus on the methods of human interaction because humans are not self-sufficient and must rely on fellow humans for maximum gain. The primary methods of human interaction include the utilization of either cooperation or coercion. Humans can cooperatively work together or they can resort to force. And the scope of this cooperation or coercion can be narrow or broad. The scope of human interaction can range from primitive reliance on only the interaction of a very small group, such as family, clan, or tribe, or it could include a very complex and sophisticated interaction with virtually all humans globally. In answering our question about human progress, it is important to analyze the extensiveness or reach of the human interaction and the ultimate accomplishments.

The rise of each major and minor civilization was generally precipitated by changes in the methods of human interaction that caused humans to work together more effectively, at least in certain ways and for distinct periods of time and in specific geographies. These new methods might have been obvious or subtle; they might have been comprehensive or strictly limited. The most noticeable result of these methods was an enhanced cohesiveness and orderliness. These civilizations were able to bring their people together and harness a combined productiveness of which less organized societies were incapable. The methods of organization in these civilizations were always based primarily on the use of coercion, but so were those of less civilized societies. The difference was in the organizational and motivational skillfulness.

These civilizations were able to use more successful methods of human interaction to build the civilizations to a grander degree than other lesser developments or remaining hunter-gatherer tribes at the same time and in near proximity. This resulted in the construction of physical structures, the accumulation of wealth, and the recording of culture to the extent that we have the artifacts necessary to partially understand that those civilizations existed and what they accomplished. The scholarship of studying each of the ancient and classical civilizations provides us a specialized understanding of human progress in that particular specialty. Unfortunately, it does not necessarily provide an understanding of universal progress or the flow of history over time across differing geographies. Such an understanding requires a much more expansive evaluation of the human condition.

What Have Been the Prevalent Views of Universal History?

Analysis and discussion of universal history has proceeded in many ways over the course of the past few hundred years since the beginning of universities and historical studies in the modern tradition. Sometimes it was discussed directly. More often, it was simply a product of how people viewed history at any given time and how philosophers dealt with the thoughts and positions emanating from the context of historical views.

Giambattista Vico produced one of the first modern universal histories in the early 1700s as a professor at the University of Naples. He discussed historical methodology and he developed a cyclical theory of civilization growth and maturation that outlined specific developmental stages of all civilizations. Vico probably did not influence many of the thoughts that flourished on the subject in the late 1700s and early 1800s, because he was a relatively obscure figure. However, the cyclical theme of universal history has always been prominent.

The concept of an inevitable *life cycle* of civilizations was based on the fact that grand civilizations of the past had peaked and declined. In particular, the historical event of the decline of the Roman civilization has greatly impacted modern thought concerning universal history. This is to be expected since the tradition of modern university-based scholarship was established in the West and the culture of the West directly descended from the remnants of the Roman Empire.

The influential work of Edward Gibbon titled *The Decline and Fall of the Roman Empire*[8] (first published in 1776) chroni-

---

8. Gibbon, Edward. *The Decline and Fall of the Roman Empire*. Paperback ed. New York: The Modern Library, 2003.

cled the fall of Rome in remarkable and voluminous detail. His work impacted the assumptions of historians for most of the following two hundred years. The fall of Rome and the descent into the Middle or "Dark" Ages, as so extensively described by Gibbon, was enough to convince many latter-day scholars that history was not progressing in any discernable pattern. It appeared to be more or less cyclical.

The opinion of many observers was that history progressed in the rise and fall pattern over time (cyclical), perhaps occasionally advancing humankind overall (spiral), but not dramatically so. For every rise, there was a fall. In the view of many philosophers and historians, the philosophical and material accomplishments of the eighteenth, nineteenth, and twentieth centuries might appear significant, but they too were destined to fall.

Nevertheless, in the grand tradition of many Enlightenment participants, Immanuel Kant developed an opposite, more optimistic and linear universal history in 1784 with his *Idea of Universal History With Cosmopolitan Intent*.[9] He believed humankind was progressively moving away from barbarism to an ever-greater reliance on rationality that would eventually result in eternal peace. Kant emphasized the importance of improving methods of human interaction by harnessing the selfish nature of humans and their "unsocial sociability."

The reasoned optimism of Kant may very well have represented the height of the Enlightenment, but the optimism was short-lived. Johann Gottfried Herder, a contemporary and one-time student of Kant, simultaneously developed a more pessimistic and relativist approach to universal history with *Another Philosophy of History*[10] in 1784. Herder minimized the influence of reason and overemphasized the importance of nationalism.

---

9. Kant, Immanuel. "Idea for a Universal History with Cosmopolitan Intent." *Basic Writings of Kant*. Ed. Allen W. Wood. New York: The Modern Library, 2001.

10. Herder, Johann Gottfried. *Another Philosophy of History and Selected Political Writings*. Indianapolis: Hackett Publishing Company, 2004.

Then in the early 1800s, George Wilhelm Friedrich Hegel greatly influenced future generations in many various directions by describing the complex activity of progress in a manner that was left largely to interpretation. Hegel was brilliant in his concentration on human freedom and participation, but he was not straightforward enough to keep future theorists from misinterpreting his conclusions. His work, in turn, influenced the ideas of Karl Marx and Friedrich Engels, who were heavily impacted by the social disruptions of the Industrial Revolution.

The disruptive impact of the Industrial Revolution began a more widespread disillusionment with the optimism of substantive human progress. This is best illustrated by the overwhelming philosophical negativity of Friedrich Nietzsche in the late 1800s and Sigmund Freud in the early 1900s. The negative world-view continued to grow thereafter. The subsequent horror of World War I was evidence to many of the universal aspect of inevitable cyclical decline. The pinnacle of this thought was the universal history put forth by Oswald Spengler in 1918 with his book *The Decline of the West*,[11] which obviously focused on the negative aspects of the then-dominant western culture. A few decades later, Arnold Toynbee became a slightly more optimistic universal historian in his important work *A Study of History*,[12] but his focus on the causes of the rise and fall of past civilizations still implied a negative outcome of the Modern West and a modified-cyclical pattern to history.

The prominence of the cyclical theory, along with the negative implications of the decline of the West, is to be expected. Variations of cyclical theory have dominated cultural thought throughout the history of humans. A simplistic cyclical view of history was prevalent in virtually all ancient civilizations and it is easy to understand why this was true. The cyclical rhythm

---

11. Spengler, Oswald. *The Decline of the West*. Abridged Edition ed. New York: Oxford University Press, 1991.

12. Toynbee, Arnold J. *A Study of History* (Abridgement of Volumes I-VI). Abridged ed. New York: Oxford University Press, 1987.

of life is such a substantial aspect of our world that it is only natural to project it onto all aspects of life and thought.

The cycle of everyday life permeates our very existence. This occurs in the seasons of the year, the lunar cycle, the tides of the sea, day and night, the movement of the stars, and on and on until it is difficult to view life or history in anything but the cyclical manner. Yet, as will be discussed throughout this book, the flow of history has not fit neatly into the cyclical pattern. This is especially true over the past five hundred years and particularly with our advantage of twenty-first century hindsight.

Have Pessimistic Cyclical Views of Universal History Been Proven Correct?

The cyclical theory of civilization appears most rational when examining each of the ancient and classical civilizations individually. This is because they all eventually *declined* in some way. Some of them essentially disappeared, while others merely lagged in comparison to more modern accomplishments. However, the viewpoint is different when we study them in combination and begin to appreciate the improvements they represent, however temporary.

The first civilization in Mesopotamia around 3500 B.C.— which was actually a conglomeration of several separate developments in the Fertile Crescent—appears as an interesting period of experimentation where virtually all development represents some new form of human improvement. This is also true of Egyptian civilization beginning around 3100 B.C., Indian civilization from about 2500 B.C. and Minoan and Chinese civilizations shortly thereafter.

The growth of agriculture and the rise of these ancient civilizations changed the pace of human development. All of the prior key human improvements in prehistory certainly aided the betterment of the human condition. Yet those events occurred over many tens or hundreds of thousands of years. Change during prehistory was primarily a product of slow genetic evolution.

31

The advent of agriculture and the appearance of civilizations began to shift this process toward faster adaptation based upon human behavior and human interaction, rather than genetics.

The population of humans before the spread of agriculture was small, scattered, and isolated. The activity of each small tribe or group of humans was directed toward the daily process of sustenance. There was little contact outside the small geographic area inhabited by each group. Most contact between groups was random because humans at the time generally did not have a stable geographic base to call home. Disparity among differing peoples was less a matter of technical achievement and more a matter of local adaptation to climate and geography.

From this perspective, the differences in the cultures of the ancient civilizations are likewise similar. Each of these ancient civilizations has fascinating and valuable contributions worthy of our interest. However, it is untenable to claim that one was more advanced than another. It is with the civilizations of the next period that greater distinctions appear. Beginning in the Classical Era, there is considerably deeper thought with much greater emphasis on individual morality, thought, and action. This trend is perhaps best represented by classical Greek philosophy where the outline of the use of *reason* is clearly delineated and foreshadows the Enlightenment of nearly two millennia later. Yet the maturation of human thought is also found in India and China at nearly the same time. The thoughts expounded by Lao Tzu, Confucius, and Buddha add complexity to the level of thought witnessed in those societies. The Romans then add to this tradition by more fully exploring legal systems and attempting to administer codes across a wide array of cultures and geographic locations.

The assessment of human progress during the Classical Period from 500 B.C. to 500 A.D. is clouded by our modern vantage point. This is also true of the Islamic civilization in the period beginning around 700 A.D. We have difficulty perceiving improvement in the living conditions of average people during those times because even the best of those societies still utilized widespread slavery and were based on hierarchical social structures we find rightfully abhorrent today. And although this viewpoint is understood, one can certainly observe the progress of human thought. Humans were thinking more deeply and these thoughts were being recorded. All of this was to set the stage for the later improvement of humans.

It is common historical scholarship to combine the Greek, Roman, and Modern Western civilizations into one continual development of Western Civilization, intimately dependent and connected. This continual development of civilization, with primary origins in Greece and with substantial expansion in the Roman Empire, eventually contributed to the rise of Modern Western Civilization. This new civilization is now quickly consuming the entire global community. From this perspective, an argument could be made that Western Civilization began well over 2,000 years ago in Greece and has continually progressed to the dominance of today. Such an argument would have to include an appreciation for dramatic phases of discontinuity throughout that process.

The case for a progression of Western Civilization is compelling, but that is not the focus of our inquiry here. Instead, we will concentrate on merely the later stages or the past five hundred years or so of that development. This is because the inherent *human progress* created by the Modern West dwarfs those classical and ancient civilizations despite the aspects of grandeur associated with the Greek and Roman societies, as well as those of India, China, and all the other civilizations that arose between 3500 B. C. and 1500 A.D.

The rise of the Modern West over the past five hundred years is substantial and self-evident. This is where the cyclical pattern so obviously breaks down. The Modern Western Civilization has not fallen or declined as did past civilizations. On the contrary, it has now expanded into the Modern Global Civilization. The cyclical theory of historical progression has been dispelled. There is objective evidence of substantial and sustainable improvement in the methods of human interaction resulting in the progress of our species.

The counter-argument could certainly be made in 1500 A.D., or perhaps even during the revolutions of 1776 and 1789, that the advancement of humans as a whole was negligible or difficult to quantify. A clear sign of progress was hard to find in 1500, given the previous dissolution of the Roman Empire — as well as the Byzantine and Islamic empires that followed — and the very gradual rise of powerful nation-states in Europe. Later, in the twentieth century, despite considerable material advancement in the West during the proceeding two centuries, human-created disasters gave understandable cause for continued pessimism in regard to human progress. This included the massive warfare and unprecedented depravity associated with the two world wars and the totalitarian regimes in the Communist Bloc.

On the whole, historians and philosophers over the past two centuries, since the optimism of Kant, had every reason to be pessimistic and many of them were pessimists of the first order. This pessimism extended to both the idea of historical progress and philosophical progress. The prevalent view of historical progress was of the cyclical pattern. In this view, even though modern scientific progress had created dramatically superior physical inventions and machinery, it was destined to bring us to another decline and fall of civilization via nuclear war or environmental holocaust. Likewise, the prevalent view of philosophical progress was of the moral deficiency of humans. In this view, even though modern scientific progress had produced incredible prosperity, it was destined not to increase human happiness or satisfaction because of the innate moral deficiencies of humans.

The idea of sustainable and measurable human progress was difficult to claim in 1500 and it was unpopular to argue from the Progressive Era until 1989. Pessimism was the prevailing and socially sophisticated point of view. However, with the benefit of our twenty-first century retrospective, the case for a modern record of sustainable and measurable human progress is now overwhelming. Regardless of whether there had been a discernable pattern of history over the several millennia of recorded history of civilizations until around 1500, one can see there has been an obvious and progressive advancement of human civilization since at least the Renaissance.

The specifics of this measurable human improvement will be discussed in detail in the following chapter and beyond. The primary focus throughout this book is on the implications of how and why this human improvement fits into the universal history of the species.

THREE

The Scorecard of Human Progress

"The great end of all human industry, is the attainment of happiness. For this were arts invented, sciences cultivated, laws ordained, and societies modelled, by the most profound wisdom of patriots and legislators. Even the lonely savage, who lies exposed to the inclemency of the elements and the fury of wild beasts, forgets not, for a moment, this grand object of his being."[1]

—David Hume, 1741

How Can the Progress of Humans Be Objectively Measured?

This question causes us to consider the very meaning of human life. What is important? What matters to us? What was of consequence to our ancestors? It is beneficial for our purposes here to establish core objective criteria without becoming immersed in esoteric philosophical arguments. The meaning of human life has been the subject of philosophy and theology since the beginning of recorded history and it is easy to become absorbed in the unlimited nuances of philosophy. The discussion here will be limited to those aspects that can help us determine core objective criteria of human well-being.

Discussion of *individual* well-being is complex enough, but how can one describe or discuss the well-being of *humankind*? Humankind is merely the sum of its constantly changing parts; that is to say, individuals with different minds and environments, hence different motivation and goals. Therefore, all dis-

1. Hume, David. *Essays: Moral, Political, and Literary.* Revised ed. Indianapolis: Liberty Fund, 1985. 148.

37

cussion concerning the progress or well-being of humankind is theoretical and valuable only as an aggregate, mosaic picture of our world. This is the point where history, anthropology, sociology, biology, psychology, political science, and philosophy merge. It is where the physical and social sciences interlock.

Humankind can only be understood as the sum of all humans at any given moment. This point is absolutely crucial in our discussion. Any understanding of humankind or society must concentrate on the basic building block of society: individuals. There are such conditions as group dynamics and social trends, but they are all based ultimately on individuals. The basic fulfillment of individuals is therefore an appropriate starting point for this discussion.

What Is the Natural Interest of Individuals?

The general aspects of human interest can be broadly categorized into selfish and unselfish characteristics. The tendency of humans to be absorbed with self-interest is well documented. Self-interest is a natural aspect of all mammals and it begins with the instinct of survival. Self-interest is hard-coded in our genetic composition and it permeates our human cultures environmentally as well. Yet despite this obvious and natural tendency, it can also be observed that humans are one of the few mammals that regularly subordinate individual selfish instinct to the needs of the group, beyond just family. Unselfish behavior can be found in other mammals, but humans appear to exhibit more unselfishness than other mammals.

The key observation here is that the most preponderate characteristic of humans is self-interest, but there remains a strong and healthy desire to help our fellow humans. Therefore, to circumvent extensive discussion as to the motivation of individuals and for humankind, the issue will be distilled here to those two concepts, self-interest and helping fellow humans (humankind-interest). These two categories must be better understood for our purpose of analyzing human history. They assist us in considering the basic goals and achievements of humans.

What Are the Core Goals of Human Self-Interest?

Every individual has his or her own understanding of personal goals and aspirations, his or her *interest* with which to be *self-interested*. These goals and aspirations are based upon personal motivation and individual definition of the meaning of life. Personal motivation and goals are as diverse as the population and almost always go far beyond the needs of basic living. One person may desire a healthy family and successful childrearing, while another person yearns for an Academy Award. Then one person may long for a fancy sports car, while someone else wishes for an antique rocking chair. A great number of individuals in the Impoverished World (Third World) may merely hunger for enough food to survive another day.

It is only in the area of basic, core goals that generalizations can be made. Even within the elementary goals, any attempt to describe universal truths is extremely problematic. However, most observers could agree that basic goals generally center on the sanctity of life, the quality of life, and the freedom to pursue happiness as defined individually for one's self and family. The first and third aspects — the sanctity of life and the freedom to pursue happiness — are relatively obvious in meaning. It is the concept of *quality of life* that requires more detail.

The definition of quality of life is much more difficult to describe because it is so personalized. Again, it is necessary to be general. The definition can be divided into two broad categories, the physical and mental aspects of life. Both physical comfort and mental happiness must be more clearly defined. Each includes key attributes that are widely recognized by the public.

The key attributes of physical comfort are the easiest to identify. They include extending life expectancy, maintaining good health, obtaining reasonable food/clothing/shelter, and achieving relative security from violence, as well as security of possessions. All of these attributes could reasonably be extended to the needs of the immediate family. Of course, further clarity is always possible within each one of these attributes. What constitutes *good* health? Extend life by how much and compared to what? What constitutes *reasonable* food/clothing/shelter? These are important and detailed discussions which are not crucial to the premise here and will not be discussed at length.

The key attributes of mental happiness are much more troublesome to identify, but they are dependent upon a certain minimal level of physical comfort. At the base level of survival instinct, all possibility of mental happiness is put on hold until a certain level of physical survival is achieved. This can be identified as the issue of leisure time, defined here merely as the times available after the basic necessities of survival are secured. It is essential for humans to first obtain the basic necessities of physical survival before they have the leisure time available to enjoy mental happiness, including aspects of arts, festivity, and spirituality.

Once the basic necessities are secured, how humans utilize leisure time to enjoy life and increase mental happiness is highly individualized. This is so individualized, in fact, that the core attributes of mental happiness can only be distilled into the two facilitating aspects that create the conditions to allow for individualized mental happiness. The first of these is the necessary leisure time itself. The second is the freedom to use the leisure time to pursue individualized happiness.

The achievement of adequate leisure time and the freedom to use it to pursue happiness usually results in the process of *striving to thrive* or, said differently, the process of advancing beyond mere survival. One aspect of mental happiness is the achievement of self-worth and recognition that often comes from the act of striving and the accomplishment of *thriving*, as it will be described in more detail later. Although this process of thriving may sound exclusively selfish, it should be noted that it might very well include striving to help others.

It is also helpful to reiterate that the leisure time discussed here is not the traditional definition of leisure time, normally described as being "time not spent on the job earning a living or performing necessary family responsibilities." Instead, leisure time is defined here as "all time beyond which is necessary to meet the basic level of survival." In other words, some individuals might choose to use their leisure time (newly defined) to actually work more hours in striving for more remuneration or recognition because it meets their individual goals.

For the purposes of discussion here, it is preferable to clearly assign specific goals to individual self-interest, both physical and mental, despite the complication of interpreting billions of individual viewpoints. The achievement of these specific goals can then be measured and analyzed in determining the success of different methods used to achieve individual self-interest.

The physical and mental goals are identified below in chart form. They represent the generalized objectives inherent in basic self-interest.

Core Goals of Self-Interest

- **Life expectancy**
- **Health**
- **Food/Clothing/Shelter**
- **International security (peace)**
- **Domestic security (from crime)**
- **Leisure time**
- **Freedom**

What Are the Core Goals of Humankind-Interest?

The concept of humankind-interest or *helping fellow humans* is also difficult to specify. Everyone has a different opinion of what constitutes the interest of humankind. The definition of humankind-interest inevitably reverts to an individualized and selfish determination because it is defined in the eye of the beholder. This, once again, brings us to discuss the goals of self-interest highlighted in the previous chart. The categories listed as the goals of self-interest are all positive in nature. What about *negative* self-interest? What about the negative attributes that we have seen manifested by some individuals throughout history, such as violence, subjugation, and thievery? This is where the concept of humankind-interest materializes. Humankind-interest inevitably revolves around the restriction of such negative attributes of human behavior.

The entire concept of humankind-interest is inherently contradictory, unless it is defined in terms that relate to the sum of individualized self-interest. Otherwise, each person's opinion of what constitutes humankind-interest is likely to contradict, at least in small degrees, every other viewpoint. Majoritarianism or the rule of the majority is not suited to solve such a complexity. It is possible for a bare majority to severely restrict the positive self-interest of a very large minority; perhaps even to do so in a vicious and brutal manner.

The solution is rather to embrace the complexity. The only natural, non-contradictory definition of humankind-interest is "to help the largest possible number of human beings achieve their individual positive self-interest." This in turn requires the simultaneous restriction of negative self-interest. In this case, negative self-interest is being defined as self-interested acts that involuntarily coerce and harm others. Stated more directly, humankind-interest is simply helping the largest possible number of people achieve their positive self-interest. This concept has been traditionally expressed as "the greatest good for the greatest number." It is unfortunate this terminology has been grossly misinterpreted and misappropriated in the past by Marxists and tyrants of various stripes. Yet there is no valid reason we should resist raising this banner again for more admirable purposes.

What Are the Objective Measurements of Human Progress?

The analysis of the progress of *humankind* or *universal history* can best be undertaken by specifically measuring the seven core objectives of human interest previously listed. These will serve as our objective measurement tools.

Establishing the attributes to be measured is merely the beginning of the dilemma. Next, we must determine how to structure the measurements. Statistics can be structured in many different ways, often misleading the casual observer. In particular, *averages* can be calculated utilizing differing methods and should be carefully clarified. The most perplexing structural element is how to measure all individuals around the world, despite the vast differences across continents and countries.

The most illustrative analysis is *by country*. The country measurements can be added together to provide global statistics, but viewing the statistics by country provides unique insight into human progress. The measurements should help us answer the question of whether or not there has been human progress and, if so, where and when. If progress or regress has occurred, these same measurements should help in the process of determining the cause by examining the differences between times and places to identify trends and circumstances.

Amassing these relevant measurements by country over long periods of time is the most problematic task of all. Specific measurements have only become reliably available around the world during the past fifty years or so (with few exceptions). Additionally, the borders of countries have constantly changed over the centuries with the incessant formation and deformation of nations. This makes the analysis all the more complex.

And emigration across borders is another complicating factor. These obstacles make the task of analysis exasperating, but not impossible.

After deciding the geographical boundaries, the most illustrative measurements would include the agreeable units of measure, the total amount of units per person in the time/place, the total number and percentage of people below an agreeable minimum threshold in each category, and a measurement for each country and each decade for at least the past one thousand years. Obviously, all of these measurements are not available. However, obtaining the best available estimated measurements within this framework and estimating the others should aid greatly in the understanding of the topic.

What Are the Units of Measure?

It is manifestly impossible to have accessibility to detailed statistics as to the life expectancy, health, amount of food/clothing/shelter, peace, domestic security, leisure time, and freedom of every society around the world for the last few thousand years or more. However, there is ample evidence that many of these particular categories are very closely correlated with the measurement of *prosperity*. The relative prosperity of societies has been chronicled and analyzed extensively. The comparable conditions of internal and external peace have also been carefully studied. Finally, the condition of freedom (political, social, economic, and philosophical) is also well known.

Therefore, we can discuss the progress of humankind, as recorded by the preponderance of scholars, by highlighting the progress of prosperity, peace, and freedom around the world over time. This includes a look at the distribution of these conditions, not only geographically by country and region, but also within each segment of society. If the sanctity, quality, and freedom of *each and every* human life are the keys to our definition of progress, then it is imperative to review all sectors of society. We must guard against giving unequal weight to the elites of societies as many historians and scholars have done until the most recent times.

The prosperity of medieval European nobles is of little consequence if the vast majority of the citizens of those societies were destitute. The incredible wealth of modern Middle Eastern oil sultans is of little consequence if the people of their societies are not developing independent methods of sustenance. The overwhelming beauty of the Chinese Forbidden City is of little consequence if it was built on the backs of masses on the edge of starvation at the time. The grandness of the antebellum southern plantations in the United States is of little consequence considering the vast numbers of slaves required to build and maintain the lifestyle.

We must also take pains to include all societies on Earth. All humans are to be considered of equal importance in our analysis. The majority of scholarship conducted until the mid-twentieth century concentrated on European history because Europeans or people of European descent performed most of the scholarship. This does not negate the fact that humans from the Americas, Asia, Africa, Oceania, or other previously neglected areas should be considered equally in our analysis because we are concerned with *human* progress, not merely *European* progress. A special attention will be paid to European history only in an effort to understand the causes of the rise of the modern, global civilization.

What Are the Primary Findings Concerning PROSPERITY?

If we look at the progress of humans in terms of prosperity — as representative of life expectancy, health, food/clothing/shelter, and leisure time — then the progress of the Modern West stands out. Certainly there was sporadic progress in ancient history and in specific civilizations at specific times. However, even at the height of the previous civilizations, the progress of humans pales in comparison to modern times. This is especially true once we carefully attempt to measure *all* of the participants in those civilizations.

We may appreciate the democratic experiments of ancient Greece, as well as their contribution to philosophy, until we recognize their considerable use of slavery and we include the well-being of the slave component of the population. We may be astonished by the pyramids and tombs of the ancient Egyptians, but we know that only the elite of their society lived well. We may marvel at the accomplishments of ancient Rome, even their widening prosperity, yet we also recognize their subjugation of multitudes of peoples. We may be awed by the artistic beauty and philosophical advances of ancient China, yet we are also well aware of the incredible hardship of their masses over time. Objectively, there is no historical example of an overwhelming, widespread, and sustained increase in the average prosperity of humans until modern times.

If we can imagine for a moment a visual mathematical representation of the prosperity of humans over time, we can develop a very useful understanding of history. The data is interesting. There are clear patterns. The visual representations of the statistics are striking, in that most of the quantifiable measurements of human prosperity record a similar pattern. There are representations of long periods of negligible or unsteady progress, followed by rapid improvement in the most recent time periods, except for what remains of the Impoverished World. In other words, the pattern follows the track of *modernity*.

This is certainly not unexpected, nor revolutionary. In many respects, it is obvious. One would expect prosperity to facilitate modern progress and, in turn, facilitate basic human benefit. All this really means is that we could have substituted wealth as a generalized attribute in place of many of the core objectives of self-interest and come to the same statistical findings. This validates the relative importance of wealth or prosperity.

It is understood that the term *prosperity* has obtained a negative connotation in some quarters, but it should be recognized as a positive force behind human progress at the individual level. And it should not be limited to merely selfish concerns or physical well-being. Prosperity can include the leisure time necessary to pursue altruism of all types. It can include the leisure time necessary to pursue spirituality and the arts. Even when considering merely the selfish and physical aspects, prosperity is a key to individual progress. It is easy for prosperous interventionists in the developed world to pontificate about how the mental and spiritual components of life are so much more important than the physical and material components. They should try explaining that concept to an individual in some impoverished distant land who is on the edge of starvation.

The most prosperous nations of today have recorded very dramatic improvement during the last century or two. And not just for the elites of society. Overwhelmingly large and affluent middle classes have developed. The evidence supports the common perception that those of us living in the Prosperous World have improved our living conditions considerably. This progressive advancement has included an explosive growth in knowledge and prosperity, albeit temporarily interrupted by the devastations of war and totalitarianism in the first half of the twentieth century. The force of this progress is powerful. This power is dramatically reshaping our world in all aspects of life, in politics, science, philosophy, economics, business, arts, and social interaction.

Examples of this progress abound, but some of the sharpest examples involve those in transportation and communication. In transportation, less than 200 years ago and *for most of recorded history,* travel was relegated to the speed of a horse and a sailboat. James Madison in his struggles during the War of 1812 could not travel appreciably faster than could Pericles managing a burgeoning Greek empire approximately two thousand years earlier. Today, humans can circumnavigate the globe in a few hours and send spaceships traveling beyond our solar system.

Likewise, in communication, less than 200 years ago and *for most of recorded history*, a relatively small number of books and poems were available only to the privileged elite of societies and knowledge was difficult to communicate from one society to another. The intellectual forefathers of the Enlightenment (Bacon, Descartes, and Newton) did not have access to appreciably more knowledge than did Confucius in ancient China approximately two thousand years earlier. Today, there are hundreds of millions of books and periodicals, readily available to virtually every citizen of the Prosperous World, and capable of being forwarded *en masse* within minutes to any corner of the globe via fiber optics and the Internet.

These examples are just the beginning. The miracle of the modern age has been very extensively researched and is widely available through many scholarly books and journals. This does not mean you will hear about it on the nightly television news or see it on the best-seller lists, but with just a little research, you will find statistical trends irrefutably proving the significant advancement of humankind. The most important of these statistics is that of life expectancy, which improved by 30 years — a huge 64% increase — during the twentieth century alone in the United States.[2] Statistics of this kind are readily available in most other prosperous countries, a few going back hundreds of years.

Statistics and scholarly journals can be tiresome for many people and it is always helpful to explain these things in more human terms. One of the best illustrations can be found in the following straightforward comparison. The majority of humans throughout history had to struggle daily to obtain enough food to survive. Now, in the Prosperous World, one of our most prevalent health problems is that of obesity. One of our biggest concerns is how to avoid the overabundance of food supply with which we are *burdened*. And, lest anyone argue this food supply is unevenly available in the Prosperous

2. Moore, Stephen, and Julian L. Simon. *It's Getting Better All the Time*. Washington: Cato Institute, 2000.

World, the statistics will show obesity is most prevalent among those with the lowest incomes.

What Are the Primary Findings Concerning PEACE?

Widespread peace has been a scarce commodity throughout recorded history. The building process of ancient civilizations generally included the combining together of smaller societies by the force of violence. Those civilizations then often enlarged their realms by further subsuming nearby lesser civilizations and hunter-gather tribes, usually resulting in annihilation or slavery. Internal leadership transitions were often bloody affairs. Conditions of peace were rare and in no way sustainable. The emergence of more modern nation-states in Europe toward the end of the Middle Ages did not immediately improve on this ancient tradition of warfare and coercion. The close proximity of numerous nations of relatively equal strength in Europe created hyper-competitive conditions between the time of the Norman Invasion of 1066 and the second fall of Napoleon in 1815. This made warfare the norm in Europe for three quarters of a millennium, even as European civilization was fast becoming the most dominant civilization in the world.

There was no evidence through 1815 that the prospect for international peace and cooperation had improved in the world. The primary military change throughout history, at that point, had been the recent development of guns and cannons, as well as the continued perfection of steel production, that greatly increased the military destructive power of European nations. This created a considerable disparity in armament compared to other civilizations around the world. The European powers used this disparity to conquer or dominate many other civilizations and societies in other parts of the world and enhance their global influence.

It was at the end of the Revolutionary Period and the Napoleonic Wars that unusual change began to occur. There proceeded three incredibly surprising and atypical periods. First, there was the period of great European peace from 1815 to 1914.[3] During this period, the primary powers of Europe lived together in remarkable peace for one hundred years, the equivalent of four generations.

Thereafter, this incredible peace was disrupted by a period of warfare unparalleled in history. The warfare that erupted between 1914 and 1945 was so extensive and devastating that a new term had to be coined to describe it. The first of the *world wars* was so shocking that participants concluded it could never happen again, that it was "the war to end all wars." Unfortunately, this prediction was premature and the second of the great wars was even more extensive and devastating.

Then, beginning in 1945, the third of the unusual periods began and it has not yet ended. This is another period of great European peace,[4] which has exhibited increasing European harmony, now even including Eastern Europe after the collapse of the Soviet bloc. This same peace has currently extended throughout the Prosperous World globally.

The statistical representation of international peace is remarkably similar to the findings of the physical well-being attributes described in the previous section. There are long historical periods of negligible or unsteady progress, followed by rapid improvement in the most recent two hundred years, except for what remains of the Impoverished World.

There is one glaring exception to this statistical representation: the unparalleled period of war from 1914 to 1945. This period deserves closer scrutiny. First, the two world wars were separated by over two decades. It is therefore misleading to group them together as one long period. They equal a period of only about 13 years of elapsed time.[5] Europe has enjoyed 177

---

3. This peace was only interrupted by the isolated Crimean War, fought mostly by European powers on territory in Asia, and the short eleven-month Franco-German War beginning in 1870.

4. This was interrupted only by the civil war within the former Yugoslavia.

5. This is utilizing the widely accepted date of 1939 as the start of WWII, obviously

years of widespread international peace compared to 13 years of devastating warfare during the past 190 years. More importantly, these wars were not perpetrated on behalf of freedom and liberty, but against the concept. As each year goes by, the devastation of the two world wars is beginning to appear more as an anomaly, rather than a trend. This does not negate the incredible importance of these wars in the history of the world, but the fact that they are anomalous actually increases their importance and our interest.

Large-scale international peace is now the norm. It has been sixty years since the Second World War and there is no longer the threat of the Cold War lingering over our world. Nevertheless, there still remain many smaller and localized concerns. There are the concerns associated with the violence from the international Islamic fundamentalists that will be discussed in more detail later. There are constant civil wars and separatist activities in Africa and some other isolated areas. Yet, on a global basis, there is more and broader international peace and cooperation than can be documented during the past millennium. More nations are cooperatively engaging and trading with one another. There is little evidence to be concerned about possible groups of countries aligning against other groups of countries as occurred in the world wars and in Europe prior to 1815. The scale of discord and disagreement has been minimized and localized.

All of this good news may be surprising to hear for those who are avid readers of newspapers and frequent watchers of television news. We are inundated with stories of crisis in news reports from war zones. News agencies have modern tools that allow for almost constant coverage of virtually any conflict around the world. This broad coverage serves a valuable purpose of reminding citizens everywhere of the horrors of war. Unfortunately, it also obscures the fact that multilateral conflict has mostly withered away over the years.

---

excluding the militaristic advances of the Japanese beginning in 1931.

What Are the Primary Findings Concerning FREEDOM?

The trends of freedom follow the same statistical patterns as prosperity and peace. The ancient and classical civilizations were rarely bastions of freedom. They maintained a pervasive use of slavery, as well as widespread restrictions on the individual freedom of freepersons, especially women and children.

It was not until the advent of the Modern Western Civilization that slavery became abhorrent in the minds of the masses. Slavery had mostly disappeared in Europe by the time of the Enlightenment. European involvement had been relegated to outposts in the New World and even there the practice was mostly abolished throughout North America, with the exception of the southern colonies, by the time of the American Revolution. An unprecedented philosophical abolitionist movement developed in Europe and the northern United States in the nineteenth century. This movement was not only instrumental in the eventual abolishment of slavery in the southern United States, but it also established the precedent of including universal freedom (anti-slavery) as the philosophical hallmark of modern society. This attitude is now taken for granted in the Modern Global Civilization. Slavery only continues today in some isolated corners of the Impoverished World.

One of the most important developments in the history of freedom is the changing role of women in society. Women were treated as virtual slaves in most societies throughout history. They are still treated as such in most of the Impoverished World today. The countries of the Modern West began changing that practice. Women are now expected to have equal political and social rights in the Prosperous World. This has become one of the standards within the concept of universal freedom. It represents a monumental change in human interaction because whereas the slave component of humankind rarely exceeded over 25 percent of the human population, the female component was usually very close to 50 percent of the species. The widespread inclusion of women more broadly in the interaction of society has dramatically increased the overall capability of humans.

Individual freedom (male or female) was a rare commodity in ancient and classical civilizations. The concept of freedom or liberty was, at first, considered largely only in the context of certain sectors or groups within society, not individually. This was seen in terms of which elite groups were allowed to participate in the guidance of society or which others were to receive certain common benefits of society. This was not an extension of freedom to an individual; rather, it was freedom based only upon group classification.

There were some temporary experiments with democracy, republics, and individualized freedom, but there was no sustainable progress. Widespread and sustainable progress with individual freedom only began in the Modern West. It was only during the Enlightenment that the concept of inalienable individual rights became prevalent.

The concept was widely heralded by the great Enlightenment thinkers (and their immediate intellectual forefathers), although not very commonly practiced. Traditions of individual freedom became customary in England and other isolated parts of Europe first. Then they began expanding elsewhere throughout the Revolutionary Era. The tradition of individual freedom continued to develop, albeit with limitations, until the later half of the twentieth century, when our current appreciation for widespread individual freedom became the norm throughout the Prosperous World.

How Can These Three Trends of Progress — Prosperity, Peace, and Freedom — Be Summarized?

We have seen the progress in the Modern West in the broad areas of prosperity, peace, and freedom. These categories are representative of the progress in all seven of the objective measurements of human progress. The improvement in all the categories maintains a similar trend. The progress appears to have begun very slowly a few hundred years ago and has dramatically accelerated in the past few decades.

Methodically accumulating the statistical trends across all nations for hundreds of years is a challenging enough process. It is also difficult to appropriately develop the proper analysis and interpretation of the data. Thankfully, numerous experts and distinguished economists have spent considerable time and attention on the topic.

A fine example of such work is from Nobel laureate Robert Fogel in his work *The Escape from Hunger and Premature Death, 1700-2100.*[6] In this work, he reviews detailed statistics showing substantial improvement in nutrition, health, and life expectancy in the modern world, especially in the Prosperous World. The data is fascinating and conclusive. Yet there is one statistic discussed by Professor Fogel that illustrates the comprehensive story of humans more than any others. It concerns the population of the world. To see historical population growth in graph form is astonishing. (See chart at right.)

Many scholars have studied human history extensively and have been relatively cognizant of the growth of population. Yet seeing it on such a chart brings a much different perspective than simply considering the numbers theoretically. The initial reaction of most people is one of shock, probably a defensive shock. Most observers start with the frightening question, "How can we survive with all these people?" Yet, once we get beyond the shock, it is important to ask a different question. Does this statistic prove that something incredibly revolutionary occurred in the past couple hundred years of human history? The answer is self-evident.

The scholarly findings of economists and statisticians are useful in our quest for understanding this flow of history. However, non-economists find it helpful to discuss the topic in less statistical terms. Let us consider this topic in personal terms

---

6. Fogel, Robert William. *The Escape from Hunger and Premature Death, 1700-2100.* Paperback ed. Cambridge: Cambridge University Press, 2004.

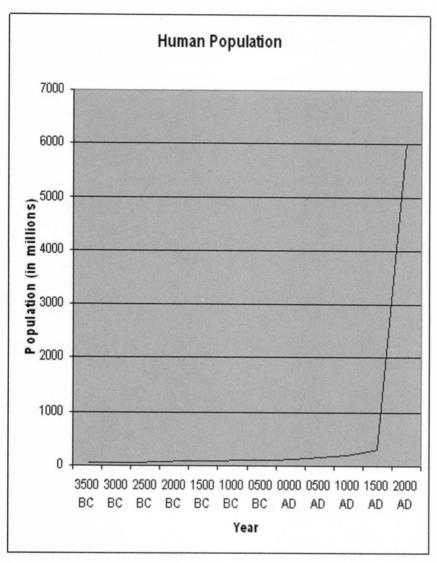

based on what we see and feel as laypeople.

There has certainly been an observable trend of human progress during the past couple of centuries. As discussed in Chapter One, the progress has been pervasive and considerable. In the Prosperous World we live longer lives, we are healthier, we incur less risk, and we enjoy more leisure time. We are safer, we are more peaceable, and we cooperate more widely. The scope of our advance and the number of humans included has mushroomed. We have improved the human condition. It can be definitively declared that at least a large portion of the world has experienced substantial and sustainable human progress. The next question must address the cause.

PART TWO
Structural Causes

FOUR

Searching for the Cause

"Enlightenment is man's exit from his self-incurred...incapacity to use one's intelligence without the guidance of another."[1]

—Imanuel Kant, 1784

How Do We Search for a Cause of the Phenomenon of Modern Progress?

The search for a cause should begin with traditional techniques of scholarship. It is advisable to study the data, look for trends, and examine the evidence. Which countries advanced and when? What did they have in common? How do these success stories differ from the countries that lack success? The answers to these questions should enable us to understand the cause.

These are not partisan questions. This is not an exercise in designing an argument in favor of a particular political opinion. This is a matter of objective analysis and sincere inquiry. It is an exercise of human interest in human progress or regression. There is no advantage in being naïve or unrealistic. On the contrary, there is much to be lost by following paths of ignorance, superstition, or fashion if those paths are not warranted by historically proven value.

---

1. Kant, Immanuel. "Answer to the Question: What is Enlightenment?" *Basic Writings of Kant.* Ed. Allen W. Wood. New York: The Modern Library, 2001. 135.

To Be Self-Evident

Which Countries Advanced and When Did This Occur?

Toward the end of the Middle Ages a series of competitive nation-states emerged in Europe. This most likely was the result
of having a number of semi-civilized and roughly equivalent
societies in close proximity to one another. These societies were
within an advantageous stretch of geography that had once
been dominated by the Roman Empire. They were now independent and competitive.

This development of modern nation-states is a watershed
event in history. It occurred very slowly and unevenly across
Europe. The area had been dominated by localized and rural
social structures after the fall of Rome. Forms of serfdom became the most prevalent type of society. Eventually, the rule
of important families over larger domains began to create mi-
cro-empires of constantly changing scope due to outcomes of
marriages, inheritance, and conquest. Slowly, these micro-em-
pires became absolute monarchies with set geographical desig-
nations, often based on the language and cultural distinctions
of the people.

These European nation-states developed certain advantages—notably guns, germs, and steel—that enabled them
to explore and subjugate the native populations of the other
continents.[2] This included the easily conquered populations of
remaining hunter-gatherer tribes in Africa, the Americas, and
Oceana. It also included the more advanced civilizations in
Asia, Africa, and the Americas, such as Persia, China, Japan,
India, Egypt, Inca, Aztec, and Maya.[3]

Despite the aggressive use of guns and steel, as well as the
accidental spread of devastating disease, these Europeans were

2. As previously noted, see Diamond, Jared. *Guns, Germs, and Steel.* Paperback ed.
New York: W. W. Norton & Company, 1999.

3. The fact that the Europe of the fifteenth and sixteenth centuries began to develop
and exploit a temporary strength over other civilizations does not in any way negate the great contributions of those other civilizations and the importance of their
own histories.

only moderately and temporarily more advanced than the civilizations they conquered or dominated (hunter-gatherer peoples excluded). The European nations of the sixteenth and seventeenth centuries were also incredibly diverse and highly competitive with one another. Their temporary global advantages could have quickly dissipated due to inter-European warfare or the rapid and aggressive perfection of guns and steel by China, Japan, India, or others.

Perhaps the peak of the era of absolute monarchs occurred with the reign of Louis XIV, (*the Sun King*). Louis ruled France from 1643 until his death in 1715, although the first eighteen of those years were administered by others on his behalf during his childhood. This was the longest and most successful of all the monarchical reigns of Europe, rivaled perhaps only by the reign of Elizabeth I (1558-1603) in England.[4] Louis became the epitome of the absolute monarch and has been attributed with the remark "L'Etat, c'est moi" or "I am the State." In the early years of his reign, he was an enlightened dictator who sponsored trade through the use of mercantilism. He created effective taxation and maintained proper financial reserves, all the while subsidizing grand arts and establishing Versailles as a lavish royal palace on a scale that would have made Julius Caesar jealous.

Louis can be seen as the peak of the burgeoning European civilization. Although he helped to transform the largest of the European states into a period of glory, it would have been typical and plausible to see the civilization degenerate after his death. Such a decline would have been reminiscent of all previous historical civilizations. Yet this did not happen. The phenomenon of European progress was just beginning. The reign of Louis XIV was not representative of the result of the progress and it is certainly not representative of the cause of the progress. Prosperity would be brought eventually to a much wider

---

4. The reign of Queen Victoria of the Great Britain (1837-1901) is also noted as a magnificent era but was far beyond the age of absolute monarchs.

body of citizens than merely the elite at Versailles and it would be extended far beyond France. This new European civilization was to be different.

Jared Diamond and others intelligently explain the geographical reasons for the development of Europe as the dominant power capable of *conquering* the remaining populations in the sixteenth and seventeenth centuries. However, the more interesting and provocative questions are as follows. How was this civilization different from all the past civilizations? Which of the European powers were to eventually become dominant internally and then expand human progress much more rapidly than even seventeenth-century Europeans could imagine?

The rise of Europe as a significant contributor to human development occurred gradually over a very long period of time. It is only after about 1500 that Europe[5] can be said to be a civilization worthy of being compared to the great civilizations of ancient and classical times. Northwestern Europe was a backwater region during Roman times and for hundreds of years thereafter. The use of the term *Middle Ages* is not very descriptive of the period in that region between the fall of Rome and more modern times. Northwestern Europe was only marginally included in Roman civilization and was mostly comprised of barbarian tribes, as they were to become known in history. The period known as the Middle Ages was actually a period of steady, but slow, growth and development. It is in this period that Europe began developing into the more mature nation-states and absolute monarchies previously mentioned.

The most obvious difference in this new "civilization" was that it was not a singular, cohesive society. It was a group of numerous disparate states. France and England were two of the first nation-states of the region to control territory roughly approximating their later contours. Denmark and Sweden emerged out of the Viking heritage. In the fifteenth century, Spain suc-

---

5. The term "Europe" in this period is commonly used as a reference to those countries in western, mostly northwestern, Europe.

ceeded in the Reconquest by expelling the Islamic civilization from Iberia. Then, Spain and Portugal took the early lead in the process of external exploration and colonization on other continents. They also were the first to gain quantities of gold and silver from the New World. Yet this initial advantage did not allow Spain and Portugal to build a sustainable advantage in Europe. All of the European powers of the sixteenth century had access to the same military weapons that allowed Spain and Portugal to subjugate much of the New World. Weapons and warfare were certainly important, but such weapons alone could not provide the advantage necessary to advance beyond the relatively equal developmental stage of many European nations at that time. Scholars such as Jared Diamond present plausible geographic reasons why these emerging nation-states grew to this level of dominance. However, it is the next level of dominance that is ultimately more important and intriguing.

The potential for the development and progress of Europe in the sixteenth and seventeenth centuries was spread widely from the city-states of the Italian peninsula to Denmark and Sweden of Scandinavia and from the Atlantic coasts of France and England through the fields of Russia (Muscovy). There existed Poland, Hungary, Prussia, Switzerland, the (United Provinces) Netherlands, and the remnants of the Holy Roman Empire. Much later there was the important emergence of Germany (subsuming Prussia and others) as a political entity. Nations were forming throughout the continent out of the many varied local societies. These various new nations had differing advantages and disadvantages. Some had better ports. Others had superior soil or weather conditions. Some had amassed more technical prowess. Others had aggressive and organized royalty capable of strong leadership.

It would have been very difficult for prognosticators in 1500 or 1600 to predict which of these new nations, if any, would take the lead in further development. Few observers would have wagered that a spectacular advancement was about to occur in the island corner of Europe known as Great Britain. Yet

63

it was in the Great Britain of England, Wales, and Scotland that conditions emerged to significantly leapfrog the living standards of the rest of Europe and other developed civilizations around the world.

Historians have categorized this event as the *Industrial Revolution*. The term Industrial Revolution is adequate enough. Names must be given to such large-scale phenomenon in order to identify them for discussion purposes. Yet no simple term is capable of the full imagery necessary to properly evoke an understanding of the human change occurring in the Industrial Revolution. It was not a singular event that can be traced to one shining moment in time. It was an evolution of immense material advancement amongst an evolution of staggering social change. It has been alternately identified as either *westernization* or *modernization*. We can see the physical results of the evolution, but the causes are much more troublesome to identify.

Many historians have chronicled the myriad of physical changes leading up to and creating the dramatic rise in living standards in Great Britain beginning approximately around 1760. There were advances in agriculture and food production, without which it is certain no other advancement could have occurred. There was the growth of the factory system and the use of steam power. There was an increase of inventions and the advancement of scientific methods. There was the continual perfection of machines to increase productivity. There was the expansion of ports and canal systems. There was the growth of trade and the increase of the middle class. All of these developments did not occur in any single year or decade. They came together over long periods of time, often decades before the arbitrarily designated commencement date of this so-called revolution.

The Industrial Revolution clearly began in Great Britain, but there was no theoretical geographic restriction. Knowledge of steam power, factory systems, transportation waterways, agricultural improvements, etc., is impossible to keep in any one nation, especially a nation of rapidly expanding external trade. Great Britain only halfheartedly attempted to maintain the mechanical secrets of the Industrial Revolution. They often openly hosted visitors from other lands seeking to understand the causes of the phenomenon. Of course, such understanding did not necessarily come easily.

We still debate the causes hundreds of years later. It was even more difficult for contemporary observers to analyze the events of those days and draw conclusions about the causes. Most problematic of all would be any attempt to implement similar changes in other societies necessary to raise living standards in the manner accomplished in Great Britain. Technical inventions and procedures were easily copied by others, but Great Britain made rapid progress toward our modern age far faster than most of the rest of the world. The Netherlands, Switzerland, and Denmark made the next notable improvements in living standards early in the nineteenth century. Comparable, and only slightly delayed, progress occurred in the former British colony of the United States and, eventually, in the other English-speaking colonies of Canada, Australia, and New Zealand. France, Belgium, and Germany made similar progress later in the nineteenth century. Nevertheless, Great Britain clearly surpassed the rest of the world in the race to modernity.

Why Did the Industrial Revolution Begin in Great Britain?

We are very familiar with the proximate causes of the Industrial Revolution. However, innovations such as factories and steam engines might have been utilized in many other countries to kick off the Industrial Revolution. Scientific knowledge, intelligence, and ingenuity were not the exclusive domain of the English, Scottish, and Welsh. The advantages of the printing press, the changing conditions brought forth by the Reformation and the Renaissance, and the advent of the scientific method were widely available beyond the British Isles. Why did the revolution occur specifically in Great Britain and why was it so difficult for other societies — especially those outside of Europe and English-speaking colonies — to imitate these successes? Why was the United States able to replicate the advancement with relative quickness as compared to other more mature nations? The answers lay in terms of human interaction and participation. The ultimate cause of the Industrial Revolution was not the technical achievements most often associated with the advancement. The cause of the Industrial Revolution was the people who made those achievements happen. It was caused by the unleashing of the unprecedented power of people. Larger numbers of people were essential ingredients in the phenomenon. Larger numbers of people were needed to be involved in inventing new machines and methods of productivity. Larger numbers of people were essential to relocate and work in new industries. Larger numbers of people were vital to invest their time and savings into new ventures. Larger numbers of people were necessary to produce, trade, sell, and ultimately purchase new products and services. This explosion of people power is the key to understanding the Industrial Revolution.

This issue of human participation is complex. France, China, India, and some other societies had more population than Great Britain when the Industrial Revolution began. What was different about the human participation in Great Britain to enable that country to progress beyond others? The answer has to do with liberty and human motivation. Virtually all other societies at the time were still relying mostly on a small fraction of their population for guidance, innovation, and productivity. Some were still mired in systems of serfdom and mercantilism that severely restrained the freedom of most common people to participate more fully in the possibilities of life. Still other societies were subject to the increased uncertainties of even more archaic systems. Great Britain was different. It had conditions that encouraged wider human participation.

Great Britain still had some restrictive traditions of behavior, but less so than others. This society allowed for more flexibility and change. Great Britain had succeeded in simultaneously centralizing a consistent rule of law and had fostered a society with an exceptional amount of individual autonomy. The basic structure was in place that allowed for law and order. This provided for a steady sense of certainty regarding the rules of human interaction. At the same time, there was an established political history that limited the government control and there was a social history that created less strict hierarchical boundaries for individuals. All of this amounted to more individual flexibility and opportunity. And the result was an explosion of human activity that is better characterized as the *Human Productivity Revolution* than the Industrial Revolution.

The royalty of Great Britain did not design, nor did they sanction the beginning of the Industrial Revolution. They might very well have opposed the development if they had completely understood it and if they had the power to stop it. They did not have the power to prevent the change. The fact that they did not have the power is the very reason the change occurred. Their royal ancestors, as well other social authorities, had ceded the ability to strictly control most aspects of human interaction. This had occurred during the previous few centuries, sometimes with small steps and sometimes in larger leaps. They had not done so with this result in mind, but nevertheless, they had opened up the possibility of a new world.

The presence of a stable environment where the rules of order were (relatively) consistently and fairly applied was very important. This happened alongside the limitation of the *visible* hand of government and social authorities. The gradual rise of this broader social freedom allowed for the simultaneous expansion of the *invisible* hand as described so well by Adam Smith. The Industrial Revolution began in Great Britain because it was there that the conditions of freedom and liberty had most successfully coalesced to enable a larger percentage of the population to participate in the advancement of their lives. This unleashed the productive capacity of people far beyond what other contemporary or previous societies were capable of accomplishing. This does not mean that the Great Britain of the early 1700s had developed into a perfect form of liberty. Actually, they were still far from it. However, the aspects of liberty in that culture had evolved to a more considerable degree and in wider distribution than in other contemporary circumstances.

None of this is to say that the aspects of liberty were not present to some degree in other nations. There were similar conditions growing throughout northwestern Europe, but they merely advanced in Great Britain sooner than elsewhere. The nations that came closest to immediately replicating the conditions of widespread freedom and liberty, such as Switzerland, Holland, and Denmark, were able to progress at speeds relatively close to that of Great Britain. Other proximate powers, such as France, Belgium, and Germany, took somewhat longer in establishing similar conditions, but then rapidly caught up about a century later. Still other nations that lacked widespread freedom and liberty, such as Spain, Portugal, Italy, and Russia, were destined to fall far behind the leaders for an extended period of time.

This differing journey of the European nations (as well as others) entering into the modern age has been astutely researched and chronicled by David S. Landes in his two most successful books: *The Unbound Prometheus* and *The Wealth and Poverty of Nations.*[6] Professor Landes came to the conclusion that the Industrial Revolution was caused—among numerous causes—by a growing autonomy of intellectual inquiry, an adversarial method of inquiry, and the routinization of research.[7] He emphasized the growth of free markets. Most decidedly, the genesis of the modern world was caused by a break from the restraints of the pre-modern world that had previously held individuals back.

---

6. Landes, David. *The Unbound Prometheus*. Cambridge: Cambridge University Press, 1969. Landes, David S. *The Wealth and Poverty of Nations*. New York: W. W. Norton & Company, 1998.

7. Landes, David S. *The Wealth and Poverty of Nations*. New York: W. W. Norton & Company, 1998. 201.

The Europeans knew much less of these interferences. Instead, they entered during these centuries into an exciting world of innovation and emulation that challenged vested interests and rattled the forces of conservatism. Changes were cumulative; novelty spread fast. A new sense of progress replaced an older, effete reverence for authority. This intoxicating sense of freedom touched (infected) all domains. These were years of heresies in the Church, of popular initiatives that, we can see now, anticipated the rupture of the Reformation; of new forms of expression and collective action that challenged the older art forms, questioned social structures, and posed a threat to other polities; of new ways of doing and making things that made newness a virtue and a source of delight; of utopias that fantasized better futures rather than recalled paradises lost.

How Was This Civilization Different from Other Previous Civilizations?

Great Britain was a leader in this remarkable journey of human progress. Some other European states could join in the progress relatively quickly because they had already developed many of the conditions necessary to excel. And still other nations on other continents were able to join the club, some taking longer than others. It was the development of the other nations in the trend of liberty and prosperity, including much of Europe and North America (then elsewhere later), which made this civilization different from the ancient and classical civilizations. This was a civilization created by a new structural form, not a ruling entity. This was not a new civilization grounded at a specific geographical point and guided by a centralized ruling elite group.

Although Great Britain was a leader, this was not a British civilization. It included other countries very early on and it has continually added more countries over time. This was a *diffused* civilization. It was not based on geography or religion. It first had the appearance of being "European" or "Christian," but it

69

has proven to be completely diverse. It is not a civilization built upon the rule of an elite group that can die out, nor is it one that relies on religious zeal for constant energy. It is simply the unleashing of human potential.

This new civilization was first known as the British Empire, and sometimes more generally as Western Civilization. Now it is obvious that there are no geographic limitations. It is global and, most distinctively, it is cooperative. This new structural phenomenon that began in earnest in Great Britain was based on human cooperation.

Unfortunately, this cooperativeness was at first restricted to cooperation internal to each participating country. It slowly began to include external relations as well. Eventually the phenomenon began to expand until it reached a global status. That expansion period was often awkward and sometimes horrendous. This issue of expansion will be covered in more detail in Part Five, but first, let us review the structure of this new civilization.

How Can We More Extensively Describe These Successful Social Conditions That Were Based on Freedom and Liberty and That Resulted in the Unleashing of Human Potential on a New Scale?

The individual freedom and liberty discussed in the broad conclusions above are not merely *political* liberty in the traditional sense of the word. The liberty being discussed is *social*, it is *political*, it is *economic*, and it is *philosophic*. The social component includes freedom of association, movement, and action. The political component includes individual-minority rights, rule of law, limited government, and democratic representative leadership. The economic component includes free enterprise, private property, and free trade. The philosophic component includes freedom of belief and expression.

These disparate components of liberty have one thing in common. They are all concerned with *freedom of the individual* or the prevention of *coercion* against an individual. Together as

70

a comprehensive framework of individual freedom and liberty, these conditions represent a fundamental change in the method of human interaction. This change was from a primary reliance on coercion to a primary reliance on cooperation. This is not merely a reference to the reduction of coercion by political authority, but also the reduction of coercion by fellow citizens and other social forces.

The comprehensive framework of individual freedom needs careful description because it is much more than simple democracy or the overthrow of monarchy. Liberty was defined in the French *Rights of Man* as consisting of "...the power to do whatever is not injurious to others; thus the enjoyment of the natural rights of every man has for its limits only those that assure other members of society the enjoyment of those same rights..."[8] Yet the forces behind the development of the *Rights of Man* were often confused about how to implement such a unique theoretical framework. It is easy to talk about freedom and liberty, but it is much more complicated to design it and implement it in a way that is both practical and successful.

In fact, design and purposeful implementation is at the heart of the matter. The conditions of liberty and freedom are not based on a specific *design of outcome*. These conditions are the rules of engagement, not the rules of outcome. They are the generic bases establishing a rough structural framework of human interaction that then fosters great results. Such results cannot be specifically predicted because they are created by individuals in coordination with other individuals with which they do not conspire, but with which they cooperate for their own interest.

Friedrich Hayek succinctly defined liberty as the "...condition of men in which coercion of some by others is reduced as much as possible in society."[9] The essence of this definition is

---

8. "The Declaration of the Rights of Man and the Citizen." *The Portable Enlightenment Reader*. Ed. Isaac Kramnick. New York: Penguin Books, 1995. 467.

9. Hayek, Friedrich A. *The Constitution of Liberty*. Paperback ed. Chicago: The University of Chicago Press, 1978. 11.

that coercion is reserved for the negative. The collective power of society should be used primarily for *restricting* unnecessary coercion. This is where the aforementioned positive and negative aspects of self-interest come into play. Comprehensive liberty is the protection of the positive (freedom and progression) and the restriction of the negative (coercion and regression).

The use of the term *coercion* here tends to emphasize the negative aspect of the discussion, but the restriction of the negative results in a positive. It results in cooperation and voluntary coordination. Humans are not self-sufficient, so they must interact to survive and thrive. Humans can interact in ways that provide extremely positive results, but only if peace, law, and order are maintained to facilitate voluntary, cooperative interaction. This interaction includes social, political, economic, and philosophic activity. All of the different aspects of life are included and they cannot be easily compartmentalized. This is why it is imperative to emphasize yet again that the liberty being discussed here is not merely political liberty.

This comprehensive view of liberty became the subject of much debate in the seventeenth and eighteenth centuries. It was discussed in political terms within the context of governmental struggles, but was also discussed philosophically by Bacon, Hobbs, Locke, Montesquieu, Voltaire, Hume, Rousseau, Smith, Kant, and others. Kant summarized it in this manner: "Right is the limitation of every man's freedom so that it harmonizes with the freedom of every other man..."[10] Kant then expanded the description to:

> *Therefore; ... I will state the freedom of man as man as a principle for the constitution of the commonwealth in the following formula: No one may force anyone to be happy according to his manner of imagining the well-being of other*

---

10. Kant, Immanuel. "Concerning the Common Saying: This May Be True In Theory but Does Not Apply to Practice." *Basic Writings of Kant*. Ed. Allen W. Wood. New York: The Modern Library, 2001. 420.

men; instead, everyone may seek his happiness in the way that seems good to him as long as he does not infringe on the freedom of others to pursue a similar purpose, when such freedom may coexist with the freedom of every other man according to a possible and general law...[11]

Such a social framework tends to benefit both individuals and society alike. Humans grow faster and stronger under these conditions and their improvements tend to benefit each other with a *positive-sum effect*. The positive-sum effect occurs when many multiples of people benefit beyond merely the ones that appear to be most successful. With proper safeguards of these basic conditions, the effect is the continual improvement of individuals and the result is the greatest good for the greatest number. This result can be seen in the broad conclusions drawn from the investigation of objective measurements of human well-being over time and around the world.

---

11. Kant, Immanuel. "Concerning the Common Saying: This May Be True In Theory but Does Not Apply to Practice." *Basic Writings of Kant.* Ed. Allen W. Wood. New York: The Modern Library, 2001. 420-421.

FIVE

Understanding Libertas

"In early society, originality in life was forbidden and repressed by the fixed rule of life...An ordinary man who wished to strike out a new path, to begin a new and important practice by himself, would have been peremptorily required to abandon his novelties on pain of death; he was deviating, he would be told, from the ordinances imposed by the gods on his nation, and he must not do so to please himself...The quaking bystanders in a superstitious age would soon have slain an isolated bold man in the beginning of his innovations...the desire of man to better his condition — was not then permitted to work; man was required to live as his ancestors had lived...Toleration is of all ideas the most modern..."[1]

—Walter Bagehot, 1872

How Is It Best to Describe This Societal Framework of Personal Freedom?

There is no term in modern usage that clearly portrays the concept of comprehensive liberty. Unfortunately, most people associate the term *liberty* primarily with political freedom. Therefore, for the purposes of clarity, the more complete framework of individual liberty and freedom will be referred to as *Libertas* (pronounced Lee-bear-taz), utilizing the Latin term to be distinguished from the traditional concept of liberty in the English language. A more visual representation of the components listed together is shown on the following chart:

---

1. Bagehot, Walter. *Physics and Politics.* Paperback ed. Chicago: Ivan R. Dee, 1999. 141-144.

Basic Components of Libertas

- **Rule of law**
- **Rights of association, belief, and expression**
- **Limited government and separation of powers**
- **Physical security from aggression**
- **Protection of private property**
- **Free enterprise**
- **Free trade**
- **Enforcement of contracts**
- **Protection against fraud**
- **Democratic representative leadership**

What is the Relative Relationship of Each Component to Another?

These various components are all crucial. They are interrelated and interdependent. It is difficult to segregate them and even more problematic to rank them in importance (with the relative exception of democracy, which will be discussed later). The complex and intricate relationship among the separate components combine to form a state of Libertas which is much more comprehensive than any of the individual components provide separately.

The use of this Latin term is a concern. It is used for the purpose of distinguishing between this broad definition of Libertas and the many traditional thoughts of liberty. It is a gamble to utilize a Latin term because of potential confusion, but the alternative is probably riskier. The alternative would be to choose another word in wide use, such as "liberty" or "freedom" or to form a completely new word for this purpose.

It is of vital importance for us to understand that the Libertas referenced in this work is a comprehensive liberty. It is not restricted. It includes social, economic, and philosophical liberty, in addition to political liberty. Modern scholarship has a tendency to segregate these areas and treat them separately, but they blend together seamlessly because of individual preference. When individuals have considerable freedom, they may choose to utilize that freedom in any of the areas and may decide to alternate back and forth between categories without warning. Libertas constitutes general freedom. The segregation into categories of political, social, economic, and philosophic represents our artificial attempt at classification. It helps us explain the circumstances because we are familiar with this process of categorization.

Most academic discussions of Libertas concentrate on only one of these categories at a time. Yet the categories are interrelated in ways that are difficult to fully appreciate. For instance, economic freedom and free enterprise are merely freedom of association exercised in a way that incorporates the exchange of goods or labor. That same freedom could just as easily have been used to exchange social contact or philosophical ideas. In combination, and only in combination, all of these categories form an immensely powerful force. This powerful force has fundamentally altered the progress of humankind.

These conditions, which seriously began to critically amass in Great Britain in the seventeenth and eighteenth centuries (and later elsewhere), resulted in the process of more individuals gaining exposure to knowledge through books, newspapers, and community conversation. They also resulted in more individuals expanding their skills and attempting new ventures, including those at the very bottom of the social order who left the agricultural fields for the uncertainty of harsh factories. There was more experimentation and more mobility. All of these conditions and many similar aspects of Libertas began to feed on themselves in ways that continued to expand and encourage even further participation. And very little of this has to do with voting and democratic participation in political processes.

Unfortunately, the changes wrought by these conditions did bring extensive disruption in the short term. Large scale changes of all types normally do bring disruption. Substantial agricultural improvements and population growth caused the widespread displacement of agricultural workers. Shopkeepers and artisans grew in number and many new enterprises were conceived, while others became insolvent. These new enterprises began utilizing displaced agricultural workers as hired laborers. The early stages of the Industrial Revolution brought the discontinuance of old industries and the resettlement of large numbers of people into different social and economic relationships. It was an awkward transition from an agricultural-based barter economy to an industrial-based money economy.

The temporary conditions associated with this stage were sometimes ugly and disconcerting, but they were temporary. And they were temporary because the conditions were largely voluntary and they were based on cooperation. The voluntary choices in these early industrial times were much more limited than we have today. We often look upon these severe limitations as if they were not cooperation. This misunderstanding is only created by the comparison to a later time. Those early times may appear dismal to our modern eyes, but they represented societal progress in action. The normal process of striving caused continual improvement and the outcome was substantially positive, even though the outcome was not planned in advance.

Why Has Libertas Been Such a Powerful Transforming Force, Capable of Altering the Progress of Humankind?

The structure of Libertas allows individuals (in aggregate) to create more, to experiment more, to grow more in their experience of life, to produce more, and to think more. The human being is, by far, the most capable and productive organism on the planet. No other living organism comes close to the capability of our species. Yet, every individual, every one of us, is a work in progress. Our ability to combine together in productive ways is very fragile and tentative.

It is not as if the ancient civilizations were based solely on coercion. No large-scale organization, beyond the size of a prison, can be successful by relying only on coercive force. Those civilizations were based, however, *primarily* on coercion, with only limited amounts of Libertas, even in Greece and Rome. The primary force of the emperor and/or the ruling classes was coercion. The coercion used by ancient leaders may have been indirect, in that it was based on legend or superstition, but it was still coercive in nature. The emperors and rulers of the most successful civilizations flourished because they inculcated the populace in ways that did not require the daily force of violence to operate. They were the leaders who could most effectively coordinate large-scale activity for productive purpose, but they still relied primarily on coercion.

The ancient civilizations were more successful than other lesser-known societies of their time because they had resourceful leaders and leadership structures. These leaders had designed or inherited social structures that allowed their personal mental power — or the mental power of their elite clique — to coordinate the activity of their subjects in relatively productive ways. This productivity did not take full advantage of the brain power available in those societies, but was limited mostly to the brain power of the controlling elites of the civilization. Many of the people were fully or partially subjugated. Their productiveness was limited to mostly that of pack animals used almost exclusively for brute force.

The primary advantage of the human species is our brain. The use of our brain is maximized when we are given the freedom to pursue our own interest, while simultaneously restricted from coercing others. Maximum freedom for individuals allows us to cooperate in ways we cannot anticipate or fully plan. When we cooperate in an open condition of freedom, we begin creating a dynamic positive-sum effect. This starts as individualized self-interest, then is transformed through the open market of ideas and economics into progress that produces far more than the individual efforts could have achieved in a coercive environment.

In a cooperative environment, we are able to specialize in what we do best and in what fits our individual attributes and circumstances. Sometimes that results in temporary displacement, but we continue to strive. We are motivated by individual self-interest to advance ourselves. We are able to grow personally and learn from our mistakes. We are able to be more flexible and react to changes more effectively. All of this allows us to collectively produce dramatically more than we would have under coercive direction where individual motivation is subdued and where collective coordination is limited to the brain power of the few who rule us and where flexibility is minimized.

There is a tremendous positive-sum effect to this cooperative environment. Production (economic or non-economic) is much more effective when Libertas is in place. It is imperative to understand that the collective product of society is not a static sum that must be *distributed* according to some formula. The collective product of society is the sum of the productiveness of individuals; it is earned by people. The total grows as people increase their productivity. The relative amount of production is determined by the overall structure under which those individuals operate.

Under the opposite conditions, the *coercion* of people generally results in zero-sum or even negative-sum outcomes. Even the great achievement of the Pyramids (and similar ancient successes) was the direct result of the labor of multitudes that was taken away from their ability to build a better life for themselves and their descendents. The temporary productivity orchestrated by the elite Pharaoh leaders created phenomenal artifacts. Unfortunately, it did not allow for a widespread growth of individual productiveness. It did not take advantage of individual human motivation. The ultimate result was not broad human progress.

On the other hand, a structure of Libertas and cooperation results in a positive-sum outcome. The collective product is much larger under a system of Libertas. Our productiveness is enhanced under Libertas by all of the advantages previously discussed. We are motivated by the positive and negative consequences inherent in Libertas. We are able to learn and grow from the experience of our successes and failures. We are able to change and be flexible based upon momentary circumstances. All of these advantages work together to create a collective product far greater than if these individual brains were minimized by coercive force. It is a positive-sum effect. This positive-sum effect is crucial to our understanding of history.

Was Accumulation a Greater Cause of Progress Than Libertas?

In some respects, the effect of Libertas on prosperity and human improvement has been too obvious, so obvious that it becomes unrecognizable background noise by blending into the landscape of history. This has tended to create the misconception that the recent progress of mankind was inevitable even without the conditions of Libertas. One of the very common misunderstandings within our complex world is the mistaken belief that *historical accumulation* is the primary root cause of the progressive pattern of history. This is simply not true. It has a secondary impact, but it is not the primary root cause.

This concept of historical accumulation is readily apparent. Every generation enjoys the fruits of previous generations. On the physical side, there are inventions, public infrastructure, roads, bridges, ports, machines, equipment, buildings, etc., all accumulating and adding to the value of future generations. On the intellectual side, there is knowledge of all types that certainly adds cumulative value to the thought and inventive powers of future generations.

This is what most people refer to as *progress*. It is the cumulative result of the societal adaptive process. Libertas takes greater advantage of this phenomenon because it includes dramatically more people in the process. This includes more people at higher levels of thought and production with the freedom to produce more and obtain the benefits thereof.

Some people skip the impact of freedom and Libertas. They chronicle the explosion of *progress*. They envision that such *progress* is self-generating and would have occurred at the same preordained rate regardless of the societal structures in place. In this mistaken vision, inventiveness and productivity continue progressing without regard for the creative, super-achieving individuals and the common hardworking individuals who are the impetus behind such progress. Not considered are the effects on individuals of social frameworks that either take advantage of human nature or work against it. Also not considered are the results of the positive-sum effects as compared to traditional zero-sum coercive environments.

Explanations of this misconception of *inevitable progress* usually highlight major inventions as the root cause of modern progress. In these reports, it is the discovery of the scientific method, the printing press, Newtonian physics, the steam engine, the assembly line, or similar creative efforts as the root cause of the explosion of modern human progress. While significant inventions are important and needed, there have been inventions throughout history. The printing press, gunpowder, and additional important discoveries were invented in other civilizations before they were discovered in Europe. It is not the inventions that created progress. It is the *people* that created the inventions and the progress. The inventions were created and used by people. The conditions under which these people interact began to change significantly in the past few centuries. The change in those conditions is the cause of the progress. The inventions are merely one of the side effects of the changing conditions.

In other reports, some scholars highlight the unique advantage of climate, the availability of coal as a fuel supply, or other such geographical features of Europe that are seen as the root cause of modern human progress. Like the explanation of spectacular inventions, the emphasis on geography fails to concentrate on the most important ingredient in the mix, that being humans. There may have been geographical advantages, but the conditions of Libertas were necessary for *humans* to more fully utilize those advantages.

Professor Diamond's conclusions (discussed on page 25) about the reasons for European supremacy at the time of the conquistadors are quite plausible. The geographical advantages on the Eurasian land mass were substantial. These are good reasons why Eurasia developed the advantages of guns, germs, and steel instead of Africa, the Americas, or Oceania. However, the explanation is most valid in explaining the developmental differences up until the sixteenth century. Our primary focus here is to concentrate on what followed. It includes some vexing questions. Why did the temporary European advantages of the sixteenth century create an explosion of prosperity in the following centuries? And why was this spectacular development led by Great Britain instead of Spain, the home of the original conquistadors and recipient of the precious metal treasures of the great American civilizations (Inca, Aztec, and Maya)?

There was a difference in this new civilization, which began in Great Britain. The difference was in the way it utilized the advantages of inventions and geography in more productive ways. The difference in the modern example is the advent of more comprehensive — but not absolute — Libertas. This is a superior method of human interaction that encourages extra inventions. It then continually adds to them. It also takes greater advantage of geography and natural resources. More importantly, the condition of Libertas utilizes inventions and natural resources much more extensively for the benefit of virtually every human living under most conditions of Libertas and even some living outside of such conditions.

83

What Has Been the Most Important Invention Since the Advent of the Civilized Age Five Thousand Years Ago?

There is one invention in the past five thousand years that is closely associated with establishing the critical mass of Libertas in the modern age. It is the one invention that most often gets confused as the cause of Libertas or modern progress. It is Johannes Gutenberg's printing press and the innovative use of movable type. The development and adoption of the Gutenberg printing press in Europe, starting in the 1450s, had enormous impact. This technology was used by the societies in Europe in ways that could not have been anticipated.

The printing press accelerated the trajectory of the growth of Libertas. It allowed for the spread of new thoughts and the proliferation of knowledge to a much wider percentage of the population and began the slow extension of literacy. This new technology provided a liberating effect. The forces of Libertas were already growing throughout northwestern Europe prior to the printing press, especially in Great Britain, but this new technology had a dramatically positive effect.

The conclusion that the printing press alone could not produce Libertas or a Human Productivity Revolution is evident in the fact that similar devices were first invented and used in Korea and China without the same effect as in Europe. However, the use of printed material in Europe helped expand a phenomenon that was already growing. The press helped expand the amount of education available to a widening group of citizens. This, in turn, helped create a greater diversity of thought and discussion. The result became a cycle of increasing knowledge and the sharing of that knowledge to ever widening audiences. The acceleration of the amassing of the components of Libertas was a natural outcome. The advent of the printing press proved to be a key lubricant in the growth of Libertas. The components of Libertas grew much faster after the spread of the printing press and they tended to grow in the very areas that accepted the widest use of the press.

The conditions of Europe after 1000 A.D. were already conducive to the establishment of Libertas. The early traditions of common law in England are examples of the growth of Libertas in the region. The dissolution of the Roman Empire had left numerous disparate societies in the region with minimal centralized control and coercion. The vacuum was filled by emerging nation-states that began the process of establishing centralized control within their own territory. These emerging nation-states were highly competitive with one another. The competitiveness, combined with conditions of relative lack of central control, caused the emerging monarchs to utilize numerous tactics to establish centralized control of their realms. This included the sanctioning of a certain amount of decentralized local control as exemplified by the concession of King John to the barons in the Magna Carta of 1215. Some of these conditions eventually — and often excruciatingly slowly — led to the creation of broader individual liberties throughout much of northwestern Europe.

The introduction of the Gutenberg printing press in the mid-1400s allowed the relatively slow progress of Libertas to explode into an expanded Renaissance and a new Reformation, eventually culminating in the Enlightenment. This explosion of thought and change, tremendously facilitated by the Gutenberg printing press, resulted in the attraction of the critical mass of Libertas. This represented the amount of Libertas that was necessary to release unprecedented human potential, kick off the Industrial Revolution, and begin the process of propagating the conditions of Libertas around the world.

SIX

The Ultimate Proof

"The history of the world is none other than the progress of the consciousness of Freedom; a progress whose development according to the necessity of its nature, it is our business to investigate."[1]

— G.W.F. Hegel, 1820

Can the Impact of Libertas Be Proven?

History is a social science, not a physical science. It is impossible to create perfectly controlled case studies of historical analysis as can be provided in most physical sciences. We must therefore rely on historical cases that provide the most viable evidence of the causes and results of social alternatives. We must also guard against leaping to conclusions based on concurrent factors that may appear to have a causal relationship, but actually are unrelated other than by coincidence.

The impact of Libertas has been regularly and incontrovertibly proven by the difference in progress between nation-states with significant Libertas and those without. A common example used to illustrate this difference in progress with and without significant Libertas is the comparison between the United States and the USSR during the period from 1920 to 1990. Although this comparison provides a reasonably good example, there are widespread differences between the starting points of the two countries that are cause for some observers to question the impact of Libertas in this comparison.

1. Hegel, Georg Wilhelm Friedrich. *The Philosophy of History.* New York: Dover Publications, 1956. 19.

However, there are other more exact comparisons that indisputably illustrate the impact of Libertas. The two most telling examples are that of East Germany and West Germany from 1945 to 1989 and that of North Korea and South Korea from 1955 to 2005. An even larger and longer example is the comparison between North America and South America between 1600 and 1975. Even though Libertas was not completely evolved in West Germany, South Korea, and North America, it is clear that Libertas was much more comprehensive in these locations than was the case in East Germany, North Korea, and South America during those same time periods.

The difference was their differing degrees of Libertas. It was not the innate character, culture, or intelligence of their citizens, but their basic framework of human interaction. There is no other logical explanation for the incredible disparity of outcome. These examples offer much more than mere coincidental factors. They offer case study results that are almost perfectly controlled environments of experimentation. It would be much more tenuous to draw conclusions and much less *self-evident* if these natural experiments were not available to us.

Such was the case when the Industrial Revolution first began and other societies had the ability to copy the physical inventions and methods from Great Britain, but they did not understand that those inventions and methods were of little advantage without the social conditions of Libertas. Such was also the case when Karl Marx and other Anti-Libertas prophets admired the technological and material progress of the Industrial Revolution but were impatient with the temporarily unequal outcome of the prosperity. They mistakenly believed you could discontinue Libertas and yet maintain the substantial material progress through illiberal elite management.

Despite the clear success of Libertas, some observers concentrate attention on the gaps or the lack of certain liberties within the nations exemplary of the most Libertas. They highlight the imperfections — of which there were many — as if these imperfections somehow disprove the hypothesis. These imperfections are concerning, but they in no way negate the fact that, in comparison and on average, the substantial difference in Libertas is clearly the deciding factor of outcome.

It may be true that the South Korea of Syngman Rhee was a partially illiberal autocracy, but that does not negate the fact that the country later liberalized substantially. More importantly, it does not negate the fact that North Korea was a brutal totalitarian regime and thoroughly illiberal throughout the period.

It may also be true that there were grossly illiberal exceptions in North America, slavery being the obvious egregious example. Yet, this does not negate the fact that North America (excluding Mexico) had substantially more Libertas for the common person than did the colonies and countries of South America. North America during that time period was comprised mostly of societies based on individual freedom, while South America was based mostly on an inequitable hacienda society that resembled serfdom.

The case for Libertas, as shown in these clear cases of more-Libertas versus less-Libertas, is overwhelming to the point of being self-evident. Our best historical case studies, all of which were only completed in the past few decades, prove the point. They prove the incredible power of Libertas. Both the successes and failures in these examples had equal opportunity to take advantage of historical accumulation. The structures of Libertas use the most effective method of human interaction to take best advantage of historical accumulation, while the structures of anti-Libertas squandered the same opportunity. This very basic problem of squandered opportunity still exists everywhere in the world where destitution and despair reigns.

All of this is not meant to suggest that Libertas is the only factor in human outcome around the world. There are certainly other factors. Geography remains one of those factors, not only in pre-modern times, but even today. There is sufficient evidence to suggest that impoverished nations in tropical zones, particularly those without ample seaports, are at a geographical disadvantage to most of the rest of the world. However, the geography of a nation is not a humanly controllable variable. The amount of human Libertas is controllable. The creation of conditions of Libertas or Anti-Libertas is the most important controllable variable in the outcome of the long-term improvement of human conditions in any nation.

What Effect Does Historical Accumulation Have?

As with most misunderstandings, there is a grain of truth in the one about *inevitable progress* that helps perpetuate the misunderstanding. First, historical accumulation can be a positive force even in a social framework devoid of Libertas, although dramatically less positive than it would be in a more effective framework. This includes a dimension of reliance on foreigners and forefathers. Even societies that have very little Libertas have access to the accumulated intellectual capital of other societies and past generations that were benefited by Libertas. Second, historical accumulation is certainly a secondary factor in the progressive historical pattern of modern history. Historical accumulation is a primary reason why the pattern is steeply progressing in Libertas-based nations rather than merely ascending. Assuming a relatively strong and consistent framework of Libertas, the factor of historical accumulation creates a condition of advancement that is not linear, but exponential, and is therefore speeding up in a manner that is irreversible, short of some earth-shattering catastrophe.

This is also the reason why Libertas-based nations continue to get so much wealthier in comparison to Anti-Libertas nations. It is not because this is a zero-sum event. The impoverished Anti-Libertas nations are not impoverished because of the actions of the wealthier Libertas nations. They are impoverished because they fail to take advantage of the human capacity within their own society. While the Anti-Libertas nations are squandering their human potential, the Libertas-based nations are racing further ahead and the disparity between rich and poor nations continues to widen. The gap between the richest and the poorest nation will widen for as long as any one nation continues to reject Libertas. Such a nation will remain at a level near destitution, while the progress of the nation with the greatest Libertas will increase exponentially. Although this sounds pessimistic, the great news is that more and more nations are joining the club of human progress and fewer remain in the depressed conditions of Anti-Libertas.

The advent of Libertas set the stage for dramatic patterns of advancement, and then it was the effect of historical accumulation—along with the continued evolution of Libertas—that caused the pattern to progressively gain speed. This is why most visual representations of the historical pattern of human improvement, regardless of the component being measured, almost always maintain a similar shape in graph form. These representations show a steep and dramatic improvement in the past two hundred years (or more recently for newer adherents of Libertas), compared to the previous five thousand years of civilization. This includes objective measurements of life expectancy, health, food/clothing/shelter, peace, security, leisure time, and freedom. The population graph on page fifty-five is visually representative of the curve for all of the individual components.

What Detailed Research is Currently Available That Tracks the Increasingly Improved Conditions of Libertas Over the Years?

An analysis based on historical documents and accounts can give us a reasonably accurate portrayal of the level of Libertas in different countries and different times throughout recorded history. The eventual establishment of a critical mass of Libertas in Europe after 1500 leads us to concentrate on the slow gathering of that critical mass. This history of Libertas will be chronicled in Chapter Nine.

The components of Libertas are generally well known. The amassing of these components follows the path previously discussed. They first reached a critical mass in Great Britain, then elsewhere in northwestern Europe, the English-speaking British colonies, and eventually throughout much of the world

This trend is obvious, even if specific measurements before the twentieth century are sometimes difficult to find. Fortunately, our measurements of the most recent thirty years are much more precise. Numerous professional research studies have become available since the early 1970s that provide annual statistical ratings of most of the components of Libertas. These include two studies that provide a very comprehensive measurement of Libertas when they are combined together. One study is *The Annual Survey of Political and Civil Liberties,* which includes two statistical ratings (political liberty and civil liberty), and is published annually as *Freedom In The World.* The second study is a survey of economic liberty published as *Economic Freedom of the World.* Both of these highly respected annual reports have undertaken extensive research across the globe in the detailed components of Libertas.

The findings of these studies present us with evidence that is not at all surprising, yet extremely confirming. Upon examining the 102 countries (with greater than 5 million population in 2003) that existed throughout the time period of 1970 – 2000, only fifteen were rated highly in political, civic, and economic freedom throughout the entire time period.[2] These countries are also *exactly* the top fifteen nations (over 5 million in population) in *gross national income per capita* in 2003.[3] The findings show that the fifteen large countries with the most consistent Libertas are the fifteen large countries with the most prosperity. There

---

2. Sources: Freedom House. *Freedom in the World 2004.* New York: Freedom House, 2004. Gwartney, James, and Robert Lawson. *Economic Freedom of the World 2004 Annual Report.* Vancouver: The Fraser Institute, 2004. Category includes nations of size that rated 5.0 or above in economic rating (scoring system is ascending) and rated FREE in both Political Freedom and Civic Freedom.

3. Source: *Economic Freedom in the World 2004* (as above), based on information from the World Bank. Also includes only nations with a population greater than 5,000,000 in 2003.

are no exceptions. There is an absolute and direct correlation!

The countries on the list of the Elite 15 are familiar and expected. They include: Australia, Austria, Belgium, Canada, Denmark, Finland, France, Germany, Italy, Japan, Netherlands, Sweden, Switzerland, United Kingdom, and United States. These countries include the traditional stalwart Libertas-based nations whose liberal traditions date back to the early nineteenth century or beyond, along with the rehabilitated Axis powers of World War II. The relationship between Libertas and *well-being* is obvious from this data.

A more extensive review of the data proves the same point. Norway and Ireland would be added to the list if we included nations with populations between one and five million. That would create a new list of an Elite 17 with the exact same features. The correlation goes both ways. The countries with the most consistent Libertas are the countries with the most prosperity and vice versa.

All of the Elite 15 or 17 countries rate highly in both economic and social freedom. We must go beyond the Elite 15 or 17 to find any interesting anomalies. One is Singapore and another is New Zealand.[4] Although Singapore rates relatively high and evenly on prosperity and freedom, their freedom was not evenly divided between economic and social freedom. Singapore consistently rated at the very highest levels of economic freedom, but rated rather poorly on social freedom. In an opposite way, New Zealand was rated very high in social freedom, but rated rather poorly on economic freedom during the 1970s and 1980s (although they more recently have improved to one the very highest economic freedom rankings in the world). Both Singapore and New Zealand are very prosperous, even though they each rank slightly below the prosperity levels of the Elite 15 or 17. Although we should hesitate to draw conclusions from the examples of countries with populations under five million,

---

4. It should be noted here that Hong Kong is not included in this list because it is now formally within the authority of China.

there is evidence to support an obvious and straightforward assumption that *economic* freedom is more important than *social* freedom in the impact on prosperity. Singapore, in particular, has been used as a theoretical model of how to build prosperity within a relatively rigid and illiberal social structure.

A secondary observation about the data has to do with the issue of *timing*. There are nations (of size) today that have scored higher in Libertas than some of the Elite 15 in recent years, but they did not score as consistently over the entire 30-year time period. They also are not in the current top 15 in per capita income. The tradition of Libertas in most of the Elite 15 nations goes back hundreds of years. Even the defeated Axis powers on the list had some strong experience with Libertas long before their illiberal manifestations in World War II. This should lead us to conclude that there is a relatively long lag time for Libertas (newly established) to lead to increased prosperity.

We certainly do know from historical experience that many people become impatient with this lag time and attempt illiberal short cuts. Such attempts have often proved to be devastating and counter-productive. However, the most encouraging trend observable by reviewing these new statistical data sources is the rapid and broad growth of Libertas around the world in the most recent years.

Actually, "rapid" and "broad" are probably understated adjectives. The global growth of Libertas in the past fifty years — in comparison to even the previous 450 years — is phenomenal. It is a trend of huge proportion that receives precious little attention in our age of 24-hour news coverage. This trend will be discussed in detail in Part Five. The implications of the trend have led to much of the unbridled optimism shared throughout this book. But first, let us turn to the human dynamics that cause Libertas to be so important in the progress of our species.

PART THREE

Human Causes

SEVEN

The Green Zone
Between Liberty and Slavery

"A man who chooses between drinking a glass of milk and a glass of ...cyanide does not choose between two beverages; he chooses between life and death. A society that chooses between capitalism and socialism does not choose between two social systems; it chooses between social cooperation and the disintegration of society. Socialism is not an alternative to capitalism; it is an alternative to any system under which men can live as human beings."[1]

— Ludwig von Mises, 1949

A View from Within a Green Haven Between Libertas and Slavery:

You could consider it a national park or a special wildlife preserve, although it was never designed for such a purpose. This "wildlife preserve" is approximately 1.5 miles wide and 155 miles long. This long strip of land had once endured through centuries of agricultural production and had suffered immeasurable destruction through wartime. Now it has enjoyed over fifty years practically untouched by humans.

This *green zone* now holds one of the richest ecological bounties anywhere in northeast Asia. Stretching from the Yellow Sea to the Sea of Japan, the zone is home to hundreds of different animal species and thousands of plant species. These include

---

1. Mises, Ludwig von. *Human Action*. Scholar's ed. Auburn: The Ludwig von Mises Institute, 1998. 676.

many species that are endangered in other parts of northeast Asia. It runs through the Dae-am-san and Dae-u-san Mountains, includes Hwajinpo Lake, and holds the highest elevation of swampland in the region. The Major Yongneup and Minor Yongneup Swamps are virtual treasure chests of biodiversity.

The area is preserved without immediate threat from developers or encroaching farmers. There is no manufacturing or traffic congestion. In fact, humans do not regularly enter the *green zone* except for rare circumstances and only under careful supervision. This sort of ecological isolation is very unusual for any inhabitable locale with a longstanding history of human cultivation. The fields have been left to return to the wild and the old dirt roads are hardly even distinguishable after more than fifty years of peace.

Peace, that is, for the plants and animals. The humans are still technically at war. The *green zone* is more formally known as the De-Militarized Zone (DMZ) that separates the Republic of Korea (South) from the Democratic People's Republic of Korea (North). The war officially started in 1950 and it has not yet ended. A cease-fire was established and the DMZ was created in 1953 to serve as a one-mile temporary buffer between the troops. It has become a seemingly permanent "no-man's-land" and now the temporary buffer has become an inadvertent ecological experiment. This was not the intention of the individuals originally responsible for creating the DMZ. It was an accident, an unintended consequence. The plants and animals have taken advantage of that accident to show the incredible resilience of nature by bouncing back quickly and flourishing in this unplanned "park."

Humans are also part of ecology. The DMZ happens to be one of the great unintended human experiments of all time. It is an experiment that shows both the amazing resilience of humans and the overwhelming importance of their method of interaction. The DMZ is the dividing line between two very distinct methods of human interaction. The results of the experiment are dramatic.

The Green Zone Between Liberty and Slavery

Korea is a beautiful country. It has over four thousand years of civilized history and a wealth of culture. Unfortunately, the Koreans were overshadowed throughout much of that history by their larger and more aggressive neighbors, most specifically China, Mongolia, and Japan. Although that interaction included some positive influence such as the Confucian tradition, it also involved more detrimental and brutal invasions and subjugations. The Japanese invasion in the late 1500s and the Mongol invasion of the 1600s set the stage for the Koreans to shut themselves off from the rest of the world and thus they became known as *The Hermit Kingdom*.

The Japanese began a more modern domination of Korea late in the nineteenth century that continued through World War II and included unspeakable acts of cruelty. The influence of liberal democracies elsewhere in the world during that time was not helpful. Great Britain and the United States acquiesced to Japanese domination of Korea at the end of both the Sino-Japanese War and Russo-Japanese War. These were some of the darkest examples of the diplomatic strategy of *realpolitik* that began with Bismarck/Metternich and peaked with Nixon/Kissinger. Korea became a pawn in world politics. After World War II, the torch of Korean interference was passed on from Japan to the Soviet Union and the United States.

When the USSR overran the peninsula in 1945, the same philosophy of political "realism" convinced the liberal allies to agree to a division of the country along the 38th parallel. The Soviets were to influence the north and the Americans were to influence the south. The wishes of the Koreans certainly did not appear to be of concern. It was the beginning of the Cold War and the circumstances were to turn very hot in 1950.

After more than half a century, many people forget the importance and the scale of the Korean War. It was the first large-scale confrontation between the new competing superpowers. It was costly and it ended in stalemate. Westerners tend to think about the fatalities in terms of the non-Korean UN forces, which numbered less than forty thousand. However, the total war fatalities exceeded four *million*. Of these, three million were Korean (military and civilian on both sides), representing ten percent of the entire population.

The Korean War devastated the peninsula. The competing troops volleyed back and forth across the nation a number of times, literally scorching the earth. The populace that survived was left in ruins. With those conditions, in 1953 the DMZ was established, leaving nature to repair the ruins within that thin strip of land and leaving humans to repair the ruins to the north and to the south. The grand experiment was inadvertently created because the humans on opposite sides of the DMZ ended up utilizing vastly different methods of human interaction.

Now, in the new millennium, the Republic of Korea is a liberal democracy with a government and laws very similar to those in Europe, North America, or Japan. The citizens enjoy widespread liberty, despite having had to struggle through early decades of various regime types. They have worked hard and they have prospered phenomenally during the past two generations.

The results in North Korea represent the polar opposite of the south. The Democratic People's Republic of Korea is a brutal dictatorship with a totalitarian government. The citizens have virtually no liberty. Their level of malnourishment is hardly much of an improvement over the hardships experienced at the end of the war.

The difference in the level of human achievement between the two countries is stark. The Gross Domestic Product (GDP) per capita is fourteen times higher in the south. Infant mortality is over three times higher in the north. The percentage of the GDP required in agriculture is ten times higher in the north. It is as if the north is still living in pre-modern times and the south is an integral part of the twenty-first century. The Republic of Korea is in the top ten percent of the nations of the world in GDP and North Korea is in the bottom ten percent. Stark difference indeed!

The disparity was not created by a difference in "starting

points." It was not created by a contrast in the historical tradition of the people prior to 1945. It was not created by a variation in the homogeneity or genetic makeup of the people. Instead, it was created almost exclusively by the difference between utilizing Libertas or Anti-Libertas as the guiding factor in human interaction after the country became divided. The reasons for the overwhelming success of Libertas will be discussed in detail throughout the following chapter. For now, it is valuable to consider this unusual human experiment that created a thin green zone between liberty and slavery.

EIGHT

The Advantage of Libertas

"The effective limitation of power is the most important problem of social order."[1]

— Friedrich Hayek, 1981

Why Has Libertas Proven to Be the Most Effective Social Framework?

We have seen a dramatic advancement of human progress and we have identified the root cause as Libertas. However, there is still the underlying question of why Libertas has proven to be the most effective social framework. What is it about Libertas that allows it to be so successful? Why is Libertas more effective than the Anti-Libertas alternatives? Why is cooperation more effective than coercion? Why is freedom more effective than subjugation? The answers to these questions require an examination into the psychology of humans individually and why we interact in different ways.

What Is the Importance of Human Interaction?

Both individual self-interest and the overall interest of humankind are ultimately facilitated through *human interaction*. Thus, the structure of human interaction is the most important element in understanding universal history. How efficiently and effectively human interaction is conducted determines the

---

1. Hayek, Friedrich A. *Law , Legislation and Liberty Volume 3.* Phoenix ed. Chicago: The University of Chicago Press, 1979. 128.

amount of ultimate self-interest (therefore also humankind-interest) that is achieved.

The history of human interaction is one of the primary focuses throughout this book. As astutely noted by Will Durant, Socrates had long ago identified the two underlying principles necessitating human interaction. First, humans are not self-sufficient and, second, humans differ from one another.[2] These are important observations. In the first case, we need each other; it is hard to survive on our own and it is impossible to achieve advancement on our own. In the second case, we are different from one another; we have different capabilities and different motivations.

The first basic concept requires humans to interact in order to accomplish sustainable improvement in the well-being of ourselves and, ultimately, the species as a whole. The second basic concept requires that we interact in ways which maximize our individual capabilities and motivations. These concepts and subsequent requirements may sound simplistic to us in the twenty-first century, but they have bedeviled our ancestors for all of recorded history.

The definition of human interaction is very simply how we work with or against one another to achieve our self-interest. Human interaction involves the utilization of either cooperation or coercion in our effort to gain the services of one another for the purpose of sustaining and advancing sufficiency. Cooperation and coercion manifest themselves in familiar forms such as peace or war, freedom or slavery, trade or confiscation, religious freedom or religious intolerance, free speech or restrained discussion, etc. This dichotomy between cooperation and coercion is the core aspect of all human interaction. It is the basis for understanding universal history.

2. Durant, Will. *The Story of Philosophy*. First Pocket Books ed. New York: Pocket Books, 1953.

What is the Basic Motivation Behind Human Interaction?

The tenets of biology teach us that all animals have an instinct for survival. Humans certainly contain that instinct, but humans have an instinct beyond mere survival. It is an instinct to continually improve and thrive. This desire to thrive was aptly characterized by Adam Smith in *An Inquiry Into the Nature and Causes of the Wealth of Nations*, when he said that humans have a "desire of bettering our condition, a desire which, though generally calm and dispassionate, comes with us from the womb, and never leaves us till we go into the grave..."[3] This instinct can be characterized as the instinct of *thrival*. In this vein, human self-interest is motivated by two basic instincts: survival and thrival. The aggregate result of these instincts by all humans is a constant adaptive process. The aggregate adaptive process is not a conscious phenomenon, it is not a chosen method of humanity, but it does represent the cumulative effect of individual action.

The aspect of *thrival* can be interpreted many ways. Hegel and others describe this as the desire mostly for recognition. This characterization is accurate to a degree, but such a description might not be clear enough. The *thrival* referenced here is very expansive. It starts with attention on the basic goals of self-interest previously listed; thriving in the areas of life expectancy, health, food-clothing-shelter, security, leisure time, and freedom. It may then expand to include the desire to thrive in the economy, arts, sciences, theology, or philosophy. It may include the desire to thrive in one's own eyes or in the eyes of others. It may include rational desires or irrational (in the eyes of others) desires. It may include the strong influence of morality or it may not. Most dynamically, it is not only individualized to every separate human being alive, but it is also changing every minute of every day as each individual changes.

3. Smith, Adam. *An Inquiry Into the Nature and Causes of The Wealth of Nations.* 1994 Modern Library ed. New York: The Modern Library, 1994. 372.

The two basic instincts of humans can create two very different dynamic functions of human change, although they are often confused. One is usually referred to as *survival of the fittest*[4] and the other should be named the *thrival of nearly everyone*. The concept of *thrival of nearly everyone* is dramatically different than *survival of the fittest* because the latter is a zero-sum game, while the former can be a positive-sum game.[5] This is a very important distinction.

The *survival* of the fittest generally implies the extinction of the less fit and the survival of the more fit. The *thrival* of nearly everyone generally implies an ever-widening improvement. Depending on the political-economic-social structure in place, the process of thrival is capable of not only improving the circumstances of individuals who thrive the most, but also improving the circumstances of virtually every individual. Even the people who thrive the least can enjoy a residual improvement effect from their counterparts who have been more successful at thriving. However, the opportunity to thrive and the residual benefits of thrival depend in part on a structure of human interaction that takes advantage of the natural instinct to thrive and to be self-interested.

The positive, residual effect that is possible from the thriving of others can be illustrated by the example that even the multitudes of people that thrive at an average or below average level enjoy the benefit of a great scientific or medical discovery by a high achiever. This is merely an easily recognizable example. There are many more examples. The most common is that of standard employment. The employer attempts to thrive by hiring and paying the most appropriate workers at the best price. The workers attempt to thrive by seeking the highest wage for their skills, usually entertaining job offers from nu-

---

4. Although this phrase is usually associated with Charles Darwin, it was actually coined by Herbert Spencer and was not used by Darwin.

5. This concept was the central point in the fascinating book titled *Nonzero* (meaning: not zero-sum) by Robert Wright. Wright, Robert. *Nonzero: The Logic of Human Destiny*. First ed. New York: Pantheon Books, 2000.

merous other potential employers even while working for an existing employer. Some of these workers eventually move on to begin their own enterprise. Another common example of the residual effect involves the ever-widening availability of new products at lower prices that are created by entrepreneurs but are available to everyone. The examples of the shared benefit created by the selfish thrival instinct are endless.

One very important historical perspective involves this thrival instinct. It became the instinct of most significance once humans progressed beyond the hunter-gatherer epoch. It became even more so once humans progressed into our current era of Libertas with unprecedented peace and prosperity. Thus, the concepts of *thriving* and human progress are inextricably linked and must be more carefully considered.

What Are the Building Blocks of These Instincts of Human Nature?

The issue of what constitutes human nature has become controversial in recent times. The controversy involves a conflict between those who maintain that cultural environment influences the basic human nature of individuals and those who support a significant influence of genetics or heredity. Current evidence suggests both aspects contribute heavily to the basic human nature and motivation of individuals. The amount of each influence is likely to provide a very lively debate for centuries to come.

The very discussion of hereditary characteristics of human nature frightens many people at this time. There is some hesitancy in acknowledging the influence of genetics in the equation because of the past abuse of genetics by madmen who espoused theories of racial superiority. This hesitancy is understandable, but the influence of heredity has been proven as a fact and it need not lead to gross misuse.

The influence of genetics in physical characteristics is obvious. Genetics are the primary determinant of eye color, height, hair types, skin complexion, etc. Heredity determines the physical starting point of a human being at conception, including initiating the building process of the brain. External physical influences, such as nutrition, begin to influence the brain and the whole body development throughout the prenatal cycle. After birth, the development of the brain continues, including components that affect preferences toward action-based characteristics.

The human brain is an incredibly complex organ that physically controls human thought and action. Aside from the genetic starting points, each and every intricate brain is affected moment by moment from birth to death by both physical and mental (environmental) influences. The physical aspects include coming in contact with actual physical impact such as bumps, fractures, and surgery, as well as the chemical reactions of ingested chemicals. The environmental or cultural influences are obvious and substantial, most importantly including childhood development, but continuing until death through all interaction encountered by the individual.

The complexity of each individual brain on earth is phenomenal. When we understand that these subsequent physical and environmental factors can change every minute of every day, we begin to appreciate the overwhelming complexity of the individual and of individual motivation. This makes any one brain or individual absolutely impossible to completely understand. Yet this complexity just describes one individual. Once we multiply that by the number of living humans, the complexity mounts towards the unimaginable.

The environmental influences on an individual extend far beyond merely the contact with other humans, such as family, peers, and the larger society. The environment includes the often-overlooked factor of non-human interaction. This consists of the interaction with weather, geology, astronomical events, and non-human creatures interacting in ways that affect the individual and each other. The wind blows, storms brew, the earth quakes, volcanoes erupt, mountains slide, rain causes flooding, droughts ravish the land, an eclipse occurs, sunspots erupt, meteors crash, ants adapt to insecticides, flocks of birds change migration patterns, a snake decides to strike, a pet becomes rabid, and on and on until our individual brains are incapable of fully understanding the complexity of all these chaotic and mostly uncontrollable, even unpredictable, events as they interact with billions of humans also being effected by genetics and human environment at the same time.

This indescribable complexity will be very important later as we attempt to understand the ability of humans to predict, plan, and control activity within the world. It also helps us understand basic or average human nature and human motivation. Although the complexity of life highlighted above is enormous, it is not ignored. From the standpoint of human thought, it is the basis of all spirituality and philosophy. From the standpoint of academics, it is a primary focus within many disciplines and it has spawned the relatively new disciplines of chaos theory, game theory, and sociobiology.

How Do Individuals Improve Their Condition?

People and societies make progress and thrive through adaptation to the environment. This concept is not referencing a Darwinist *survival of the fittest* genetic adaptation, but rather a more simplistic day-to-day mental adaptation based upon self-interested decision-making caused by an innate desire to survive and thrive. This distinction has everything to do with the difference between humans and other animals. Humans are partially rational beings. Humans can *reason* and this allows for more progressive adaptation.

This process of progressive adaptation involves a continual loop of failures and successes, followed by adjustment, followed by more failures and successes, resulting in positive advancement on average, though not guaranteed in every circumstance. This is what makes life difficult, challenging, and wonderful for individuals in their daily lives and it is what has made history interesting at the societal level. It is the marvel of life, the beauty of the unknown, and the grace of existence, but it is not without difficulty.

The process of navigating through human existence is complex and requires serious thought, careful analysis, hard work, and sacrifice. Scott Peck brilliantly described this condition using the theme of *life is difficult* in his runaway bestseller *The Road Less Traveled.*[6] Individual adaptation within this complexity of life is most successful when people appreciate, rather than ignore, the inherent obstacles of life. Once an individual overcomes the natural reluctance to tackle the complexity and problems of life, then they must put forth the serious thought, careful analysis, hard work, and sacrifice that are necessary to build a positive and productive life. The need for complex problem solving and thoughtful decision-making are very important in the discussion about adaptive strategy, both individually and within larger social organizations.

What Is the Importance of Decision-making?

Individuals are primarily making decisions to facilitate their own prosperity and the prosperity of their families. Although most individuals will sometimes act unselfishly, it is not human nature to act that way consistently. The preference for individual decision-making (selfish by definition) is a successful adaptive strategy in a complex world. This is because of the complexity of the decisions and the need for increasingly careful thought about these decisions.

It is hard enough to make good decisions for one's own self, but it becomes much more difficult to make good decisions for larger groups. One person, regardless of intelligence—some-

---

6. Peck, M. Scott. *The Road Less Traveled.* 25th Anniversary ed. New York: Simon & Schuster, 2002.

110

times because of it—has problems enough in making the decisions they face personally, even though they generally have the most information about the specific aspects that may be unique to their personal circumstances. Going beyond the individual or the family and making decisions on behalf of other individuals or larger groups becomes exponentially more problematic and less likely to be successful. Therefore, decision-making is generally most successful at the lowest level (self) and least successful at the highest level (global, species-wide). This is not necessarily true in every specific instance, but it is decidedly true on average.

This point was very aptly described by Friedrich Hayek when he said: "The more men know, the smaller the share of all that knowledge becomes that any one mind can absorb. The more civilized we become, the more relatively ignorant must each individual be of the facts on which the working of his civilization depends."[7] This is the essential cause of the universal truth of decision-making being most successful at the lowest level. Knowledge and complexity continue to expand, therefore making any one individual relatively less knowledgeable of the whole of knowledge (and especially in regards to specific, individualized circumstances of others). Therefore, individualized decision-making becomes increasingly more successful than centralized decision-making on a relative basis.

A somewhat natural reaction to the expanding complexity of life is to reject the universal truth about decision-making being most effective at the personal level. Many people are overwhelmed by these circumstances and, because of feelings of inferiority, they assume that other individuals or groups would be better prepared to make decisions on their behalf. This would probably be true if other individuals or groups were able to exist as an *alternative self* or *invisible surrogate* of each person as they go about their daily routine. Yet this is obviously not possible.

---

7. Hayek, Friedrich A. *The Constitution of Liberty*. Paperback ed. Chicago: The University of Chicago Press, 1978. 26.

There is no way for alternative or centralized decision-makers to absorb the unlimited specific circumstances of individuals and there is no way for them to plan for the responsive flexibility necessary to successfully make decisions for an individual on a minute-by-minute basis throughout their life.

The universal truth about the most successful decision-making being at the lowest level has become even more applicable and relevant in the modern age. In pre-modern times, when only elites had ready access to education and when the common person was illiterate, a monarch or emperor could more effectively make widespread decisions impacting a broad range of individuals. Such a structure failed to take full advantage of comprehensive human potential, but the process of centralized decision-making was at least more understandable because the structure of life was much simpler, more static, and involved less decision-making.

Centralized decision-making became much less effective and increasingly counter-productive as the structure of life became more complex and volatile. At the same time, centralized decision-making became less necessary once ordinary individuals became educated — either formally or informally — with ready access to societal information and alternatives. The complexity of life continues to steadily increase. Therefore, the universal truth gains in importance as each day passes.

Does the Issue of Responsibility Play a Role in the Truth About Decision-making Being Most Successful at the Lowest Level?

While the points about the individual knowledge in relation to decision-making are very compelling, that represents only one half of the story. The other half involves the issues of motivation, responsibility, and personal growth. The very notion of the innate individual instinct of *striving to thrive* is predicated on the motivation of the individual and on acceptance of the responsibility for actions, both positive and negative consequences.

112

This core aspect of human psychology is a key factor here. The motivation provided by positive consequences is severely retarded when decision-making and the consequences thereof are taken away from the individual. Individuals are much less likely to continue to strive if the positive reinforcement of immediate and individual rewards is not obvious. Similarly, the substantial motivation provided by negative consequences is severely retarded when decision-making and the consequences associated with wrong decisions are taken away from the individual. Individuals are much less likely to continue to *strive* if the negative reinforcement of immediate and individual consequence for failing to strive is not obvious.

This is not exactly leading-edge psychological theory. This has been a basic tenet of psychology since the beginning of the field of study. It is *self-evident*. The motivation of positive and negative consequences is the key to understanding everyday human action. The more these consequences are removed from the direct control of individuals, the more skewed, unpredictable, and unproductive will be the results on average.

The issues of motivation and responsibility have more than just a short-term impact on the results of human endeavors. The existence of reasonable motivation and responsibility — in the framework of positive and negative consequences — creates an environment where most individuals can personally grow. All individuals have a great deal to contribute to our world. This contribution is maximized by the personal growth of individuals caused by the life experience of attempting to thrive in society, especially where conditions of Libertas are prominent. Human potential is expanded when human interaction is conducted under conditions allowing for individual responsibility and, therefore, personal growth and the resultant individual contribution over a lifetime. Human potential is restricted whenever individual responsibility is unnecessarily curtailed, as it is under human interaction based on conditions of coercion and centralized decision-making.

Why is Human Potential So Important?

Humans are considerably different than all other life forms. The human body, especially the human brain, is the most remarkable physical entity in the world. The human brain is capable of extensive creativity and reasoning. It also serves as a nerve center that controls a very flexible and amazingly adaptable human body. It is not at all surprising that, despite huge advancements in computer technology, we continue to fail at attempts to build truly human-like robots. There is good reason for this failure; humans are spectacularly complex and capable.

Therefore, humans are the deciding factor in history, not only because we write the history and because it is a history mostly about our own species, but also because we are the dominant productive force on Earth. Under conditions of coercion for most of recorded history and before, the tremendous potential of humans was minimized. The cooperative conditions of Libertas have unleashed much of that potential.

What Are the Key Human Traits That Cause the "Libertas Advantage"?

The very essence of human psychology and human physiology are at the center of understanding universal human history. Humans are motivated by a selfish instinct to thrive, but they cannot do so alone. They must interact. That interaction is complex and requires incessant decision-making. The decision-making is most successful at the individual level because of both human physiology and human psychology. First, there is the limitation of human physiology to absorb complexity beyond the individual. Next, there is the limitation of human psychology in the ability to maintain motivation and responsibility without specific positive and negative consequences.

It is a successful adaptive strategy for individuals to prefer individual decision-making and conditions of cooperation rather than centralized decision-making and conditions of coercion. It is also a preferable strategy for larger social organizations. This is a simple deduction from the previously stated point that humankind is merely the sum of its parts.

What Is the Most Effective Societal Framework?

The most effective social-political-economic framework has proven to be a structure that allows for the greatest flexibility and takes best advantage of the human desire to thrive, the predominant nature of self-interest, and the successful adaptive preference for individual decision-making. Such a structure contains universal inclusion of citizens for the opportunity to thrive and contribute to society. This requires extensive freedom, but also a solid societal framework to protect that freedom.

Human advancement has been greatest when individuals have obtained the most substantial liberty to pursue their self-interest, when they have acquired the freedom and responsibility to make decisions themselves, and when they have the most substantial motivation to enjoy the fruits of their efforts via extensive property rights and the security of their person and possessions. The opposite negative point is also true. Advancement has been hindered when liberty is hindered or whenever decision-making has been unnecessarily centralized, regardless of the intentions of that centralization. These are proven facts backed by a multitude of irrefutable examples, especially the specific historical cases previously discussed in Chapter Four.

This determination that Libertas has been the social structure with the greatest success in the advancement of humans means it is also the most moral structure. It has created the greatest good for the greatest number. Immanuel Kant summed up the concept precisely in the eighteenth century when he stated definitively: "We have finally reduced the definite conception of morality to the idea of freedom."[8]

---

8. Kant, Immanuel. "Fundamental Principles of the Metaphysics of Morals." *Basic Writings of Kant.* Ed. Allen W. Wood. New York: The Modern Library, 2001. 205.

NINE

Why It Took So Long

"Custom ruled everything originally, and the area of free argument was enlarged but very slowly. If I am at all right, that area could only be enlarged thus slowly, for custom was in early days the cement of society, and if you suddenly questioned such custom you would destroy society...In this manner politics or discussion broke up the old bonds of custom which were now strangling mankind, though they had once aided and helped it."[1]

—Walter Bagehot, 1872

What Have Been the Primary Alternatives to Libertas?

If we describe the forces of freedom and cooperation as Libertas, then it would be best to describe the primary alternative forces of coercion, conflict and control as Anti-Libertas. The forces of Anti-Libertas have a very long history, having been the primary organizational force of humankind throughout the ages. Anti-Libertas has taken many macro forms, including, but not limited to, dictatorship, feudalism, absolute monarchy, theocracy, fascism, socialism, and communism.

The differing motivations of the elite rulers behind the many varied forces of Anti-Libertas have been extremely diverse. Sometimes the motivation has been merely the personal aggrandizement of a monarch or dictator. Other times the motivation has been the desire to serve religious dogma. Sometimes the motivation was a desire to help better the condition of the

---

1. Bagehot, Walter. *Physics and Politics.* Paperback ed. Chicago: Ivan R. Dee, 1999. 163-164.

117

impoverished. Other times the motivation was the twisted immorality of a totalitarian. Regardless of motivation, all of these forces have one thing in common: disregard for individual decision-making and disrespect for the common person. This has been true at all levels of society, whether at the national level, lesser district level, or small community level.

The conflict between Libertas and Anti-Libertas has always centered on the conflict between cooperation and coercion, or between elite, centralized decision-makers and individual decision-making by the masses. Much of the dramatic twentieth century history was centered on this conflict when it included some the most hideously barbaric elites, especially those of Joseph Stalin and Adolph Hitler. Yet, even within Libertas-based nations — such as France, the United Kingdom, and the United States — there is always a more subtle conflict between the philosophy of centralized elite decision-making and decision-making by common individuals for themselves.

Why Did it Take So Long for Humans to Adapt to Libertas?

The superiority of cooperation over coercion is substantial and the historical success of Libertas is overwhelming proof of this fact. Yet we should legitimately ask: "if Libertas has proven so superior, why did it take humans so long to adapt toward this structure and why is it still under constant assault?"

The primary answer is straightforward and logical. As so correctly pointed out by Louis Menand: "Coercion is natural, freedom is artificial."[2] The brute force of the caveman is only slowly replaced by the rational intelligence and superior social cooperation of the reasoned individual. Even now, when Libertas is clearly the preferred method of societal organization, there will always be attempts to revert to the brute force of the caveman. In this way, Libertas is active and progressive, while

---

2. Menand, Louis. *The Future of Academic Freedom*. Chicago: The University of Chicago Press, 1996. 3.

Anti-Libertas is reactive and regressive.

The complete development of this obviously productive framework of Libertas has been and will continue to be delayed or temporarily reversed by the destructive power of elite control. This occurred most notably in the extreme twentieth century examples of fascism and communism, but it can also occur in much more benign settings. The destructive power of elite control is not limited to the dramatic, large-scale elite control as represented by Stalin and Hitler. The evolution of Libertas has involved much more than those large-scale struggles.

What Is the History of Libertas?

The exquisite quote by Walter Bagehot is perfectly appropriate to introduce the history of Libertas: "Man, being the strongest of all animals, differs from the rest; he was obliged to be his own domesticator; he had to tame himself."[3] The widespread emergence of Libertas was the culmination in many ways of humans taming themselves. The process is certainly not absolutely complete and there obviously had been some limited *taming* earlier in history. But the special mixture of the components of Libertas came together more fully and in more substantial combination in Europe and North America between 1500 and 1800. This served as the root cause for the dynamic explosion of human progress from 1800 to today as described in the previous chapters.

Limited aspects of Libertas had been known to humans throughout recorded history, but did not thoroughly come together until the last several hundred years. This development reached a theoretical *tipping point* in England and Scotland, although it simultaneously grew within other parts of Europe as well. There is no clearly defined starting point in time or place, nor is there a definitive explanation of exactly how and when

---

3. Bagehot, Walter. *Physics and Politics*. Paperback ed. Chicago: Ivan R. Dee, 1999. 48.

the tipping point was reached. It would be impossible to precisely quantify the impact of each and every instance of the growth of Libertas. What we can do is observe the cumulative effects of the growth and list some of the more obvious events leading to that growth.

An important advancement, perhaps the most important advancement, was the establishment of a common legal tradition in England from about 1000 onward. This tradition helped establish a series of civil and political rights, as well as customs of tolerance. It began in a very crude form during the Middle Ages and was continually enhanced over time. An early significant milestone was the signing of the Magna Carta in 1215 and the subsequent First Baron's War. This represented a formal limitation on monarchical power by the force of an elite group of barons. It was certainly not widespread liberty, but it was a seminal beginning of the growth of Libertas.

The concepts of individual rights, philosophical toleration, limited government, separation of powers, and constitutionalism continued to evolve from that point on for over four hundred more years. The crucial story involves the development of a common law that was not devised by a central authority, but developed over time through *traditions* to become a unifying and liberating social structure. This social structure created by British common law was developed over the course of several centuries and, unlike the creations of the great philosophers of Greece or the powerful Emperors of Rome, it was essentially an unplanned phenomenon.

These conditions set the stage for much more turbulent events in the seventeenth century. The English Civil War from 1642 to 1651 and the Glorious Revolution in 1688 represented more obvious structural changes. During this time, the issues of individual rights, religious toleration, the role of government, and the control of government took dramatic turns. It was during this time that the English public began to fully appreciate the fact that the advance of Libertas required much more than merely controlling a monarch. They found that Parliaments could also be tyrannical. They found that their religion might soon be out of political favor and that they may require the toleration of others with which they did not philosophically agree.

This period of strife in the British Isles resulted in the Bill of Rights of 1689 and the merger of England and Scotland into a formalized Great Britain in 1707. In many respects, this is evidence of Great Britain struggling through the societal experience that would envelop much of Europe a century later in the period sparked by the French Revolution.

Great Britain had a long tradition of liberal evolution and experimentation dating back at least to 1215. This maturity of experience in liberal traditions allowed the nation to abandon feudalism and establish many of the conditions of Libertas much sooner than on the continent. The people of Great Britain were well underway with the process of using their Libertas to build unprecedented prosperity while France and most of Europe were in the midst of tumultuous and devastating revolutionary machinations. The other European societies had also been evolving in certain aspects of Libertas prior to the Revolutionary Period, but in a slightly lesser amount than in Great Britain, marking a delay in the formation of the necessary critical mass of Libertas.

At nearly the same time, the Americans were in the midst of establishing an even stronger form of Libertas, although they had to endure a debilitating war of independence that was fought on their home soil and that divided their people. Afterwards, the Americans still had to struggle with establishing the formal mechanisms to rule themselves and create a united nation out of fiercely independent states. The Americans certainly contributed greatly to the experimentation process of increasing Libertas, as did the French and other Europeans. Yet while these events were substantial developments in the progress of Libertas, they were relatively late in comparison to the contributions of Great Britain. This is true despite the fact that the American drive for independence was in direct opposition to

Great Britain. That battle was a drive that improved the structure of Libertas from the best to even better.

In addition to these legal and political developments, there were important social and intellectual improvements being made in the direction of Libertas. The Renaissance, the Reformation, and the Enlightenment were also crucial movements in the growth of Libertas. These movements are as important as the purely political revolutions because Libertas is so much more than mere political freedom. The Renaissance, the Reformation, and the Enlightenment paved the way in social, philosophical, and intellectual arenas. Many philosophers have noted that all action is first rooted in thought. The action of Libertas taking hold is rooted in the explosion of thought and discussion about Libertas that culminated in the late 1700s.

First, the Renaissance represented a general broadening of philosophical thought and intellectual inquiry that created greater opportunity for discussing the alternatives of social organization. Then, the Reformation seriously weakened the influence of a centralized church and—whether intended or not—eventually resulted in the conditions of wider religious tolerance in the future (such as represented by the Peace of Westphalia) and greater receptivity to new social conditions.[4] Finally, the Enlightenment represented an explosion of modern thought about both physical and social science. At the height of the Enlightenment, a crescendo of thought about Libertas permeated enlightened discussions to the point of substantially changing public opinion toward action. This resulted in big revolutions, but also caused much larger numbers of people (and their future generations) to look at human interaction and social organization in considerably different ways.

Throughout the entire period of 1500-1800, the basic com-

4. It should be recognized here, of course, that the Church of England had already broken from the Roman Catholic Church by the time Martin Luther made his stand. However, the Protestant Reformation on the continent had philosophical and social ramifications that widely influenced thought and action throughout Europe, even within England.

ponents of Libertas began to be assembled together more completely than in previous historical periods, such as in the Greek or Roman civilizations. This new assemblage of Libertas in Europe and North America was far from exhaustive or complete, but it was unparalleled in volume and scope in comparison to previous historical times and places.

Did Libertas Come Together in One Bright Spark of Ingenuity?

It is not of crucial importance whether we consider the establishment of the critical mass of Libertas as beginning with the Magna Carta, the English Civil War, the Peace of Westphalia, the Glorious Revolution, the American Revolution, the French Revolution, or at any other specific time and place. The evolution of Libertas is exactly that — an evolution — not a singular event. It is not a specific revolution or identifiable *movement*. It has developed mostly as an unplanned, spontaneous order.

Libertas was not completed or perfected in any specific time or place, nor has it yet been completed or perfected. Libertas can never be completely perfected on a large scale because the human environment is entirely too complex and often too uncontrollable for such an accomplishment. The emergence of Libertas, as it was extolled during the Enlightenment, was based mostly on the recognized advantages of the use of reason. The Enlightenment was the Age of Reason. The popularity of the *use of reason* began an ever-widening belief in the perfectibility of human societies and the desire to produce *certainty* through group action. Later, this concept of perfectibility would spur numerous visions of utopias. Yet the most fervent supporters of reason often failed to appreciate that many aspects of human interaction would always be subject to forces beyond reason.

However, the popularity of reason and freedom during the Enlightenment did create a strong impetus for strengthening the Libertas components. Libertas did reach a certain critical mass — a tipping point — during the late 1700s. This was transformation enough to fundamentally change the structure of human interaction in those times and in certain places. This structural change began a chain reaction of increasing expansion of Libertas elsewhere over time and the resultant explosion of prosperity and human progress in its wake.

The process of assembling the components of Libertas proceeded in building-block fashion, without a centralized plan or a specific philosophical movement. Some components were emphasized more than others in different nations and in different time periods. That process continues to this very day. The concept of democratic, representative government garnered the most attention, but all of the components of Libertas were crucial to the ultimate mixture that created the explosion of progress. The development of the rule of law based upon written constitutions was obviously very important. The establishment of greater religious tolerance and the break-up of a central western church had considerable impact. Perhaps one of the most important ingredients was the evolution of free enterprise and relatively free trade, which developed without a philosophical movement and was hardly recognized intellectually until the groundbreaking works of Richard Cantillon in Ireland, Anne Robert Jacques Turgot, Jean-Baptiste Say, and Claude-Frederic Bastiat in France and Adam Smith in Scotland.

It is perfectly fitting that Smith's *An Inquiry into the Nature and Causes of the Wealth of Nations*[5] was published in 1776, the year that Libertas took its most declarative form in the *Declaration of Independence,* culminating eventually in the more permanent establishment of the United States of America through its Constitution in 1787. The historical circumstances peculiar to the rise of the United States will be discussed in greater detail later, but Libertas continued evolving, in differing degrees, from that point until today, throughout many portions of the world, far beyond the basic beginnings in England and the rest of Europe.

---

5. Smith, Adam. *An Inquiry Into the Nature and Causes of The Wealth of Nations.* 1994 Modern Library ed. New York: The Modern Library, 1994.

Did Libertas Develop in a Steady and Predictable Way?

There is no doubt that the progress of Libertas in the world since 1500 has been unsteady. Great Britain reached the tipping point of Libertas first. It had a long evolution of liberal improvements that culminated in more substantial changes during their revolutionary periods of the seventeenth century, although there remained some relatively strong components of monarchy and aristocracy. France and most of the continent did not reach that level of Libertas until the late eighteenth century and, even then, was still saddled with some vestiges of feudalism and consequently burdened with the chaos associated with violently cutting all ties to feudalism. This made the transition to Libertas much more difficult for France and delayed much of the progress until well into the nineteenth century. Meanwhile, the Americans were still saddled with the task of designing and implementing a new government without monarchy and aristocracy, deprived of a great depth of personal experience in political governance. The Americans had to accomplish this task while remaining under the ominous military intimidation of the British for another thirty years.

Even after the eighteenth century, the progress of Libertas within these countries was unsteady. In most historical cases, some aspects of Libertas were applied, while others were ignored. The illiberal aspects of the Reign of Terror and the resultant Napoleonic reaction often made a mockery of Libertas in France, despite the establishment of order under Napoleon and the continued revolutionary rhetoric. The grossest Libertas contradiction resided in the United States with the use of slavery until the mid-nineteenth century and the restriction of the rights of black Americans until the mid-twentieth century. A definitive Libertas contradiction was also true for a time in the United Kingdom during the twentieth century when the component of free enterprise was substantially muted by heavy-handed socialistic practices. Similar examples of the unsteady progress of Libertas abound within most all of the stalwart nations supporting Libertas. And yet, on average, Libertas continued to grow and expand until it reached the unique challenges of the twentieth century.

A primary aspect of this new civilization was not merely the rise of the nation-state, but the acceptance of other nation-states. The ancient and classical civilizations were usually ethnocentric, sometimes even xenophobic. They often expanded until they exhausted their resources. This was the cause of the collapse of some civilizations. Even when they did tolerate other coexisting civilizations, it was usually caused by remoteness and their own sense of superiority. This was especially true of China, the grandest of all civilizations in longevity and population.

By contrast, the new Modern Civilization developed a tradition of acknowledging the equal sovereignty of others. This required a long process of acclimation. The early history of the two most prominent participants in the rise of Europe—France and England—began with the invasion and conquest of England by the Normans in 1066. These two participants were to frequently battle each other for another 750 years, including the famous Hundred Years War. In general, Europe after 1066 was rife with international conflict. Some of these conflicts, such as those of Napoleon and Hitler, were attempts at complete continental domination, but there were also many examples of peaceful coexistence over time. From all of this there eventually arose a tradition of acceptance of other nations as equals in sovereignty.

Prior to this acceptance of equal sovereignty, an essential contradiction of the early movement toward Libertas was that it was almost exclusively internal. The components of Libertas were often growing within some of the aforementioned countries while at the same time, these countries were sometimes undermining Libertas externally. External cooperation between nations was slow to materialize. There was still strong external competition, especially in areas outside of Europe. Even once greater acceptance of European sovereignty materialized, the

European nations did not immediately extend that concept to other parts of the world.

The first sign of significant external cooperation of Libertas — at least cooperation among equals — was within the stalwart Libertas nations of northwestern Europe, North America, and Australasia. Most of these nations created an enduring peace among each other after 1815. However, at the same time, these same nations often ignored the promotion of Libertas in their foreign policy and colonial endeavors. The most obvious example is found in the overt colonialism of these nations, but some additional examples of this behavior will be discussed later. The cause of this type of contradiction is rarely contemplated. Most critics assign the cause to myopic national self-interest and shortsightedness. While this is undoubtedly true in part, it does not explain the full story.

There is also an element of the gross misunderstanding of the success of Libertas. The nations with historical Libertas success often failed to appreciate the structural strength of Libertas that resulted in their spectacular prosperity and power. There is still a tendency to give devotional lip service to the conditions of Libertas, while subconsciously believing the success was actually due to a superior breed of people, to the special protection of religion, or to simple luck. This helps to explain, but not excuse, the relatively frequent early tendency of Libertas-based nations to conduct external relations in contradiction to the growth of Libertas.

This original trend of *internal* Libertas development did not necessarily help speed the process of extending Libertas around the world. It certainly did help create the erroneous impression that the advantages of Libertas were somehow "British," "American," "European," or "Western" cultural traits and were not applicable to other humans. The most enduring *reversal* of this early trend of internalization of Libertas resulted from the extreme cases of direct confrontation that required the first-adopter nations to begin banding together more closely for the sake of survival. The twentieth century was to provide plenty of such direct confrontation.

The most substantial challenges to Libertas developed as the forces of Anti-Libertas became violently dominant in specific places at specific times, as was true in Nazi Germany, Imperialist Japan, Stalinist USSR (and satellites), and Maoist China. In these and similar cases, full-scale philosophical and political movements developed in direct opposition to the general concept of Libertas. Virtually all components of Libertas were directly opposed by the four extreme examples listed above. These are some of the many twentieth century examples that virtually forced Libertas-based nations to support the forces of Libertas externally by bonding together with like-minded nations. The forces of Libertas proved ultimately victorious against these comprehensive challenges of Anti-Libertas.

Despite the direct challenge of huge Anti-Libertas forces — as well as the indirect challenge of illiberal gaps within the proponents of Libertas — the phenomenon of Libertas continues to evolve and advance. The structure of Libertas advanced geographically in the last quarter of the twentieth century rather significantly. These advancements include nations that share virtually no cultural heritage with the original adopters such as France, the United Kingdom, and the United States. These most recent advances have proven that the development of Libertas is a *human* phenomenon, not a "British" or "Western" event. It represents a more effective method of human interaction.

As we entered the twenty-first century, Libertas was the undisputed and preferred model of social organization, albeit a model with a perplexing array of components that often become confused with simple democracy. The progression of Libertas has also extended in another very important way. That is toward a greater appreciation for the external promotion of Libertas to those who still live without it. That process of the extension of Libertas is a key futuristic trend.

It is fascinating to research and speculate on the exact origins of the different components of Libertas and how, when, and where they came together hundreds of years ago. It is a topic of particular interest to many scholars. Yet an important focus of this book is on the *result* of Libertas, not merely the origin. A history of human progress and modern prosperity — including the achievement of the greatest good for the greatest number — mirrors the exact trail of Libertas. Wherever widespread Libertas was established, substantial prosperity and happiness followed. The antithesis is also true. Wherever there is a severe lack of Libertas, substantial poverty and despair reigns.

The broad alternatives to Libertas have been thoroughly discredited over the past century. From our vantage point in the new millennium, we can now clearly see that the relative victory of Libertas was undoubtedly the primary root cause of the radical transformation of historical progression, the incredible rise of material prosperity, and a decrease in overall human misery. This conclusion is inescapable by following the facts. This deduction is reached by observing the times and places where the components of Libertas came together most substantially and by reviewing the objective measures of human well-being in those times and places in comparison to other times and places.

This understanding of the history of Libertas, our Universal History, is important for a productive discussion of current events and policy decisions. However, overemphasis on the origins can sometimes create counterproductive ethnocentrism. It can simultaneously mislead some to think their citizens are superior (early-adopters) and others to think their citizens are inferior or are kowtowing to foreign culture (late-adopters). There are many varied reasons the first tipping point was reached in Europe, some of which were forces beyond human control, such as geography. The primary consideration should be that the improvement of human interaction created by Libertas is the means by which our species has significantly advanced and can continue to do so.

The geographic starting point of the phenomenon is no longer relevant except as benefiting our understanding of how we came to be where we are today. This is no different than with other major human innovations. Does it matter to us today that language was probably first spoken and fire was first tamed in Africa? Should those of us on other continents consider language and the use of fire to be "African"? Should we reject the benefits of language and fire as Afrocentric and as a cultural intrusion on us by Africans? Of course we should not. Should late-adopters of Libertas in the Middle East, Africa, and elsewhere reject the benefits of cooperative human interaction as Eurocentric and as a cultural intrusion on them by Europeans or European descendents? The answer is self-evident.

TEN

The Misunderstanding of Libertas

"So a principle may be put in practice long before it is understood or defined. Therefore it is not strange if the obvious fact that a high production system [Libertas] works on a long circuit of energy has not been perceived and the general laws governing its creation and maintenance have not been formulated."[1]

— Isabel Patterson, 1943

Are the Components of Libertas Consistent Over Time?

As previously identified, Libertas consists of much more than democracy. It is a complex mixture of many components that interact and reinforce each other. It is the achievement of what must have appeared to many to be merely a utopian dream when Jean Jacques Rousseau described it as: "...a form of association which will defend the person and goods of each member with the collective force of all, and under which each individual, while uniting himself with the others, obeys no one but himself, and remains as free as before."[2] The combination of Libertas components is similar to a complex chemical mixture. The presence, volume, and quality of each component are essential to the outcome. An incorrect mixture or lack of some

---

1. Paterson, Isabel. *The God of the Machine.* New Brunswick: Transaction Publishers, 2005. 280. (Author's clarification in parenthesis)

2. Rousseau, Jean-Jacques. *The Social Contract.* London: Penguin Books, 1968. 60. Although Rousseau spoke eloquently of freedom and liberty, his thoughts of implementation of these ideals mark a crucial divide (on the wrong side of history) in this universal history and the conflict of visions that will be discussed later.

components can tilt toward anarchy or totalitarianism.

Libertas is extremely complex. It is very complicated to judge the amount of Libertas from one large nation to the next, much less comparing different time periods. It can be measured in different ways depending on the circumstances, and the circumstances are constantly in flux. Perfect Libertas might not even be fully describable and it is certainly not achievable. The discussion of Libertas during the Enlightenment emphasized the use of *reason*. There is no doubt that the increased use of reason is an important aspect of Libertas. However, Libertas cannot be completely perfected because our world is not based only on the consistent use of reason. First, reason is in the eye of the beholder and what is reasonable to one person is unreasonable to another. Second, much of the activity and circumstances of our world are based on the unplanned, the unpredictable, and the chaotic beyond the reach of human reason.

Although the political structure of a nation maintains the most direct influence over the development of the Libertas mixture, there are other influences as well. The underlying culture and social traditions of each society dramatically influence the ability of those societies to create the most effective mixture of the components. Each society creates a different mixture, with more of some components and less of others. Therefore, the detailed tracing of Libertas throughout history is extremely complex.

Kant, Hegel, and others focused on Libertas (mostly referred to as *freedom*) as the defining element of universal history and rightly so. Much of history has been devoted to the search for what Kant called "a perfect civil constitution" or what might best be described as the most effective general method of human interaction. That search was concluded when Libertas became the undisputed and preferred organizational structure by the end of the twentieth century.

The fall of the Iron Curtain and the victory of Libertas signaled the triumph of cooperation over coercion as the principal method of human interaction. This emergence of Libertas was not caused by political luck in government or by military genius in battle. Libertas emerged as the superior method of social organization for human interaction because it takes best advantage of human nature. This includes the human nature to thrive, the human nature for self-interest, and the human adaptive preference for decentralized decision-making. The pre-modern use of coercion as the primary method of social interaction unnecessarily inhibited the creativity and productiveness of humans, while the transformation to the modern use of cooperation has liberated the human capacity for improvement.

What Was the Last Big Struggle with Anti-Libertas?

The last big historical struggle between Libertas and Anti-Libertas involved the confrontation with communism. The argument for communism revolved around the issue of *equality of outcome* and the concern about unequal outcome within a structure of Libertas. Yet, exact *equality of outcome* is unnatural and impractical, which will be explained in more detail later. The battle between Libertas and communism — aside from that nasty little issue of the personal aggrandizement of dictators — boiled down to the conflict between the desire for near universal prosperity (albeit unequally) against the desire for near equality of outcome (albeit at levels much closer to destitution).

Here is where Libertas won the battle on both moral and practical lines. Despite the concern from some about the selfish motivational underpinnings of Libertas, the result of these underpinnings has been an unprecedented increase in unselfishness, including a much heightened sensitivity for the sanctity of life, for the equality of opportunity, for the treatment of the disabled, for the protection of the environment, and for the nourishment of children.

Using any Libertas-based nation (whether one chooses Austria, the United States, or any of the other Elite 15 in between) as an example of a Libertas-based nation and comparing them to any non-Libertas nation in the world, such as Myanmar or

North Korea, one can quickly witness the signs of these self-less examples within a Libertas nation. There is considerably more emphasis on safety devices and preventative medicine; near obsession with equal opportunity by ignoring ethnic and religious barriers; incredibly sensitive and supportive treatment of the disabled; significant advancement in improving pollution problems; and genuine care and concern for children. This is no claim that these issues are resolved or that continued advancement is not possible, only that the Libertas-based nations are way ahead of Anti-Libertas-based nations on these accounts. More generally and more significantly, Libertas has harnessed the power of individual selfishness to build a much better world for all.

At the same time, the inferiority of communism — as one of the primary Anti-Libertas alternatives — included: a destructive abolishment of the incentives necessary to harness self-interest, an ineffective use of centralized decision-making, and an inevitable loss of freedom associated with the drive to equalize outcome. These three negative components had tremendously detrimental effects. The first two components caused a dramatic comparative lag of productivity and output for the entire society. The third component caused an inevitable abuse of the enlarged political power.

The superiority of Libertas is found in the fact that it works *with* human nature to tap the inherent self-interest of individuals. It takes advantage of the effectiveness of individual decision-making to gain the greatest good for the greatest number, including increased unselfishness overall. It cannot deliver exact equality of outcome, but it has tangibly been proven to deliver near universal outcome success, especially in one very significant and moral area — that of improving the life of humans in the most direct and tangible of ways.

The case for the superiority of Libertas can be stated clearly and concisely. For the benefit of nearly everyone living within Libertas-based nations, Libertas has virtually conquered the *Four Ds* that have plagued humans since the beginning of civilization: Disease, Destruction, Destitution, and Death (prematurely). This is the ultimate proof of the progressive advancement of civilization. There is no legitimate, broad alternative to Libertas in the world today because no legitimate philosophical or social belief system should prefer disease, destruction, destitution, and death more than health, peace, prosperity, and life!

Does Libertas Preclude All Use of Centralized Decision-making?

Libertas is essentially the absence of coercion, and coercion is essentially the forcible replacement of self decision-making by the decision-making of others. In essence, all decision-making is conducted at the individual level, in that individuals are the building block components of all groups. The distinction is that centralized decision-making, although administered by individuals, is seeking to make decisions on behalf of others. Although individualized decision-making has a natural advantage, some degree of centralized decision-making is necessary within the conduct of society, both in public and private affairs.

Centralized decision-making that is private and voluntary may be good or bad, efficient or inefficient, depending on the circumstances, but it is not coercion. Coercion is involuntary by definition. Private coercion is generally what we think of as crime. Public coercion is what we think of as government restrictions or interference.

The action of government might be good or bad, efficient or inefficient, but it is a form of centralized decision-making. Any centralized decision-making by government is quite different from voluntary-private action because government enforces those decisions not only with the power of a gun, but also with the power of legitimacy within the society. Therefore, centralized decision-making by government is a very crucial aspect of human interaction that should be given the highest level of scrutiny. Centralized government decision-making is the most prevalent form of coercion remaining in the world today.

What is the Most Effective Extent of Legitimate Public Coercion?

Libertas has proven to be the most effective social-political-economic framework. If the goal of Libertas is to reduce the coercion of some by others and if government is the only legitimate coercive force in society, then the specific objectives of government should be twofold. First, it should protect society from illegitimate coercion (crime and foreign aggression) and second, it should limit its own use of legitimate coercion to mostly the first objective. This concept was a primary consideration of the American Founding Fathers. James Madison stated this clearly and directly in the *Federalist Papers*: "In framing a government which is to be administered by men over men, the great difficulty lies in this: you must first enable the government to control the governed; and in the next place oblige it to control itself."[3]

A political and societal framework that protects the ten components of Libertas is most likely to achieve these objectives. This is much easier to conceptualize than it is to put into practice. Libertas is not the absence of government. It requires the presence of government. It requires limited coercion. It must provide the protective framework of society. This includes establishing and administering the *rules of engagement*. These rules are what we think of as laws. Most societies also maintain informal rules in addition to laws and those are known as *social norms*.

Creating an effective framework of laws and norms is difficult. The Libertas countries of the world have achieved this task. None of them are exactly the same, but they do emphasize the components of Libertas, some more than others. Not everyone within each country agrees completely with each law or norm. This is true even for strong believers in Libertas that are political science experts.

---

3. Madison, James. "Number 51 Checks and Balances." *The Federalist*. Ed. New York: MetroBooks, 1961. 356.

A political framework that attempts a strict construction of Libertas still has to struggle with the boundaries of where individualism stops and where social control starts. There are many questions that are perplexing to answer, such as: At what point does the individualism of one person begin to endanger another enough to need to be restricted by society? At what point of neglect or abuse should society restrict the individual rights of parental control over children? To what degree should the government provide assistance to disabled individuals incapable or unwilling to provide for themselves? These are just some of the many complicated questions that each country and each community answers differently. Yet, however different these answers may be within the Libertas community of nations, they are all roughly similar to one another in the basic primacy of individual control within the rough structural perimeters. They differ substantially from Anti-Libertas nations that tend mostly toward the absolute control of totalitarianism.

Libertas is essentially the de-emphasis of decision-making on behalf of others at the centralized, governmental level in favor of decision-making at the personal level on behalf of one's self. In this way, the coercive power of a Libertas-based government should be limited only to protecting the citizenry from coercion. Coercion is deemed to be harmful regardless of the intentions behind coercive attempts. Coercion is harmful because it works against the best interests of individuals in two fundamental ways. First, coercion contravenes the universal truth that decision-making is most successful at the lowest level and, second, even initially unselfish coercion is highly susceptible to eventual malfeasance. Stated differently, "power corrupts."

The issues of coercion and the role of government are very important. The conflict concerning the essential role of government is at the heart of most political differences. It has been argued that the use of coercion—for other than the essential use of preventing coercion—by a democratic government should be acceptable because it is essentially *voluntary* in that it is based on majoritarian vote. This argument is baseless on the surface because, even if the coercion in question were directly voted upon in plebiscite, it would be voluntary only to those who voted in favor of the coercion. Additionally, the concept of *majority* on many issues in most democratic systems is actually based on a majority of representatives that were elected by only a fraction of the citizens and may not necessarily represent majority opinion.

All those points aside, the most critical detail is that the political system constructed by the Founding Fathers of the United States is *not* pure democracy or majoritarianism, but limited democracy with careful protection of minority rights. This development was based substantially on English heritage and it is the political concept that has a fundamentally changed human interaction in all Libertas-based nations. It is a crucial aspect of Libertas. This limited use of democracy with careful protection of minority rights requires a concentrated concern about the use of unnecessary coercion, even when in favor by the majority. This is the essence of Libertas.

Coercion exists to a lesser degree in the world today than it did centuries ago, but it does still exist. This is true even within the societies with the greatest Libertas. However, the widespread emergence of increasing Libertas—and the resultant decrease in coercion—is the most important development in human history since the advent of the first agricultural civilizations more than five thousand years ago and it accounts for our universal history.

What Is the "Spontaneous Order" in Between Anarchy and Totalitarianism?

The framework of Libertas is incapable of planning exact results in advance. The effectiveness of Libertas lies in the very ability of individuals to maximize their creativity and responsiveness according the circumstances that present themselves at any given moment. It requires ultimate flexibility. Adaptability and motivation are the very heart of the superiority of

Libertas. Therefore, this framework precludes specific planning of outcome.

Instead, Libertas allows for the growth of a creative social condition that is constantly changing and is hard to describe. It has generally been referred to as a *spontaneous order*. It is *spontaneous* in the sense that it is constantly changing and unplanned. It is an *order* in the sense that it creates a condition of relative order out of the chaos of life, albeit a partially unpredictable order.

Yet this *spontaneous order* is not devoid of all planning and control. The planning and control are merely restricted (for the most part) to establishing the rules required within the definition of Libertas. This implies that planning and control are not used to determine exact outcome. Libertas utilizes a degree of restrictive control to develop the framework within which individuals interact with one another, but it then allows for creative interplay without controlling the outcome. Libertas is essentially the middle ground between anarchy and totalitarianism. This is true politically and socially.

The framework of Libertas results in an intangible spontaneous order that has proven to be the most effective structure for human interaction. It has resulted in the greatest good for the greatest number, but the intangibility of this spontaneous order makes it exasperating to describe, burdensome to promote, and arduous to track historically. It also makes Libertas troublesome to maintain; and it is to that dilemma we now turn.

PART FOUR
The Maintenance
of Libertas

ELEVEN

The Human Sacrifice

"Man, being the strongest of all animals, differs from the rest; he was obliged to be his own domesticator; he had to tame himself."[1]

—Water Bagehot, 1872

A Perspective from One of the Many Disastrous Examples of Humans Taming Themselves:

It is a beautiful little piece of Earth nestled in the rolling hills and nearby mountains of western Maryland on the border with West Virginia. It has never been heavily populated, even by the Native Americans prior to the colonial settlers. Yet the land is fertile, water is readily available, and the climate is reasonable.

There is not much history to note in this little corner of the world either, with one glaring exception. The town is called Sharpsburg and was named after the colonial governor of Maryland, Horatio Sharpe. It is a quaint and rustic town with a current population of less than 700 inhabitants, roughly the same number as were there two hundred years ago. The local county (Washington) was formally established in 1776 and it was the first county or city anywhere to be named after George Washington. The town of Sharpsburg consists of less than one square kilometer of land, none of which is covered by water. But there is both a famous river and a famous creek in near proximity.

---

1. Bagehot, Walter. *Physics and Politics.* Paperback ed. Chicago: Ivan R. Dee, 1999. 48.

143

The town was first inhabited by settlers in 1740 and was formally established in 1763. Therefore, despite the naming of the county in 1776, this little community was not engaged in the War for Independence. It was, however, engaged in another conflict some eighty years later.

The town of Sharpsburg and the nearby creek were not particularly strategic targets for military experts. Nevertheless, through historical accident, it became famous for what occurred on just one day: the day of September 17. Here is an eyewitness account from that ominous day:

When we engaged the enemy he was in a strip of woods, long but narrow. We drove him from this, across a ploughed field and through a cornfield into another woods, which was full of ravines. There the enemy held us in check till 9 1/2 o'clock, when there was a general cessation of musketry. All over the ground we had advanced on, the Rebel dead and wounded lay thick, much more numerous than ours, but ours were painfully mingled in. Our wounded were rapidly carried off and some of the Rebels'. Those we were obliged to leave begged so piteously to be carried away. Hundreds appealed to me and I confess that the rage of battle had not hardened my heart so that I did not feel a pity for them. Our men gave them water and as far as I saw always treated them kindly.

The necessities of the case were so great that I was obliged to put my whole corps into action at once. The roar of the infantry was beyond anything conceivable to the uninitiated. Imagine from 8,000 to 10,000 men on one side, with probably a larger number on the other, all at once discharging their muskets. If all the stone and brick houses of Broadway should tumble at once the roar and rattle could hardly be greater, and amidst this, hundreds of pieces of artillery, right and left, were thundering as a sort of bass to the infernal music...

The Rebel dead, even in the woods last occupied by them, was very great. In one place, in front of the position of my corps, apparently a whole regiment had been cut down in line. They lay in two ranks, as straightly aligned as on a dress parade. There must have been a brigade, as part of the line on the left had been buried. I counted what appeared to be a single regiment and found 149 dead in the line and about 70 in front and rear, making over 200 dead in one Rebel regiment. In riding over the field I think I must have seen at least 3,000. In one place for nearly a mile they lay as thick as autumn leaves along a narrow lane cut below the natural surface, into which they seemed to have tumbled. Eighty had been buried in one pit, and yet no impression had apparently been made on the unburied host. The cornfield beyond was dotted all over with those killed in retreat.[2]

The cornfield was dotted indeed. It was and still remains the bloodiest day in American history. The name of the creek is Antietam. This day claimed over 22,000 wounded and nearly 5,000 dead. These men were not fighting the British for independence, nor were they fighting the Nazis on the beaches of Normandy to help the French reclaim their liberty. These men were Americans fighting against each other. It can be said that *independence* and *liberty* were the ultimate prize to be won at Antietam, but that point certainly needs elaboration. It can also be said that this was an ugly battle in the very long struggle of humans taming themselves.

The progression of Libertas had begun earlier in Europe. By the 1860s, Europe was in the midst of the first great period of peace (1815-1914). There was rapid industrialization. Railroads were ushering in a new stage of modern life. Yet Europeans could not help but notice the huge growth across the ocean in the United States.

The United States was a bastion of the republican ideal, very

---

2. Williams, Alpheus S. "South Mountain and Antietam." *From the Cannon's Mouth.* Ed. Milo M. Quaife. Detroit: Wayne State University Press, 1959. 126-130.

unlike the vestiges of monarchy still prominent in Europe. The Constitution of 1787 had been a daring political experiment, but it had ultimately proved successful. The nation grew into an economic powerhouse with no sign of slowing down. The components of Libertas were more thoroughly installed in the United States than anywhere else in the world and they were making a difference.

Still, there remained a gaping contradiction in this new success story of the United States of America. This contradiction was obvious to the Founding Fathers, but they codified it anyway within the Constitution for the sake of unity among the states. The unity was assured in 1787 and the Constitution was later ratified. The gaping contradiction, however, was not to be resolved nearly so easily.

The southern states (and predecessor colonies) had utilized slavery for about two hundred years. The leaders of these states were not inclined to allow northern politicians to interfere on their freedom to be illiberal. They had the political tradition of *states rights* on their side. This fundamental contradiction was the basis for the Civil War. It also set up a critical showdown for Libertas.

The United States was at the forefront of the progression of Libertas from 1776 through 1860. It was fast taking over the mantle of Libertas and progress from Great Britain and other European countries. It was successful despite the oppressive institution of slavery within its midst. But the institution was too horrendous and the contradiction was too substantial to be sustained. The battle had to be fought. It was either to be an improved Libertas or the Anti-Libertas contradiction of slavery. Humans would suffer mightily to work through this chapter of the *taming* process.

The activity at Antietam Creek on September 17, 1862, is a powerful example of humans taming themselves. The citizen warriors in that battle may or may not have fully understood their place in history. Civil wars are often considered needless and the American Civil War is no exception. Nonetheless, the contradiction had to be solved and so it was solved by the use of human carnage. Libertas was eventually the victor.

The *taming* lessons learned at Antietam and all of the killing fields of the Civil War were seared into the collective consciousness of Americans. This use of modern armament factories and railroad supply chains in widespread warfare created unprecedented efficiency in destroying human life. It was a warning sign to the world of what war had become.

Unfortunately, the lessons were not complete and there was even wider taming to be completed in the next century back across the Atlantic and across the Pacific. Libertas would again be the victor, but only after far greater carnage at places such as the Somme, Verdun, Stalingrad, and Tokyo where the casualties would mount faster than anyone at Antietam could possibly imagine.

What Was the Ultimate Purpose of the Human Sacrifice and Was It Worth It?

Most of us in the Prosperous World of the new millennium understand the theory of human cooperation. We appreciate the dictum "live and let live." The philosophers of the Enlightenment could discuss the concept in depth. The difficulty was getting from there to here.

The norm of human interaction was in the midst of changing from coercion to cooperation. The initial changes in Western Europe and North America helped bring substantial material advancement. Unfortunately, the material benefits of the initial cooperation developed faster than the appreciation for the cause of the progress. Humans were still in transition.

There were still plenty of humans willing to build their interaction (or at least much of it) around coercion in 1861, 1914, and 1939. This was true of the Confederates who insisted on retaining slavery. And it was true of the supporters of dictators in the world wars and the communist movement. Our fellow humans, our ancestors, suffered in great numbers because of it. They were sacrificed in the cause of taming ourselves. Their sacrifice helped us get to the point in the twenty-first century where war is widely regarded as abhorrent and the norm of human interaction is toward the protection of life, liberty, and the pursuit of happiness.

This is not a claim that warfare has been extinguished or that some parts of the world are not still rife with coercion. It is a statement of the obvious, however. It is self-evident that warfare has ceased between and within the many nations of the Prosperous World. These nations are even reluctant to use force against external brutal dictators outside the Prosperous World.

This reluctance was demonstrated by the strong disagreements among Libertas powers as to the appropriateness of using force (the second time) against Saddam Hussein in Iraq. This was a dictator who was documented to be one of the worst perpetrators of human atrocities in recent history. Yet it is obvious that force would not have been used against him had he not first attacked Kuwait in 1990 and then had not the Bush Doctrine of the War on Terror been established after September 11, 2001.

There is no doubt that Hussein was a brutal menace to Iraqis and to neighboring countries. However, there are other brutal menaces in the world. The unusual attention on Iraq in the first Gulf War was obviously impacted by the Allied desire to maintain stable world oil supplies. Then, the unusual attention in the later Iraq War was obviously impacted by the Allied desire to fight terrorism by beginning to forcibly reform hostile Middle Eastern countries.[3] The unimpeded and even more genocidal dictators of some African nations are proof enough that the majority of citizens in the Prosperous World are reluctant to intercede and use force in the matters of others unless it directly benefits us.

Perhaps the best example of the change in attitudes among

---

3. Whether one agrees or disagrees with that strategy is irrelevant to the point here.

the citizens of Libertas nations is in the level of toleration we have for casualties in the few wars we still fight. It is very limited warfare. The citizens of the Prosperous World now insist upon minimal casualties and collateral damage whenever the use of force is reluctantly utilized. In our current wars, it takes years to reach the death tolls it once took hours to reach at Antietam and the Somme. That statement deserves repetition. We are now rightfully anguished by the death of soldiers in Afghanistan and Iraq over the course of years that our ancestors (even those less than a century ago) once tolerated in *hours*.

The death toll of Libertas powers during all the major wars of the past sixty years since World War II barely add up to the death toll suffered by the Japanese during *one night* in Tokyo on March 9/10, 1945. This is not a declaration that any death is tolerable. It is a validation of just the opposite. We now regard human life more preciously than ever before and this is proof that our species is mostly tamed. The previous sacrifices were tragic, but our newer and more humane appreciation for life is the result of their sacrifice. The evidence supports the assumption that their sacrifice, while tragic, was not in vain. As proclaimed so resolutely by Montesquieu and quoted by Bagehot: "Whatever be the cost of this glorious liberty, we must be content to pay it to heaven."[4]

What Was Gained by the Human Sacrifice Required to Tame Ourselves?

The sacrifice was not in vain. In actuality, the gain was monumental. Our species has fundamentally changed for the better. We, the adherents of Libertas, are not different genetically than our Anti-Libertas opponents, but we are different in the methods we use to interact. This difference involves cooperation, respect for individuality, and the unleashing of human potential.

4. Bagehot, Walter. *Physics and Politics.* Paperback ed. Chicago: Ivan R. Dee, 1999. 180.

This new human productivity is responsible for altering our living conditions as described earlier.

We live longer, healthier, and more fruitful lives. We respect the life and liberty of others more. We hesitate to tolerate violence, subjugation, and inhumane treatment in our midst. (Unfortunately, we do tend to tolerate that treatment outside our midst, because we are even reluctant to go to war against brutal and murderous dictators.) All of this is probably an even stronger example of human progress than the stories of how we have so dramatically altered transportation and communication. We live and let live. It is all because we have found Libertas to be the most advantageous method of human interaction.

There are still some challenges facing our species. This is especially true in the nations that have not yet developed the structure of Libertas and the tradition of cooperation. Those difficulties will be addressed in Part Five. Less obviously, there is also a substantial internal challenge within the nations embracing Libertas. The positive improvement inherent in the unleashing of human potential is threatened by a new phenomenon from within. This challenge begins with the power of the state and it is to that dilemma we next turn.

TWELVE

The Power of the State

"...[The] worth of a State...is the worth of the individuals composing it...a State which dwarfs its men, in order that they may be more docile instruments in its hands even for beneficial purposes — will find that with small men no great thing can really be accomplished; and that the perfection of machinery to which it has sacrificed everything, will in the end avail it nothing, for want of the vital power which, in order that the machine might work more smoothly, it has preferred to banish."[1]

—John Stuart Mill, 1859

What is the Most Influential Cause of the Rise of the Modern Nation-State?

The rise of the modern nation-state is a common historical topic. The nations of Europe began developing in the second millennium. There were France, England, Denmark, Sweden, Spain, Portugal, Belgium, Russia, Poland, Prussia, Austria, Switzerland, the Netherlands, and, eventually, a united Germany and a united Italy. These new "nations" (and others) emerged over a number of centuries in many various ways. Some were achieved through conquest and some were achieved through unusual alliances. Some of the nations were small and homogeneous, while others were large and culturally diverse.

It was obvious that a new European civilization had arisen, but this new civilization was decentralized. It was not cohesive. Instead, it was highly fragmented and internally competitive.

---

1. Mill, John Stuart. *On Liberty.* New York: The Liberal Arts Press, 1956. 140-1.

Each nation was essentially a new civilization amidst many other new civilizations in close proximity.

The unusual developmental conditions within Europe created an intense need for strong states. The primary purpose of any organization, especially a government, is that of self-preservation. This purpose is usually couched in patriotic terminology, such as "for the protection of the citizens," but the leaders are almost always primarily concerned with preserving their personal position first and that of the citizens second. In either case, the focus of the nation-state became that of "strength" out of necessity.

The strength of the nation-state was then used either defensively or offensively or both. The intense competition of the emerging nation-states of Europe virtually required the emphasis on strength for survival, especially among those most closely competitive of neighbors. France and England are a perfect illustration of this development. It is exemplified by their several-hundred-year history of conflict against each other. As one state strengthened, the other had to strengthen or be threatened with extinction.

The history of Europe from the twelfth into the twentieth century can be seen, at least from one important perspective, as a long, complicated arms race among multiple competitors with shifting alliances. Each national leader—whether they were called king, emperor, chancellor, or prime minister—had ample justification for increasing their power by pointing to the other nation-states as a potential threat to the security of the citizens. The build up of internal power was often a requirement for survival. Unfortunately, it was also sometimes used for external aggrandizement.

Did the Rise of Nation-States Occur Quickly and Evenly?

The modern European nation-states arose slowly. The medieval kingdoms started out very small and decentralized. The *manorial system* (or its equivalent) was the standard societal organization. The process of centralizing power was a gradual phenomenon for a very good reason. Power and control are difficult to administer. They are easiest to administer within the close horseback riding distance of the manor, the nearby fields, and the supporting village. To go beyond close proximity is very problematic.

The centralization of power away from the manor to the nation-state proceeded over time through battles, diplomacy, marriage, and inheritance. The persons attempting centralization faced the same dilemma of administration as was faced by all the ancient rulers of civilizations. The dilemma was how to administer beyond your personal ability to oversee daily operations. Some ancient and classical civilizations had accomplished centralization and enlargement of their empire, but the Roman Empire served as evidence that even the grandest empire was difficult to maintain indefinitely.

The unique competitive environment of the emerging Europe actually created a persuasive rationale for national centralization: defense against aggressors from abroad. As each nation became more centralized, it was cause for others to do so. They were each encouraged to find ways to centralize and they took varied paths. The dilemma of administering centralized control was at first overcome by utilizing many differing methods, but mostly motivated by the force of necessity. It was later overcome by the use of technological advancements. The railroads and the telegraph were some of the many tools that helped states administer centralized power across wider territory.

The English proceeded in their internal process of centralization with a greater emphasis on freedom. The English barons established restrictions on the monarchy early in the process as seen in the Magna Carta. The social order eventually gained an emphasis on individual liberty through the evolution of common law. This helps to explain why the conditions of Libertas occurred first in Great Britain.

Regardless of the varying emphasis on freedom in the dif-

ferent emerging nations of Europe, the trend toward centralization and military build-up was obvious. Successful nations
were usually required to have at least defensive power in order
to survive. Therefore, the rise of the nation-state in Europe also
coincided with the rise of Libertas, as well as other unrelated
phenomena.

Was There a Causal Relationship Between the Rise of the Nation-State and the Rise of Libertas?

Unfortunately, the fact that the modern nation-state and Libertas both arose at roughly the same time has led many to the
incorrect conclusion that they are causally related. One did not
directly cause the other. However, they do have some effects
on each other. On one side, Libertas requires the power of an
overarching civic authority to maintain the *rules of engagement*
that are the foundation of Libertas. On the other hand, the incredible power of nations beginning in the mid-nineteenth century would not have been possible without the technological
and managerial changes of the Industrial Revolution that, itself,
was contingent upon the conditions of Libertas.

Yet these simultaneous connections do not constitute a direct cause-and-effect relationship. Libertas does not require
governmental power beyond that needed to ensure the maintenance of the rules of engagement. Abundant governmental
power does not require the conditions of Libertas, as the totalitarian examples of recent history certainly illustrate. Yet the
rise of the nation-state and the expansion of Libertas at roughly
the same historical time have created an incorrect perception to
some observers that the incredible prosperity caused by Libertas was actually caused by the rise of the nation-state.

The evidence overwhelmingly proves the opposite. Central
administration of most human action by government authority has caused misery, hardship, and despair. While, contrarily,
widespread Libertas has created human improvement that can
be objectively measured. The rise of the nation-state, however,

created a tremendous rise in armament that ultimately resulted in unprecedented devastation during the twentieth century. This devastation was essentially a battle between the forces of Libertas and Anti-Libertas over who would win and over who would control this new power of the nation-state and the resultant armament.

The forces of Libertas won out against the forces of fascism and communism. Therefore, the forces of Libertas were left holding the huge power of nation-states and incredible military might. The battles of World War II and the Cold War required tremendous power. Many casual observers became confused between the necessity of centralized power for those purposes and the necessity of centralized power for the purposes of everyday life.

Centralized governmental power began to be seen as the best way to resolve all human problems. This is a natural reaction to the success of Libertas-based governmental power winning the big battles against the forces of Anti-Libertas. Observers failed to remember that the power—being principally the power of soldiers, money, and the armaments money can buy—had ultimately been drawn from the work of decentralized individuals being productive because of the conditions of Libertas. It was the unleashing of individualized productivity that created the prosperity and technology necessary to establish the strength of the modern hegemonic power.

The extension of the power of the state away from the primary goal of self-defense, law, and order toward many other social goals has been a predominant phenomenon since the end of the world wars. The success of government direction in the United States and the United Kingdom during World War II naturally gave leaders and citizens confidence that governmental power could be successful in virtually any endeavor. This led to a mistaken belief that the use of governmental action was the best (perhaps the only) way to cure social problems, irrespective of the obvious contradiction that such action required the reduction of Libertas.

This slow, methodical abandonment of the essence of Libertas has been very pronounced since World War II. However, it was well underway in all the primary Libertas nations long before the world wars. Much of the movement began in the Progressive Era of the late nineteenth century. The success of governmental direction during World War II was only one catalyst in expanding the movement. The actual root causes of not fully appreciating the advantages of Libertas over centralized governmental direction are much more complex. We next turn our attention to the cause of our incessant desire to interrupt the conditions of Libertas that have proven so successful.

THIRTEEN

The Reluctance to Embrace Libertas

"Galling as it may be to be helpless to redress the crying injustices of the past, symbolic expiation in the present can only create new injustices among the living and new problems for the future, when newborn babies enter the world with pre-packaged grievances against other babies born the same day. Both have their futures jeopardized, not only by their internal strife but also by the increased vulnerability of a disunited society..." [1]

— Thomas Sowell, 2005

Why Is There a Reluctance to Fully Embrace Libertas?

What is it about Libertas that causes the elite (and sometimes the populace) to ignore the overwhelming evidence and pursue the unsuccessful forces of democratically based Anti-Libertas governmental interference? To a large degree, it is a reaction to the factor of *chance*, along with the altruistic concept of fairness, all in combination with fear of the uncontrolled and the innate human preference for action. Many intelligent and thoughtful people are driven by a desire to eliminate the unfairness of chance circumstances in the world. They then reject some of the components of the Libertas approach because they prefer action to inaction. Action provides what appears to be a clear line that points directly to the resolution, whereas inaction appears less certain, even dangerous.

Democratically elected elites generally prefer the controlled approach of the interventionist to the uncontrolled approach

---

1. Sowell, Thomas. *Black Rednecks and White Liberals*. First ed. San Francisco: Encounter Books, 2005. 289.

of Libertas despite evidence that Libertas is superior in over-all result. This is usually true of most political parties and philosophies within Libertas-based nations. This is the crux of the dilemma. The proponents of Libertas like to suggest that "you get what you deserve," but our world is not quite that simple or certain and people tend to want to solve the uncertainties of the world. Even in Libertas-based countries, we are inundated daily with examples of the vagaries of chance. It is a reaction to this complex issue of chance and fairness that is the root cause of the development of most initiatives coming from altruistic elite forces.

What Is the "Factor of Chance?"

In order to understand the factor of *chance*, it is valuable to start the discussion with the first and most influential instance of chance in every human life, that being birth. We do not choose our parents; it is a matter of chance. Our parents might turn out to be loving and nurturing or they might turn out to be hateful and neglecting. We might be born to a patrician family in New Haven or we might be born to an underclass family in the slums of Calcutta. We might be born with the bodily attributes of an Olympic athlete or we might be born with significant physical disabilities. There is an underlying fundamental inequity associated with this process.

The complexity of this inequity at birth is multiplied by the infinite number of historical inequities that were involved in the eventual creation of the circumstances at the time of the birth. Those circumstances at that moment of birth are the product of inequities that go back to the beginning of time. This includes the inequities of each proceeding birth of every ancestor. It is as complex as life itself, with innumerable complicating factors.

The immense factor of chance within the process of birth is certainly the most important instance within an individual life, but the instances of chance continue long after birth. Every day, some people become innocent victims of accidents or disease that have nothing to do with their behavior. Similarly, every day, some people become undeserved recipients of chance windfalls. The element of chance continues deep into every human action, not just large events such as birth, but even more so with smaller events. This complexity of chance and fairness in our world dramatically influences how people approach the different alternatives of social-political-economic organization.

The concept of the advantage of Libertas is one of individual decision-making, careful thought, hard work, discipline, and sacrifice for the purpose of receiving the benefits of life, liberty, and the pursuit of happiness. That concept of "you get what you deserve" irrefutably works *on average*. It is especially successful as motivation for individuals to be upstanding and productive citizens, and it is usually even beneficial to individuals of below-average motivation and achievement. As stated before, the results of Libertas are positive-sum, not zero-sum in nature. Even those individuals who do not develop their intelligence as much or work as hard or delay gratification as substantially as others, even they tend to benefit within a Libertas-based system from the efforts of other achievers they never see.

Take a closer look at the factor of chance, however, and you can more clearly understand and appreciate why it influences how people approach the different alternatives of social-political-economic organization. The complication comes when the vagaries of chance disrupt the potent cause-and-effect structure of Libertas. Sometimes (but rarely), even within a Libertas-based society, the careful thought, hard work, discipline, and sacrifice of an individual does not result in a positive consequence. Sometimes (but rarely) a lack of individual discipline and initiative does not result in a negative consequence. These individual injustices are not caused by a deficiency of Libertas, but rather by the interruption from the forces of chance. The fact that they are anomalies from the norm does not console the participants or the observers.

Occasionally, these anomalies can be dramatic and disturbing. For instance, a wholesome, hard-working, caring person might (by chance) get cancer and die a painful death; while at the very same moment, a despicable, lazy criminal might (by chance) hit the lottery jackpot and then live comfortably in Hawaii. These are a tortuous turn of events to any observer with a sense of decency and a love of humankind.

It must be noted that these dramatic chance interruptions of the results of Libertas are rare. Yet the rarity is not appreciated. Dramatic anomalies are constantly trumpeted in the news and it is human nature to be intrigued by negative anomalies. They are a frequent topic of neighborhood and community conversation. Decent and caring people are naturally empathetic of these circumstances. Consciously or subconsciously we end up professing the old saying: "There, but by the grace of God, go I." And this is because we all experience at least a little influence of chance each day.

This circumstance creates a desire by most caring individuals to do something about it. We rarely stop to think about the causes and the alternatives. We look around and see the prosperity of the modern Libertas-world and we have an instinctive confidence that the collective force of our community — usually the government — can solve these unfortunate events. It is only natural to want to move boldly forward through government intervention to solve every problem and right every wrong. Our preference for action leads many of us toward to this conclusion.

What Explains Our Preference for Action?

It is natural to have a bias toward the tangible and against the intangible. The interventionist approach of centralized, governmental decision-making is tangible. Taking action against the vagaries of chance and the anomalous unfairness in life gives people an immediate sense of relief and accomplishment, even if the intended results do not materialize or even if negative, unintended consequences overtake the benefits of the intended consequences.

160

The internal resolve and fortitude necessary to *not* take action is much more difficult. The philosophy of *wu wei* or inaction, as first expressed by Chinese philosopher Lao Tzu thousands of years ago, is unnatural and takes considerable discipline. The collective force of society rarely exhibits such discipline. In addition to the preference for action and a natural desire to solve problems, it is also true that the most fervent supporters of intervention are generally activists who naturally exert influence, while core supporters of Libertas and individual responsibility are generally less active politically and exert less influence.

Most people within the Libertas-based prosperous nations would agree that a system that provides prosperity and well-being according to individual achievement is preferable, including the diminished results for low performers. They draw the line when it comes to what to do about the "unfortunate" few, the people who get a bad break despite their good efforts. This is when natural instinct and the bias toward tangible action usually result in intervention, even by those commonly supportive of Libertas and individual initiative.

How Can We Distinguish Between the Effects of Human Initiative and the Effects of Chance?

Our own personal behavior is controllable by our brain. This is true for all humans except a miniscule percentage with severe physical disabilities or psychosis. Most of the results we achieve in life are a direct result of our behavior and our initiative. There is no doubt that we are regularly influenced by chance events, but we usually have ample opportunity to prepare for the unexpected and react to it. This is the essence of life. We learn from experience and we grow as individuals.

There are many habits of behavior that have proven to be extremely valuable. An exhaustive account of those is not necessary for our purposes here. Most observers would include the items already mentioned in previous discussions, such as being curious and learning (education), thinking carefully, working diligently, and delaying gratification until after the necessities are secured (including insurance for the unexpected). Such behavior allows individuals to overcome the difficulties in life, including ordinary chance events.

Individual human events can be broadly categorized into those that are controllable and those that are uncontrollable (chance). Controllable human events are the driving force in our efforts to thrive. We are all impacted by chance events, but our *conscious behavior* represents our only opportunity to thrive. We cannot alter the uncontrollable aspects of our lives. That is inherent in the definition; they are *un*controllable. We can, however, alter our behavior. It is controllable. We can alter our preparation for and our reaction to uncontrollable events.

As the modern Prosperous World has developed, it has lessened the prevalence of the negative impact of chance. It has simultaneously increased the positive impact of constructive human action (behavior). This tremendous improvement in our world has been caused by the advent of the critical mass of Libertas. This occurred because Libertas provides a structure that allows for personal growth and responsibility. Yet, despite this self-evident development, we are still rightly concerned when rare instances of chance dramatically impact the cause-and-effect relationship of Libertas. We are often distraught when our fellow citizens are affected by negative events beyond their control; when they suffer from a "bad break."

Nevertheless, the genuine dilemma comes when an attempt is made to define what constitutes a bad break and how to establish a remedy. This is where elite, centralized decision-making breaks down. It is relatively easy for one closely involved individual to make a rational decision about the bad break and remedy of another individual when they are intimately aware of virtually all of the circumstances of that case, but it is much more difficult when such decisions have to be made *en masse* about strangers.

What Should Be Done About Any Residual Effect of Historical Injustice?

The aspects of chance include the residual effects of the past. As previously mentioned, the birth of each of us is the primary example of chance. We were brought into the world without our permission and into circumstances that we could not control. There is a huge difference between being born to a two-parent upper-class family in the suburbs as opposed to being born to an unwed teenager in the ghetto.

Individuals are powerless to undo the historical past and the circumstances that led to the present. They can only react to what is happening now. Individual reaction to the present represents our only genuine opportunity for surviving and thriving. If we become unduly focused on the injustices of the past, we lose much of our ability to control the present. It is far more successful and rewarding to take full advantage of our only controllable element: our behavior, our actions.

Group action is no different. It is merely the sum of the individuals of which the group is made. And yet, groups represent the most common vehicle for undue focus on the past. Group identity is often forged by hardship and such hardship regularly becomes synonymous with some groups. Prime examples of this phenomenon are found in the Jewish and African-American "groups." The term "group" is used tentatively here because no group—whether from a college alma mater, a religious denomination, or any various compositions—is homogeneous. They are merely comprised of individuals that largely defy categorization, except in very broad and superficial terms.

However defined, groups that have suffered severe historical injustice have difficulty shaking the identity associated with the injustice. This is natural. We do not want to dishonor our ancestors by ignoring their plight. Yet the real dilemma occurs when any group attempts to move beyond the act of "honoring" the suffering of their loved ones to an attempt at seeking a redress of history. This becomes unmanageably complex and counterproductive whenever the historical injustice involves large groups or whenever long periods of time have past.

Whether we seek a redress for a past group injustice or we seek to help the "unfortunate" few, the dilemma is similar. Should we strip away the proven, positive structure of Libertas to attempt unproven centralized governmental actions? Or should we continue to improve the structure of Libertas? It is to this dilemma of democracy we next turn.

FOURTEEN

The Dilemma of Democracy

"A system in which the politicians believe that it is their duty, and in their power, to remove all dissatisfaction, must lead to a complete manipulation of the people's affairs by the politicians."[1]

— Friedrich Hayek, 1979

How Has the Struggle Between Libertas and Anti-Libertas Changed?

The early portion (from circa 1500 until 1989) of this emerging Age of Libertas was characterized by the struggle against *non-democratic* elites, such as dictatorial monarchies, fascism, and communism. A primary theme of Professor Fukuyama's fascinating *The End of History and the Last Man* was that such an age has ended.[2] Obviously, he was not saying that history really ended or that progress was no longer possible. Rather he was saying that the big struggles against non-democratic elites were over and that Libertas won. Lesser fights against the few remaining non-democratic elites, such as Islamic fundamentalism, would still continue, but the outcome was inevitable.

The current portion — 1989 forward — of this Age of Libertas is being characterized mostly by the struggle against *democratic* elites. This includes the struggles within newer democratic nations that are missing many other components of Libertas. It

---

1. Hayek, Friedrich A. *Law, Legislation and Liberty Volume 3*. Phoenix ed. Chicago: The University of Chicago Press, 1979. 16.

2. Fukuyama, Francis. *The End of History and the Last Man*. New York: The Free Press, 1992.

165

also includes the struggles within older democratic nations and their well-intentioned legislative attempts that are designed to improve daily life, but that tend to curb individual-minority rights, the rule of law, the protection of private property, free enterprise, and other components of Libertas. This struggle within *democratic* elites is subtle, fought mostly with ideas, media, and votes, not with military force or guerilla violence. This is perhaps one of the crowning achievements of Libertas. Humankind has primarily advanced to a point of fighting battles of reason with ideas, rather than fighting battles of death with weapons.

What Is the Relationship Between Libertas and Democracy?

We often hear that *democracy* defeated fascism in World War II and that *democracy* defeated communism in the Cold War. Similarly, it is often suggested that western powers are deposing despotic regimes in certain undemocratic nations for the purpose of bringing *democracy* to their people. Yet it has already been pointed out that Libertas includes much more than democracy. It would be far more accurate to say that *Libertas* defeated fascism, communism, and isolated despotic regimes.

The relationship between democracy and Libertas is therefore important to understand. It is theoretically possible to establish substantial personal liberty and free enterprise without democracy, but historical evidence suggests a strong — but not absolute — correlation between the success of Libertas and the presence of democracy. The opposite is also true. There is a strong correlation between the advent of Anti-Libertas and non-democratic governments.

There is an obvious reason for these correlations. An elite governmental group that is not democratically based, no matter how devoted to other components of Libertas at a given moment, is severely hampered by a lack of internal self-control and by succession planning. Autocratic leadership has a long-term

166

deficiency. A benevolent autocrat can sometimes be helpful in establishing other components of Libertas, but autocracy cannot succeed in the long run. Eventually, the controlling elite of a non-democratic government succumbs to the corruptive force of power and abandons the other aspects of Libertas, either in the first generation or in subsequent transfers of authority.

Can Democracy Actually Work Against Libertas?

Democracy by itself does not ensure Libertas. A democratic society can easily abandon the concept of individual-minority rights, rule of law, limited government, free enterprise, free trade, and the protection of private property. As previously stated, Libertas is not just political, it is also social, economic, and philosophical. The brilliance of the Founding Fathers of the United States was their meticulous and careful construction of a constitution that establishes democracy, but also limits democracy in favor of the other components of Libertas.

Democracy can be the enemy of Libertas unless important controls are in place to limit democratic attempts to abandon the other aspects of Libertas. Worse yet, democracy may very well have an innate evolutionary bias away from certain other components of liberty. This bias arises from the proclivity of political candidates to play to the momentary whims of certain special interest groups within the electorate, against minority interests and against other aspects of Libertas. These same politicians (of all parties) tend to form a new class of elite decision makers with an image of competence and superiority. At any given time, especially on specialized issues, the majority of the electorate may not appreciate or acknowledge the limitations on government that were so important to the Founding Fathers of the United States or to the founders of other Libertas-based nations. The most important social-political-economic struggles of the twenty-first century and beyond will be the struggle of democracies to maintain Libertas.

Why Do Altruistic Elites Believe in Their Superiority?

The universal history of our species is the amassing of Libertas to the point that the majority of human interaction is cooperative rather than coercive. The revolutionary character of this triumph of Libertas and *triumph of the common individual* should not be overlooked. Still today, very large portions of the most educated and successful people in society absolutely reject this notion of individual power and control. They believe that individual choice and responsibility should be ceded to governmental control. They do not trust *the people*. They trust elite decision-makers.

There is a logical explanation of this superiority complex often exhibited by altruistic elites. Our very existence is predicated on our consciousness. As Descartes so philosophically stated: "I think, therefore, I am." The mystery and preciousness of that consciousness causes a natural admiration of, perhaps even worship of, our own ability to think and to reason. This, in turn, causes an innate predilection toward the superiority of our own thought or to the thought of a surrogate that we have chosen to support.

Some people therefore tend to support construction of society by the design of an elite group (which requires coercion) rather than by the spontaneity of individual Libertas (which requires the absence of coercion). Such elitists tend to believe in the superiority of their own thought; or, by extension, the thought of their chosen surrogate. Overcoming this natural superiority complex is not only an act of unselfishness, it is also an act of realism. It is a second stage of our species *taming* itself.

Although our universal history does not show evidence of humans fundamentally altering the predominant characteristic of selfishness, it does show evidence of humans rejecting the elite decision-making of Anti-Libertas for the individual decision-making of Libertas. This was true as Libertas evolved slowly before the Revolutionary Period in the eighteenth century and it has been true as Libertas grew more swiftly in later periods. This includes an appreciation that, although we may not always agree with our fellow citizens, we do respect their right to make their own decisions, be responsible for their own actions, and live freely.

Yet, at the very time Libertas was becoming the only legitimate social structure of humans, the idea of ceding much of that Libertas to new democratic elites also grew. The causes of this tendency have been explained and are understandable. The real question remains: Is it the best method to achieve humankind interest? The answer to that question brings us to an examination of the weaknesses of centralized action.

FIFTEEN

The Weakness of the State

"Ah, you miserable creatures! You who think that you are so great! You who judge humanity to be so small! You who wish to reform everything! Why don't you reform yourselves? That task would be sufficient enough."[1]

— Frederic Bastiat, 1850

What Is the New Challenge to Libertas?

The new challenge to Libertas is mostly from within. It is from you and me. It is the challenge of maintaining Libertas within the societies that already embrace it. At the core, yet again, this is still a struggle of the common person versus elites.

The complexity of life and society, which continues to progressively expand, creates unlimited opportunity for missteps and mistakes. Most failures in individuals occur when problems are ignored and the individual does not put forth the serious thought, careful analysis, and hard work necessary to thrive. This tendency to circumvent positive effort is generally self-correcting. It is self-correcting because individuals usually expect their actions to result in either positive or negative consequences. Individuals either self-correct or they fail to thrive. The vast majority individuals refuse to fail. They insist on *thrival.*

The dynamic role of positive and negative consequences is quite different when we move from the individual level to the

---

1. Bastiat, Frederic. *The Law*. Second ed. Irvington-on-Hudson: Foundation for Economic Education, 1998. 56.

societal level. A government that concentrates only on the strict provision of Libertas merely creates the social structure that facilitates individual decision-making and the resultant positive and negative consequences of individual action. Yet no government ever stops there, even Libertas-based governments. The history of Libertas-based governments includes inevitable attempts to intervene into societal outcomes. This includes attempts such as those designed to promote the worthy goals of education, safety, healthcare, and economic sustenance for some or all of the citizens.

Democratically elected elites are particularly susceptible to falling into the trap of attempting to solve every problem of the citizenry. This is true no matter how complex the issue and no matter how much historical evidence shows the futility of this approach. These attempts are generally not caused by bad intentions, but by misguidance and unwillingness to sacrifice the immediate superficial gratification of *doing something* for the substantive long-term advancement of actual achievement.

Governmental actions require even more care and consideration than individual actions because of the inherent disadvantages of centralized decision-making. Unfortunately, governmental actions usually proceed with less care and consideration. Serious thought, careful analysis, hard work, and sacrifice are not exactly the hallmarks of typical governmental action. And although mistakes made by individuals are often self-correcting, those made by democratically elected elites and governmental bureaucracies are often *not* self-correcting, at least not in acceptable time periods.

Why is Governmental Coercion So Vulnerable to Failure?

The ability of a government to successfully intervene beyond maintaining individual Libertas is severely hampered in many ways. Only the primary difficulties will be highlighted here, but they are overwhelming. The problems start with the process of building a *consensus* for action. They then include the process of dealing with the *complexities* of centralized action. Within these processes, centralized action is hampered by *structural* deficiencies. They are also hindered by *measurement* problems. Throughout all of these components, centralized action suffers from lack of *ability*.

The result of these difficulties is predictable, but only broadly so. There is actually an increase in unpredictability. Centralized governmental actions (beyond the protection of Libertas) do not always result in negative outcomes. However, on average, they lead to less progress for humans than would have otherwise occurred with a stricter focus on individual Libertas. The inherent deficiencies in the conduct of centralized action are the cause.

What Are the Problems of Building "Consensus"?

The difficulties of democratic governmental intervention begin in the process of building a consensus for the governmental action. This entire topic was brilliantly described by James M. Buchanan and Gordon Tulluck in their renowned work *The Calculus of Consent.*[2] These difficulties are so pervasive and complicated that the studies of Buchanan, a Nobel laureate, and others have spawned an entire sub-discipline called Public Choice. One of the primary premises of the school of *Public Choice* is that individuals (both voters and politicians) do not necessarily transform themselves magically from self-interested to public-interested as they enter into political activities.

> *Political theorists seem rarely to have used this essentially economic approach to collective activity. Their analyses of collective-choice processes have more often been grounded on the implicit assumption that the representative individual seeks not to maximize his own utility, but to find the 'public*

---

2. Buchanan, James M., and Gordon Tullock. *The Calculus of Consent.* Indianapolis: Liberty Fund, 1999.

*interest' or 'common good.' Moreover, a significant factor in
the popular support for socialism through the centuries has
been the underlying faith that the shift of an activity from the
realm of private to that of social choice involves the replacement of the motive of private gain by that of social good...No
one seems to have explored carefully the implicit assumption
that the individual must somehow shift his psychological and
moral gears when he moves between the private and the social
aspects of life.*[3]

Once the individual motivation behind collective decisions
of voters and politicians is more realistically understood, the
process of building consensus reveals many complex factors
that often work against the greatest good for the greatest number. This includes citizens voting for issues in which they benefit but with which the whole of society does not. It also includes politicians voting for items to which they are opposed,
but which will gain for them the vote of other politicians on
other matters that they favor. This latter process is known by
the unusual name of "logrolling" and it is a major reason for the
disgust most observers have when examining the intricacies of
the legislative process in detail.

The reason why consensus — whenever it is reached on most
particular issues — is usually so disappointing to individuals is
that it rarely represents the true desires of any one person because it is a compromise by definition. In private affairs within
a structure of Libertas, individuals have much greater freedom
to meet their desires more exactly than in public governmental
affairs. They are not required to purchase the best-selling food
item or clothing product in any category; they can choose to
purchase the least popular if that meets their interest. They are
not obligated to worship in the primary religious denomination; they can choose an obscure religion or none at all. They

3. Buchanan, James M., and Gordon Tullock. *The Calculus of Consent*. Indianapolis:
Liberty Fund, 1999. 19.

can choose to associate broadly in society or they can choose to be a hermit. This type of choice is severely limited in public policy where consensus is required. Choices are much more limited and they rarely match perfectly with the desires of any one individual.

What Are the "Complexities" of Centralized Action?

The complexities of centralized action are many. Four of the most common include: the issue of *participation*; the issue of *multiple sources*; the issue of *group activity*; and the issue of *moving targets*. These are not the only complexities of centralized action, but they are some of the most common and significant.

The issue of *participation* involves the difficulty of determining who receives the benefit of centralized action and who must bear the cost. This may sound simple, but it is hardly so. An illustrative example involves general welfare payments or tax credits designed to help the poor. In the United States, these are often determined by the level of income declared through the Internal Revenue Service. Any single adult (or household) with an income below a certain level might be eligible for a particular program. Yet, what if the single adult is the twenty-eight-year-old son of wealthy parents living off the generosity of his family? What if the individual is earning a virtual fortune in illegal drug trades? These questions represent merely the beginning of the complexity of participation that is almost endless.

The issue of *multiple sources* includes the many different levels of governmental jurisdiction that often cause harmful confusion when attempting simultaneous intervention into the lives of citizens and their businesses. This includes many private actions that are not the result of direct governmental orders, but are the indirect result of the fear of frivolous lawsuits. This circumstance is created by contradictory and coercive court decisions. Actions taken (or threatened) through the court, even those involving a jury made up of citizens, can be coercive and detrimental to Libertas. The impact of court decisions is merely one of the many multiple sources of jurisdiction that add to the complexity of governmental action.

The issue of *group* activity includes the effect of governmental action on groups of citizens. The everyday impact of governmental intervention is partially masked by the fact that most modern governmental bureaucracies affect businesses and institutions more directly than individuals. Businesses and institutions absorb the most harmful initial effects of the majority of governmental bureaucracy. They then pass those effects on to individuals. This problem is only slowly becoming obvious to everyday people. It has been relatively easy to gain the support of the majority of the population for excessive regulation of business because most people tend to think of businesses and institutions as abstract, impersonal, and greedy entities divorced from the aspects of actual people. However, the fact is that businesses are merely extensions of people. Individuals own the businesses, individuals work at the businesses, and individuals ultimately consume the products of the businesses. Therefore, individuals always absorb the effects of governmental, centralized, bureaucratic decision-making on businesses, even if it is not immediately obvious to them. This extra level created by groups (businesses and institutions) adds even greater complexity to governmental attempts at societal intervention.

The issue of *moving targets* includes the incredible difficulty of using written legislation, static codes, and bureaucracy to administer governmental action in a fast changing world. The activity of government is slow and inflexible, but the world changes every minute. Problems targeted for improvement by government action often change before the ink on the legislation is even dry. Those circumstances change again before administrative and regulatory bodies can interpret the legislation and act upon it. Finally, those changes pale in comparison to the changes that occur after the action has begun and after they begin to affect the issue in unintended ways. All of this adds to complexity immensely.

What Are the "Structural Deficiencies" of Centralized Intervention?

The structural deficiencies of centralized intervention are many. Three of the most egregious concerns are the use of *bureaucracy*, the *administrative overhead*, and the potential for personal *malfeasance*. These are not the only deficiencies of centralized intervention, but they are some of the most common and significant.

The use of *bureaucracy* by government is inevitable because of the span-of-control dilemma and the impossibility that a small elite group could physically make decisions throughout the span of control. Bureaucracy requires the establishment of standard procedures that cannot possibly foresee every future circumstance and therefore ineffective decision-making inevitably occurs when the circumstances and the procedures do not match properly. This is an inherent inefficiency within bureaucracy. Ludwig von Mises wrote an in-depth treatise on the nature of bureaucracy that brilliantly explained this deficiency.[4] Most observers despise bureaucracy and consider it to be a sign of "bad" government, but it is actually an inevitable tool of government that cannot be avoided. The explanations used by Mises in his book *Bureaucracy* are as valid today as when they were when written over sixty years ago. The negative effects of governmental bureaucracy are almost overwhelming in most large Libertas-based nations of today, which is essentially becoming a genuine threat to the success of Libertas overall.

The issue of *administrative overhead* is another structural deficiency of governmental intervention. It receives unusually little attention. There is often attention paid to specific examples of government waste, but less so to the overall administrative expenses of governmental programs. For example, in the United States there has developed a fine tradition of requiring private charities to very specifically identify the percentage of donated

---

4. Mises, Ludwig von. *Bureaucracy*. Cedar Falls: Center for Futures Education, 1983.

dollars that are used directly to help the recipients as opposed to the percentage that are utilized in administrative and fund-raising expenses. Unfortunately, we do not regularly require the same disclosure information of our government programs. It is obvious to even the most casual observer that such disclosures would prove that public charity is dramatically less efficient than private charity, partially because of the unusually high administrative expenses.

The concern over another structural problem, that being the potential personal *malfeasance* by governmental officials, is deservedly high. Most public employees have good intentions and conduct themselves with high standards. However, the temptation to steal from the public trough is incredibly strong because there is so much bureaucracy and inefficiency that it is hard to notice. Additionally, the "public" does not necessarily present the engaging face of a victim as would an individual in a private theft. The potential malfeasance includes much more than only the direct theft of funds. It could also include the personal use of public property, the acceptance of bribes, or merely getting public wages while slacking off the job. The deficiencies of malfeasance, administrative expense, and bureaucracy all react together with other deficiencies to add to the disadvantages of governmental intervention.

What Are the "Measurement Difficulties" of Centralized Action?

It was previously stated that the negative consequences of governmental actions are often not self-correcting, at least not in acceptable timeframes. The reason for this relative lack of self-correction is that governmental decision-makers are usually buffered from the results of their decisions and the results of such complex societal decisions are extremely difficult to measure.

The buffer exists largely because the effects — if they can be measured with any accuracy at all — often take long periods of time to materialize. The decision-makers frequently change over those periods of time, the focus of the public changes, and the societal circumstances evolve.

The measurements are extremely complicated, especially with large-scale governmental projects. The decision on what and how to measure is made through the same inefficient consensus-building process and administered through the same bureaucracy as described before. The projects are often so large and complex that the results are impacted by a multitude of related circumstances that are difficult to understand because they cannot be isolated.

The complexity and inexactness of centralized, elite decision-making almost always causes unintended consequences, often the opposite of the intended consequences. A United States senator was once heard to claim that the only item Congress always includes in every piece of legislation is that of *unintended consequences*.

What Is the "Lack of Ability" Inherent in Governmental Intervention?

As previously discussed, individual decision-making is superior to group decision-making because humans have a limited mind and the world is complex. The decisions and actions of each individual over the course of every minute of every day of their lifetime, multiplied by every individual in every society, sums up to a level of complexity that reaches near infinity. Many of those individual decisions require serious thought and careful analysis of the factors facing that individual at that particular moment. The process of decision-making is difficult for an individual and there is no doubt that some individuals are better at it than others. Yet, as hard as it is, imagine if an individual not only has to make those decisions for their own personal circumstances, but then also for a thousand other people...or a million...or a billion. It cannot succeed. No one person (or elite group) is capable of that level of intelligence. It is many times more successful to utilize the brainpower of billions through the mechanism of individual Libertas.

For those who would suggest that the age of computers now makes centralized governmental decision-making more possible, it should be noted that the opposite is true. The advent of computers adds to the complexity of the world faster than they can be used centrally to deal with such complexity. Computers are merely extensions of humans. Humans utilize computers for human purposes. Computers allow humans greater complexity in interaction, thereby adding to, not subtracting from, the overall superiority of decision-making at the lowest level.

Therefore, it is a much more successful adaptive strategy to maintain decision-making at the lowest level possible and to avoid using governmental action for other than improving the conditions of Libertas. In one way or another, elite control or Anti-Libertas is always founded on the premise that individuals are either incapable or too self-serving and must be centrally controlled by an elite governmental group. Actually, the opposite is true. It is the governmental elites that are either incapable or too self-serving and it is the elites that must be controlled by the individuals (masses).

Henry Adams very astutely recognized the limitations of centralized, elite decision-making when he said: "The effect of unlimited power on a limited mind is worth noting in Presidents because it must represent the same process in society..."[5] The point is that even the smartest governmental leaders have a limited capacity for decision-making, even if they do not succumb to personal aggrandizement or malfeasance. They have great difficulty making decisions about the complexities of life, not because of their personal level of intelligence, but because of the inherent limitations of the human mind. When this limitation meets up with an unlimited amount of governmental power to make decisions on behalf of large groups of individu-

5. Adams, Henry. *The Education of Henry Adams.* Paperback ed. Oxford: Oxford University Press, 1999. 350.

als, less-than-optimal results inevitably occur.

What Are the Direct Results of the Deficiencies Inherent in Governmental Intervention?

The deficiencies inherent in governmental intervention result in case after case where the bureaucracy in action trumps common sense. This is especially obvious to citizens as they deal with daily matters at the post office, the Office of Motor Vehicles, the Transportation Safety Administration, or a myriad of similar government operations. Yet these large examples are not isolated and they represent merely the most obvious cases. The details of the predominantly negative impact of governmental intervention have been intricately researched in a multitude of scholarly works, including *The Death of Common Sense* by Philip K. Howard,[6] *The Dream and the Nightmare* by Myron Magnet,[7] *Losing Ground*[8] by Charles Murray, and *The Tragedy of American Compassion* by Marvin Olasky.[9]

The history of the major western democracies is rife with examples of these unintended consequences. There are so many similar examples that their number cannot even be estimated, probably equaling billions if anyone could ever comprehensively research every local government around the world over the past couple of centuries. They permeate throughout the centralized governmental decision-making process, whether that is local, national, or global government. They are the inevitable result of a Libertas-based government moving beyond the primary responsibility of preventing coercion (crime and

---

6. Howard, Philip K. *The Death of Common Sense*. New York: Random House, 1994.

7. Magnet, Myron. *The Dream and the Nightmare*. First paperback ed. San Francisco: Encounter Books, 2000.

8. Murray, Charles. *Losing Ground*. Tenth Anniversary ed. New York: Basic Books, 1994.

9. Olasky, Marvin. *The Tragedy of American Compassion*. Washington: Regnery Publishing, 1992.

181

war) and creating new governmental coercion with the best of intentions.

A substantial and common unintended consequence of most interventionist action in general is the vicious cycle created by the overall process. It usually starts with the identification of a problem or crisis. Then the legislature, administrative body, or court attempts to solve the problem through legislation, policy decree, or court order. Yet that merely outlines the solution that then must be turned over to regulatory or administrative bureaucracies for more detailed planning and implementation. Then the citizens and businesses begin reacting to the new rules and processes. Their actions are often adjusted again and again depending on the results of their initial reactions. These reactions are usually complex and varied. They almost always include unintended consequences, many of which were practically unpredictable at the time of initial governmental decision. It is not at all uncommon that some of these unintended consequences actually exacerbate the original crisis. Finally, there is eventually a call for more and different governmental action due to the exacerbated circumstances that were, in some part, created by the previous governmental action. And the cycle begins again and builds on itself until the intended consequences are often far out of sight and usually unachievable. This process is like a bad psychological experiment gone awry.

Are These Negative Results a Sign of the Bad Intent or Personal Ineptitude of Those Involved?

The results are mostly unintended. The individuals voting, writing the legislation, issuing court decisions, developing the regulations, and administering the programs do not usually have bad intentions. Their intentions are honorable, often noble. Most of these multitudes of negative, but unintended, consequences are not examples of the personal ineptitude of the individuals developing or administering the regulations, policies, or programs. The problem is in the fundamental flaws inherent in governmental intervention and the unnecessary coercion of government. The intent is positive, but the effect is negative. The negative effects extend beyond merely the direct unintended consequences. The less obvious consequences are much more harmful. These include the displacement of the positive effects of Libertas and the diversion away from the maintenance and improvement of Libertas.

What Results Are Displaced When Government Coercion Replaces Individual Cooperation?

The extensive advancement of Libertas, with the inherent productive use of self-interest and individualized decision-making, does eventually "raise all boats." Sometimes the effect takes time, perhaps years or even multiple generations, but Libertas outperforms all alternatives—even good-intentioned governmental action—in the long run. The extensive advancement of Libertas actually reduces the vagaries of chance, thereby reducing the need to help future victims of such vagaries. In the business world, this is known as attacking the root cause, rather than concentrating on applying resources to the visible manifestation of the problem.

Examples of Libertas reducing the vagaries of chance abound. Today, when we think of such vagaries within the Libertas-nations, we may think of chance accidents, the acts of weather, natural disasters, rare birth defects, and the like. Prior to the more complete evolution of Libertas and the resultant rise of prosperity, the vagaries of chance were many times more common and we would worry about infant mortality, rampant diseases, food shortages, pervasive use of slavery, incessant warfare, arbitrary confiscation of property, and a much more severe lack of personal security. These are still the vagaries that endanger our fellow humans in the Impoverished World today.

Perhaps the best example resides in the most important instance of chance in the life of every individual. As previously noted, *birth* is the ultimate instance of chance. The flow of our lives moves only in one direction, as is also the case with history. We frequently talk about the decisions — or lack of decisions — that parents make in the process of having children. The children have no choice in the matter. They cannot choose their biological parents. The inequity associated with that process was overwhelmingly negative throughout most of recorded history when only a very small elite component of society lived much beyond destitution. The process of birth in those times relegated most children to short lives and miserable conditions. Now that Libertas has enabled humans to spread prosperity much more broadly, that primary instance of chance in the life of each individual within the Prosperous World is more skewed to positive circumstances.

These processes represent an important change in the lives of humans. The result of Libertas has been to make things better in this regard. Perhaps we have not really reduced the overall instances of *chance,* as much as we have reduced the negative possible outcomes of chance. We have not necessarily made our lives or our world more *certain*, but we have made our lives and our world more positive. We have improved the well-being of humans on average. This is the universal history of Libertas.

Aside from representing the difference of today from our past, these examples also accurately represent the difference between the Prosperous World and the Impoverished World today. Those of us in the Prosperous World have much better lives, much less to worry about, and we are much less susceptible to the vagaries of chance. The difference is Libertas. Our structure of Libertas allowed for significant and tangible human advancement, but the framework of Libertas is still absent in the Impoverished World. Even our chance accidents and natural disaster problems of today are minimized by Libertas. The prosperity and stability of Libertas allows for affordable insurance, personal safety devices, extensive public safety mechanisms, and limited social safety nets.

Unfortunately, the use of governmental intervention in attempts to solve broad social ills almost always requires the suspension of many aspects of Libertas. Not only are the results of these efforts often negative because of unintended consequences, but, more importantly, the very positive results of Libertas are simultaneously lessened. The amount of human and financial resources required to implement governmental intervention could have been used in private actions by individuals building a better world, one person at a time. The ultimate cost of this partial displacement of Libertas is a substantial negative consequence of interference.

What Diversion of Focus Takes Place When Government Expands to Intervene in Societal Outcomes?

The administration of national defense, law, and order is a crucial task of government. The oversight by the citizens in a democracy over the government should be of utmost importance in discussions leading into voting decisions. The growth of excessive government extension into other, less essential areas inhibits the proper focus on the core governmental processes by politicians and voters alike.

Most criticism of societal overextension is centered on the fiscal cost, the restriction of liberties, or the paucity of results. However, there is a much more dangerous consequence that is often overlooked. It is the danger of diverting focus and resources away from the truly crucial task of maintaining Libertas; that being the prevention of coercion (crime and aggression).

Maintaining Libertas is not easy. A system of laws is required that focuses on individual liberty. Fair administration of those laws is necessary. The citizens must be protected from foreign aggression. Public safety needs to be considered. All of these essential tasks require policemen, prosecutors, defense attorneys, judges, firemen, military troops, etc. Yet these essential services do not materialize without considerable effort and they do not operate justly and efficiently without oversight.

185

These crucial public tasks are administered by individuals. This small group of individuals exercises incredible power over the larger percentage of citizens. This power sometimes includes the power of life and death, sometimes the power over personal freedom, and always the power to spend public funds. The difficulty of centralized governmental administration has already been highlighted. This also applies to the provision of the services necessary to maintain Libertas. All of this makes these tasks both crucial and exasperating.

Therefore, the time, attention, and resources of the government agencies should be dedicated almost exclusively to these tasks. Great care should be given to enacting precise and proper laws. Police and judicial actions should be carefully administered. It is important to ensure that the power of law makers and law enforcers is not abused and that it is dispensed with astute fairness and equal protection. This in turn requires the focus and attention of the public. The public should be making voting decisions based largely upon the success of public officials in maintaining the conditions necessary for Libertas. Public volunteers and media should help provide keen oversight to ensure that the results of those holding the public trust are as clear and evident as possible.

The incredibly arduous task of maintaining the best possible conditions favorable to Libertas in a society is damagingly shortchanged when the government begins expanding far beyond these basic tasks. The attention of the lawmakers is shifted. The law enforcers begin to be overwhelmed by the sheer volume of codes to enforce. Important resources are diverted. The crucial oversight provided by public and media scrutiny is distracted from the primary goal.

The diversion away from the core public functions can lead to conditions adverse for achieving the best possible state of Libertas. Prosecutors may attempt to prosecute cases based primarily on the amount of publicity they will achieve, rather than on a clear violation or a danger to the community. Cities or counties may concentrate their law enforcement efforts on generating revenue by overzealous enforcement of traffic codes rather than on serious crime protection. Government agencies may arbitrarily enforce regulatory codes based upon the personal ideology of their administrators, rather than on the valid interpretation of codes. Finally, all levels of government are likely to be seriously hindered by the task of interpreting an unfathomable number of laws and regulations that—although unintended—create the inevitability of arbitrariness, even for the best of public servants.

These public servants should instead be concentrating on having a concise number of laws structured on Libertas, on enforcing those laws with the highest degree of fairness and equality, and on conducting public activity with an air of openness to scrutiny from the citizens. All of this requires intense focus and effort. Attempts to overextend into other areas of life will divert resources away from these important tasks. Therefore, such attempts at overextension are most assuredly counterproductive. Although a minority of such attempts may succeed, the majority will bring unintended consequences. The gravest of all these unintended consequences is the dilution of focus on Libertas, the primary factor of human progress.

Do the Deficiencies of Government Intervention and the Prevalence of Unintended Consequences Mean We Should Do Nothing or Stop Caring?

The fact that government intervention has a long history of failure does not negate the fact that we should still care about distressful conditions in our societies. We still care about senior citizens, the poor, and the homeless. We still care about people who harm themselves by abusing drugs and alcohol. We still care about those who cannot maintain themselves because of psychosis or severe physical disabilities.

There is middle ground. The longstanding Libertas-based nations have gone way too far down the interventionist path to be able to successfully eliminate all social interventions. It would not be prudent to attempt to do so suddenly. Yet, we should appreciate that centralized government decision-making and coercion have strong innate inhibiters to success. Therefore, we should be extremely careful before adding to the problem. And most of our efforts should be directed toward cautiously unraveling our past mistakes. Most importantly, we should appreciate that expansive centralized governmental decision-making diverts important attention away from those activities that government must perform well for the survival of Libertas.

One great example available for the modern, realistic reassessment of government action can be found in Chile. The national leaders of Chile realized that their version of a Social Security system was designed as a generational transfer scheme (similar to the United States) and was hurting the very people it was intended to help. The national leaders were not willing to revert to the pure form of Libertas of "each to their own," but they were willing to establish a much better retirement system based mostly on private investment, yet still adhering to some regulatory guidelines and including a limited safety net. In the long run, this reversion to more Libertas will greatly enhance the financial security of the citizens, especially in future generations.

This is just one of many examples of governments readdressing the programs of past interventions. It is an excellent way to channel our overwhelming desire to do something, to be active in improving the conditions of our fellow citizens. The most effective way to channel our altruistic urges is to participate in private charitable activity and to help in the collective public efforts to improve the structure of Libertas. We cannot realistically stop the desire to help, nor should we want to do so. The desire to help is actually the result of our human success. The irresistible yearning to help others is something that has only become prevalent in the modern Prosperous World caused by the conditions of Libertas.

It is because most humans care for one another that the

problems of destitution and inequality distress us. Therefore, the urge to solve problems through government intervention is almost uncontrollable. It is unrealistic to expect that no intervention will be attempted, and some intervention occasionally succeeds. However, the most prudent action requires extreme caution, careful thought, and serious discussion before taking the drastic action of utilizing the armed power of government to intervene into the structure of Libertas.

Can the "Weakness of the State" Be Overcome and Can Centralized Elites Still Make Better Decisions Than Individuals?

This pertinent question can be restated in the following way: Can elites make more effective decisions for individuals than individuals can make for themselves? The answer is a resounding *no*! This statement may be astounding to some, particularly when it comes to complex or specialized issues. It is true there are issues, such as foreign affairs, national defense, and criminal justice where we certainly would not want to administer operations based upon plebiscite. We need and want a highly competent elite group of individuals in those fields to conduct affairs on our behalf. However, the vast majority of human activity is not involved in those affairs and instead is involved in an unlimited number of other activities that are conducted by the billions of human beings on this planet. While we need a proper skeletal framework of Libertas (the rule book and enforcement that restricts coercion) and a small elite group to conduct a very limited number of governmental functions, the remainder of human activity is much more effective with individual decision-making, rather than centralized decision-making, and with voluntary-private choice, rather than involuntary-governmental coercion.

Obviously, there are examples where common individuals do not make good, rational decisions. In those cases—if they could be determined in advance—centralized, governmental decision-making might appear to be preferable to individual decision-making, but those are exceptions to the rule. In any case, it is impossible to determine those individuals and their specific mistaken decisions in advance. In the majority of cases and on average, individuals can make more effective decisions than remote elites can make on their behalf.

It should be noted very distinctly here that the remaining disagreement, in general, between the rational proponents of Libertas and the rational proponents of Anti-Libertas intervention has *nothing* to do with the relative level of compassion on either side of the argument. Both sides have compassion, both sides care about the unfortunate, and both sides want a better world. The difference boils down to the issue of strategy and tactics. One side believes in centralized, governmental coercion for the purpose of helping build a better world and the other side believes in the spontaneous order and prosperity that individuals create when coercion against them is minimized. One side takes satisfaction in pursuing immediately tangible action and the other side is confident that the more successful approach requires the patience of freedom secured by law. One side has ample evidence to show the abject failure of their approach and the other side has overwhelming evidence of the repeated and sustainable success of Libertas.

What Is the Most Important Advice to Give to Those Struggling to Maintain Libertas?

Individuals within Libertas-based nations are increasingly becoming aware of the new internal struggle to maintain Libertas. As we attempt to understand this struggle, we would do well to recognize the structural conditions related to Libertas. A great place to begin is with the study of the deliberations of the American Founding Fathers during their task of building a structure for Libertas.

Most people have a basic knowledge of the colonial struggle, the heroic efforts of General Washington's troops, the compromise to form a new national government, the formation of a democracy, the idea of separation of powers, the foundation of a written constitution, and the enumeration of basic rights. Yet the nation and the world have changed so much over time that the one permeating concern of the Founding Fathers is often neglected; that is of the *limits* of democracy.

During the past one hundred years, the structural focus in the United States and elsewhere in the Prosperous World has been mostly concerned with how to use the government for action, in a desire to solve certain economic or social problems. The focus of the Founding Fathers was quite the opposite. Their focus was how to protect individuals from government action; not merely from *bad* government action, because such judgment was subjective by definition, but from *all* government action, except that which protected citizens from illegal coercion. This permeating concept was the primary motivation for the origin of the United States and yet it is often overlooked in our world today.

The focus on *democracy* and democratic action today causes too many to overlook the genius of the Founding Fathers as seen in their result of establishing a constitution designed to provide for democratic elections while simultaneously restricting government action, even by the consent of the majority. The structural design was purposefully complex. Authority was divided between the states and the national government, then further divided within three branches of the national government, then further divided by two houses within the legislature, and, most importantly, any and all of these subdivisions were to be tightly restricted by the restraints of the constitution itself.

The key to a superior framework of society is the establishment of Libertas. The Founding Fathers understood that Libertas was much more than political democracy; they understood it was the absence of coercion. They understood the absence of coercion required a governmental structure that restrained coercion, particularly by the government itself. James Madison, the Father of the Constitution, was specifically concerned about the limits of democracy and the potential restriction of Libertas by majority rule. The following passage from *The Federalist* is attributed to James Madison as he was attempting to convince the populace that their existing state constitutions were not sufficient to restrain the potential tyranny sanctioned by majority vote:

> *The instability, injustice, and confusion introduced into the public councils, have, in truth, been the mortal diseases under which popular governments have everywhere perished...The valuable improvements made by the American constitutions on the popular models, both ancient and modern, cannot certainly be too much admired; but it would be an unwarrantable partiality, to contend that they have as effectually obviated the danger on this side, as was wished and expected. Complaints are everywhere heard from our most considerate and virtuous citizens, equally the friends of public and private faith, and of public and personal liberty, that our governments are too unstable, that the public good is disregarded in the conflicts of rival parties, and that measures are too often decided, not according to the rules of justice and the rights of the minor party, but by the superior force of an interested and overbearing majority. However anxiously we may wish that these complaints had no foundation, the evidence of known facts will not permit us to deny that they are in some degree true...*
>
> *It is in vain to say that enlightened statesmen will be able to adjust these clashing interests, and render them all subservient to the public good. Enlightened statesmen will not always be at the helm. Nor, in many cases, can such an adjustment be made at all without taking into view indirect and remote considerations, which will rarely prevail over the immediate interest which one party may find in disregarding the rights of another...*
>
> *When a majority is included in a faction, the form of popular*

government, on the other hand, enables it to sacrifice to its
ruling passion or interest both the public good and the rights
of other citizens. To secure the public good and private rights
against the danger of such a faction, and at the same time to
preserve the spirit and the form of popular government, is
then the great object to which our inquiries are directed.[10]

The result of this political concern was the establishment of
the representative constitutional republic of the United States of
America. These founders struggled mightily to create a structure that supported Libertas in all its aspects. Their result was
masterful, yet still far from perfect. All individuals desiring to
improve the lot of humans, either in a nation previously devoid
of Libertas or in a nation struggling to maintain Libertas, would
do well to study this dilemma that faced the Founding Fathers
because it is at the essence of our struggle to improve civilization.

The founders of the United States would be astonished by
the size and scope of the government today. The bureaucracy is
huge. The number of employees, the amount of annual expen-
diture, the size of the deficit, the scope of regulation, and the
intrusion into daily life is monumental. This is true in most of
the nations stalwartly supporting Libertas. The real issue here
is not philosophically a question of more or less government for
ascetic reasons. It is a practical matter. It does not work. In fact,
it works against the best interests of achieving the most benefit
for the most people.

The "weaknesses of the state" previously highlighted —
those of consent, complexity, structure, measurement, and ability — are not the only deficiencies of centralized governmental
decision-making. This is merely the beginning of many more
obstacles. An exhaustive list of these obstacles is not necessary
here because the results are self-evident. The majority of the

---

10. Madison, James. "Number 10 The Size and Variety of the Union as a Check on
Faction." *The Federalist.* Ed. . New York: MetroBooks, 1961. 129-132.

public in the Prosperous World do not usually have an intricate knowledge of these inherent deficiencies but they do have an obvious understanding of rampant government failure at solving complex social problems. They have a common sense understanding that government intervention is not working well and that excessive interference is not what their national founders intended.

We either believe in the power and primacy of individuals or we believe in the power and primacy of elite decision makers. The primacy of pre-modern dictatorial elites took thousands of years to overcome. It took hundreds of years to establish the basic conditions of Libertas in small pockets of the world. Now the strength of Libertas is being extended globally. The next adaptive improvement will be to overcome the primacy of post-modern democratic elites.

This is a nice problem to have. The Prosperous World is living longer and healthier lives with plentiful food, clothing, and shelter. In order to continue this prosperity, we have to maintain the primary conditions of Libertas. More people are becoming cognizant of this maintenance dilemma, as will be discussed further in Part Six. This makes the maintenance of Libertas very likely to succeed.

On the other hand, the conditions in the Impoverished World are much more distressful and problematic. It is in those locations that the conditions of Anti-Libertas have remained. It is there where destitution and hopelessness reign. It is to the expansion of Libertas in those regions that we next turn our attention.

PART FIVE
The Expansion
of Libertas

SIXTEEN

The Mountain Pilgrims

"The iconoclasts were too smart to be wise, too rational to be reasonable, too much enchanted with an immature science to hold fast to tested truths. They could not find the human soul when they dissected their cadavers; they could not measure the inalienable essence."[1]

— Walter Lippmann, 1937

What Is An Example of How Humans Interact in Many Obscure but Valuable Ways?

There were thirty-nine participants and they met for a little more than a week in April 1947. The setting was a mountain resort in Switzerland. This was not a summit conference of world leaders. Instead, it was an inconspicuous and odd group of people who were unmistakably out-of-step with the mainstream intellectual current of the time. The names of the participants would not have been recognizable to any of the hotel staff at the resort. Nor would they have been recognizable to average citizens anywhere.

These pilgrims were mostly obscure college professors of economics (over one-half of them). They were from ten different countries, with about one-half coming from the United States[2] and the others coming from various European countries. They could not even afford their own travel expenses. They only

---

1. Lippmann, Walter. *The Good Society*. New Brunswick: Transaction Publishers, 2005. 379.

2. Although the U.S. contingent was, by far, the largest of any nation, it should be remembered that some of them were recent immigrants from Europe.

agreed to meet after securing funds from benefactors. It would be an obvious understatement to admit they had very little influence in the world at that time.

Only a couple of the members had yet achieved any notoriety. One of the members, the principal founder, had published a reasonably successful book a few years earlier, in 1944. Another member had been an influential professor in Vienna during the early part of the century. They used their contacts to convince like-minded thinkers to come together at this meeting. The purpose was to form a kind of intellectual club.

They discussed the establishment of this club at the initial conference in 1947. The group decided that the club should be brought together whenever feasible for the purpose of encouraging intellectual discussion among members. It was not to develop policy or influence governments or to publish propaganda. It was meant merely to give these out-of-step thinkers a chance to discuss concepts together and to exchange ideas. This was necessary because there were so few intellectuals around the world who believed in the principals these participants believed.

They believed in the power of individual liberty. They had inherited the tradition of Frederic Bastiat, David Hume, Thomas Jefferson, James Madison, Adam Smith, and others that supported free enterprise, freedom of speech, freedom of association, and the rule of law. This is a heralded tradition, but by 1947, it was a position ridiculed as old-fashioned and no longer valid in the modern world.

The forces of collectivism had expanded beyond Russia and now covered all of Eastern Europe. In democratic countries, powerful governmental action had seemingly been the cause of vanquishing the fascist powers and the curing of economic depression. John Maynard Keynes and other intellectual leaders had apparently found a "middle way" between Libertas and totalitarianism. The advantages of individual liberty were now viewed as a quaint fancy of a by-gone era.

There were precious few respectable thinkers in 1947 that

believed in the continued benefit of Libertas and in the inevitable disadvantages inherent in the fashionable philosophies of the day. So few, in fact, that they felt it necessary to meet together occasionally for mutual support. These believers in Libertas had already tended to congregate in certain universities, particularly the London School of Economics and the University of Chicago. Yet, even with such enclaves, their philosophical outlook was so unfashionable that they sought to remedy their isolation by forming a new international society of their kind.

That first meeting in 1947 occurred at the Swiss resort area of Mont Pelerin. When the participants could not agree on a name for their new club, they settled on *The Mont Pelerin Society*. The name was not the only disagreement. This was not a unified and doctrinaire political party. It was a group of individuals that believed in the primacy of individual freedom. Therefore, unanimity was neither a goal nor a realistic outcome. Discussion, disagreement, and debate were the goals and the outcomes.

The agreement they could reach at the first meeting was that they enjoyed exchanging ideas and, by continuing such an exchange, they may affect the international marketplace of ideas, at least in some small way. In their own Statement of Aims, they identified a vaporous aspiration:

> *The group does not aspire to conduct propaganda. It seeks to establish no meticulous and hampered orthodoxy. It aligns itself with no particular party. Its object is solely, by facilitating the exchange of views among minds inspired by certain ideals and broad conceptions held in common, to contribute to the preservation and improvement of the free society.*[3]

The Mont Pelerin Society has remained a relatively obscure intellectual club for over fifty years. It has never lobbied governments or published material aimed at proselytizing policy posi-

---

3. Feulner, Jr., Edwin J. *Intellectual Pilgrims*. Washington: Edwin J. Feulner, Jr., 1999. XIV.

tions. It has remained true to its objective of being a discussion group. It has been a club for exchanging ideas and for being a support group for the members. It has had virtually no direct influence in the world. The indirect influence is more substantial, but very hard to document. The influence of the group has occurred only through the individual efforts of its members. Those members have, in turn, touched many others.

The founding members were obscure at the time of the first conference in 1947. In the fashionable circles of the time, they were outcasts. But the fashionable iconoclasts of the time were "too smart to be wise." The members of the Mont Pelerin Society, on the other hand, were wise and often ignored. They understood the complexities of human interaction. They observed human interaction with a keen eye and they helped to establish detailed understanding of the advantages of individual liberty and the disadvantages of coercive intervention by government. This was accomplished through a steady pursuit for the truth, not by a desire to serve a particular orthodoxy. Slowly, their ideas began to be recognized.

Over the years, the members have won an astounding eight Nobel prizes (including three members out of the original thirty-nine). They have sold countless books and contributed to innumerable periodicals. They have regained influence on many college campuses. They have established influential think tanks around the world. They have advised many governments. Most importantly, they have influenced many millions of people who, in turn, expanded that influence to many times more people.

None of this influence was more important than that in the two most powerful defeated powers of the war: Germany and Japan.[4] The influence in Germany proceeded much faster because there were German supporters of Libertas that had survived the war and were initial participants in the Mont Pelerin

---

4. The first Japanese participant became a member in 1958 and was joined over the years by a large contingent of Japanese society members that played prominent roles in the Japanese Economic Miracle.

Society. One of them, Ludwig Erhard, came to prominence a few years after the first conference in 1947. He held a variety of influential German government positions, including rising all the way to Chancellor. As an economic advisor, he helped create the German Deutschemark and, subsequently, became known as the father of the German Economic Miracle.

It is impossible to retrace the widespread impact of the members of the Mont Pelerin Society. They quietly started a war of ideas. At first they were ignored. Eventually, their ideas gained currency. It subsequently turned into a flood. Now, the ideas are ascendant in the world of ideas about human interaction, although often not widely known by the public at large.

How Was This War of Ideas Won?

The genesis of the revitalization of Libertas had started in the late 1800s at the University of Vienna. Carl Menger is generally considered the founder of what became known as the "Austrian School" of liberal thought. His first serious scholarly work resulted in the publication of *Principals of Economics* in 1871. He began teaching at the University of Vienna the next year. His influence then extended to Friedrich von Wieser, Eugen von Bohm-Bawerk, Ludwig von Mises, Friedrich Hayek, and others who spent valuable time at the University of Vienna. They were the essential ingredients in creating the Austrian School.

The Austrian School began the modern reinvigoration of liberal thought. It did so by adapting classical liberal thought to a more modern focus. Classical liberal economics had concentrated on the function of capital and broad economic mechanisms such as supply and demand. The Austrian School began to focus on individuals and the dynamics of human interaction. This direction of academic analysis allowed for a better understanding of how and why the conditions of Libertas produce dramatically superior results for humans than do the conditions of coercion.

The progress of this neo-liberal line of thought proceeded

slowly. At first, it was primarily isolated to the academics at the University of Vienna. Eventually, it spread on to many different pockets of influence around the world, especially the burgeoning offshoot known as the "Chicago School" at the University of Chicago and across the United States. Yet, despite this growth, by 1947 these pockets of influence were still quite isolated and relatively ignored by governments, policy makers, and pundits. Friedrich Hayek helped to reduce this sense of isolation by forming the Mont Pelerin Society at that time.

The members of the society, as well as many others, continued the in-depth analysis of human interaction. This resulted in many new books and scholarly articles. Sometimes they focused on examining the advantages produced by liberty and free markets. Other times, they focused on examining the disadvantages of coercion and collectivism. The best of the neo-liberal school always strived to find observable human tendencies and trends, regardless of ideological implications, that could enlighten our understanding of history and economics. They often encouraged one another and frequently served as sources of critical review.

Although these scholars are usually classified as economists, they expanded into many other fields. The books *Human Action* by Mises and *The Constitution of Liberty* by Hayek are as much works of philosophy as any other discipline. They include emphasis on political science, sociology, psychology, and economics. The broad works and extended coverage of these pilgrims harkens back to the expansive thoughts of the Enlightenment thinkers.

The findings of these scholars and their students began expanding throughout the postwar decades. The prominence of the neo-liberalism rose dramatically in 1974 and 1976 with the awarding of Nobel prizes to Friedrich Hayek and Milton Friedman. Additional Nobel prizes were awarded to George Stigler (1982), James Buchanan (1986), Maurice Allais (1988), R. H. Coase (1991), Gary Becker (1992), and Vernon Smith (2002).

The growth of the liberal ideas was also expanded beyond

academia to a wider audience. A significant boost occurred in the United States in January 1980 with the first airing of Milton Friedman's acclaimed *Free To Choose* television documentary series.[5] To a greater degree, the public began realizing the limitations of government intervention and began appreciating the advantages of the free market and free trade.

The average citizen in the Prosperous World today still has only modest exposure to the detailed analysis provided over the decades by these outstanding scholars. However, this new prominence of neo-liberal thought has filtered through to many policy makers in much of the world, as witnessed in part by the dramatic increase of free trade agreements everywhere. The growth of neo-liberal thought predated the substantial increase in the expansion of Libertas in the latter half of the twentieth century.

It is impossible to specifically prove an exact cause-and-effect relationship between the rise of "thought" with the rise of "action" on the conditions of Libertas. Yet it is obvious in many ways. We know that many of the neo-liberal advocates began to be included as governmental advisors around the world, especially toward the end of the 1970s and thereafter. We also know of numerous governmental leaders who clearly explained the influence that the neo-liberal thinkers had on them.

The influence of this line of thought was still relatively obscure from the time of the founding at Mont Pelerin through the mid-1980s. They were temporarily dwarfed by the apparent success of the communist juggernaut and the dominance of Keynesian economics. Their consistent refutation of collectivism and government economic manipulation appeared antiquated and incorrect. But then this appearance was swept away by the global recession of stagflation in the late 1970s and by the fall of communism in 1989. It was at this point the fog began

---

5. As a form of personal disclosure, the author admits this documentary was a life-changing experience to a twenty-four old graduate student at the University of Michigan.

to clear. The voices of Hayek and others were proven not to be outdated or reactionary but instead, quite ahead of their time. These voices had been predicting the disintegration of communism for over forty years.

The reinvigoration of Libertas around the world in the past few decades has been substantial and will be detailed in the following chapters. However, to appropriately discuss the challenges of how Libertas can be expanded, it is best to begin by examining the original expansion from northwestern Europe to one of the colonial outposts over two centuries ago.

SEVENTEEN

The Colonial Example

"These great events, in many respects unparalleled in all history, make a totally new, a most wonderful and important era in the history of mankind…a change from darkness to light, from superstition to sound knowledge and from a most debasing servitude to a state of the most exalted freedom…So that, in comparison with what has been, now only can we expect to see what men really are, and what they can do."[1]

—Joseph Priestley, 1781

What Has Been the Role of the United States in this Progress of Libertas?

The victory of Libertas in the struggle between the major political-economic-social structures in the world is closely associated with the United States, although it so clearly began in significant form in England and Scotland. One of the first large-scale victories for Libertas occurred with the United States at the time of the American Revolution. And the last conclusive victory occurred with the United States leading the winning side of the Cold War. However, one should not take these facts and conclude that the United States has a special mixture of superior people or leaders. In fact, even the great Founding Fathers of America should be put into proper environmental perspective before assuming their superiority.

---

1. Priestley, Joseph. "Of the Prospect of the General Enlargement of Liberty, Civil and Religious." *The Portable Enlightenment Reader.* Ed. Isaac Kramnick. New York: Penguin Books, 1995. 382-383.

There is no doubt the Founding Fathers were great individual achievers. Their special character included the determination to contribute serious thought, careful analysis, and hard work to make a very successful adaptive choice in constructing a political contract that dramatically improved the provision of the most liberty to the most people (excluding slaves and natives), while giving the people substantial motivation to enjoy the fruits of their labor.

The work of the Founding Fathers was instrumental in the progression of political science. The Declaration of Independence and the Constitution are transformational political documents. One needs to look no further than Madison's Federalist Number Ten (and the entirety of the Publius articles) to find one of the finest political arguments in all of history. His predictions of "a fractious spirit" tainting public administration, of dividing "mankind into parties," and inflaming them "with mutual animosity" rings more applicable today than it did in 1787.[2]

The Founding Fathers represented a broad group of individuals who were remarkably well educated in the history of governance. When presented with the extraordinary challenge of designing a political structure from the ground up, they were able to construct a great system of government while maintaining a relative consensus among representatives from many different backgrounds. The Founding Fathers deserve the continued attention and study they receive. Yet it should be noted that such individuals exist today and have existed during every time and in every civilization. The difference with the Founding Fathers was the time and the place. They were in the right place at the right time.

The time was ripe. It was the late 1700s. The Enlightenment

---

2. For an in-depth understanding of the political thought of the Founding Fathers see Adair, Douglass. *Fame and the Founding Fathers*. Indianapolis: Liberty Fund, 1998.

had caused a large scale blossoming of thought and ideas, particularly involving the concept of Libertas. The progress of Libertas in Great Britain had caused that country to become the new world power. Great Britain promulgated the concept of individual liberty, the rule of law, limited government, and lawmaking by representatives, albeit alongside the traditional monarchy. Great Britain had not only established these more formal structures of Libertas, but they had also evolved many more informal structures of Libertas, such as greater informal political and philosophical tolerance.

The tradition and culture of Libertas in colonial America was substantially borrowed from Great Britain. This is why the best starting point for the historical pattern of Libertas may be the establishment of English common law or the English Civil War, or certainly England and parts of Europe between 1500 and 1775, but not the American Revolution. The Americans contributed greatly by adding to these existing traditions, but we were fortunate to have the base of tradition on which to build.

The place may have been even more important. The place was a newly settled frontier, on a huge continent that was sparsely populated by widely dispersed and unorganized indigenous tribes (without modern weapons). These indigenous inhabitants had already been considerably decimated by the diseases spread through contact with the original Spanish conquistadors from Florida to the Mississippi Delta to the Southwest. This huge continent contained boundless natural resources and was capable of incredibly rapid growth. Most importantly, this new settlement was comprised of independent-minded immigrants and it was loosely governed by a relatively liberal country that remained an ocean away.

This is not meant to take any sense of achievement away from the Founding Fathers. They were remarkable leaders who created something extraordinary. However, the point is made simply to demonstrate that the creation of the first widespread, mostly liberal systematic model of governance (excluding slaves and natives) was not providential, a freak of nature, or a sign of American superiority. Instead, it was the confluence of time and place, with thoughtful and courageous individuals making very good, adaptive decisions that significantly helped the progress of humankind.

Is Libertas Feasible in the Remaining Anti-Liberty Countries?

The point about the special Colonial American advantage of time and place bodes well for the overall adaptive possibility of humankind and that is the purpose for the inclusion of it here. The remainder of the Anti-Libertas world, such as parts of the Middle East, Asia, and Africa, has individual citizens capable of progressive adaptive change and they have the fortunes of historical time-place as well. The possibility, even probability, they will successfully adapt to the Libertas model may be much greater than appears on the news headlines.

They have the good fortune of living in a historical time conducive to Libertas. The structure of Libertas has won the big battles of history. There are no legitimate alternatives for or-ganizing societies. This philosophical and intellectual condition is substantially better than even the time of the Enlightenment; it is better than any previous historical age. This condition also gives the remaining Anti-Libertas countries unique visibility today. Their depressed Anti-Libertas conditions stand out to the dominant Prosperous World and cause us to want to help, either out of altruism or fear. These facts and features should be cause for reasoned optimism despite current conflicts that seem unchangeable, intractable, and incurable.

EIGHTEEN

The History of Libertas Expansion

"How consoling for the philosopher, who laments the errors, the crimes, the injustices which still pollute the earth, and of which he is often the victim, is this view of the human race, emancipated from its shackles, released from the empire of fate and from that of the enemies of its progress, advancing with a firm and sure step along the path of truth, virtue, and happiness! It is the contemplation of this prospect that rewards him for all his efforts to assist the progress of reason and the defense of liberty."[1]

— Marquis de Condorcet, 1794

What Have Been the Methods Used in Expanding Libertas?

There is legitimate reason to raise the question as to what might be the best way, if any, to expedite the spread of Libertas to the remaining Anti-Libertas nations. This is the second most important question of our new age.[2] Here too, the choices are essentially those between coercion and cooperation. The process of *laissez-faire* — in the sense that they must do it themselves internally — has been the primary method for the recent emerging Libertas nations of East Asia, Southern Europe, Eastern Europe, South America, and Central America. The process of force or coercion was used in the more distant cases of West Germany, Austria, Italy, Japan, and South Korea, requiring relatively long

---

1. Condorcet, Marquis de. "The Future Progress of the Human Mind." *The Portable Enlightenment Reader.* Ed. Isaac Kramnick. New York: Penguin Books, 1995. 38.

2. The first, most important question of our new age is: What might be the best way, if any, to proactively protect Libertas within the nations already supportive of Libertas?

military occupations by victorious international Libertas powers.

The use of coercion in the spread of Libertas has been rare since those post-World War II cases mostly because Libertas nations tend to be incredibly cautious about expending the lives of their soldiers in the process of what is commonly called the *nation building*[3] of others. It is understandable that free and prosperous people, especially those in nations that had to build their own Libertas through their own internal struggles, would be reticent to expend the lives of their fellow citizens in foreign countries for the purpose of helping those countries establish Libertas.

The five prime examples of coercion (West Germany, Austria, Italy, Japan, and South Korea) all had other reasons for the use of force prior to the installation of Libertas. The Axis powers of World War II were imminent dangers to all other nations throughout the world and had to be defeated. The threat of international communism, particularly the theoretical threat as espoused in the Domino Theory, was enough to cause the United Nations to forcefully take back the control of the southern half of the Korean peninsula. None of these examples are cases where Anti-Libertas nations who pose no external threat are invaded by Libertas-based nations for the sole purpose of spreading Libertas and bringing eventual prosperity to the people.

There is no such example in the history of the world, although many expanding conquerors have attempted to make the claim. Some observers would suggest that the invasion of Afghanistan in 2001 and Iraq in 2003 are such cases, but that claim is clearly false. It is ludicrous to suggest that the United States, the United Kingdom, or any of the other participating nations chose to invade Afghanistan or Iraq for the sole purpose of bringing Libertas to the people of those countries. They

---

3. This term is a misnomer since the countries in question are already "nations". A more accurate term would be Libertas-building.

chose to invade those countries because of a real or perceived threat. The installation of Libertas in those two countries is merely a strategy of how best to relieve the threat in the long run. There is no evidence that Libertas-based countries are willing to expend the lives of their citizens for the purpose of building Libertas elsewhere unless they feel threatened by the Anti-Libertas countries.

Are Certain Conditions Required Before Libertas is Feasible?

The natural hesitation to proactively and forcefully extend Libertas is exacerbated by the realistic concern as to whether those Anti-Libertas nations are "ready" for Libertas without an intense decades-long occupation that essentially forces Libertas on a culture that has little or no experience in Libertas. The forceful extension of Libertas into West Germany and Japan after World War II required prolonged occupations, despite the fact these countries were already industrialized, modernized, and educated prior to the war and had some historical experience with Libertas. One might reasonably expect even more difficulty in forcibly establishing Libertas in less developed countries.

There is considerable historical evidence to support that expectation. The critical mass of Libertas was first achieved in the British Isles. The spread of this success was limited mostly to Western Europe for well over a century. This included the countries closest to the influence of the British and those who shared the most similar modernizing influences of the Enlightenment. Outside of Western Europe, the expansion of Libertas was primarily limited to former British colonies until after World War II. The conditions of Libertas had been exported to the colonies that became the United States, Canada, Australia, and New Zealand. The conditions did not exist with the native populations of the Americas or Oceania. The native Americans and aboriginal Australians did not participate by and large in this advance, except as victims of displacement.

The spread of Libertas was limited for some time to those

places where the British, with new traditions of Libertas, established burgeoning societies and countries. These special cases of the United States, Canada, Australia, and New Zealand are where the immigrant British culture and traditions were totally dominant and where native influences were minimized, usually in brutal fashion. The results were not the same in other British colonies where the native population was still the primary population in the country, even though the British ruled through military occupation, such as was the case in India.

The second and third waves of Libertas expansion occurred in the twentieth century as the result of world wars. The victorious Libertas powers usually attempted to establish Libertas in the wake of military success. This began with the Wilsonian movement after World War I. The liberal movement of the time expressed splendid rhetorical support of Libertas and created the League of Nations as a budding attempt at building conditions for worldwide Libertas. However, history has proven those steps to have been woefully inadequate at sustaining the expansion of Libertas.

Different tactics were used after World War II that proved to be much more successful. These included the complete occupation of defeated powers and the assertive installation of the rule of law based on constitutions built upon the major aspects of Libertas. These tactics created some of the world's most successful Libertas-based nations in West Germany, Austria, Japan, and Italy.

This technique of expanding Libertas by force was limited only to the defeated Axis nations, and the progress of Libertas slowed thereafter. The United States, United Kingdom, and other Libertas powers abandoned the aggressive expansion of Libertas mostly out of a sense of expediency in defending against the growth of communism and wanting to return to a post-war normalcy. In retrospect, this posture seems backwards. The Libertas powers abandoned a proven technique and began embracing Anti-Libertas autocrats, all in the name of Libertas. It may have been a questionable strategy, but it is explainable upon reviewing the historical times.

The first major battle of the Cold War— the Korean War— was obviously the primary cause for the change in tactics. The Korean War was unacceptably protracted and costly for the participating Allied Powers who were still recuperating from the devastation of World War II and were anxious for peace at nearly any cost. A negotiated cease-fire, a division of the Korean Peninsula, and a new-found fondness for non-communist autocrats were the results. The consensus foreign policy goal of the primary Libertas nations after World War II ceased to be the idealistic Wilsonian goal of advancing Libertas and instead became the practical goal of checking the expansion of communism. This goal appeared to be most practically achievable—meaning the fastest and cheapest—by embracing nearly any anti-communist regime, regardless of its Libertas credentials. As inherently contradictory as this strategy now appears in retrospect, the conditions at that time make it more understandable.

The Libertas nations were still war-weary and they had become gripped by the belief that communism would easily spread from one country to another until the force would be unstoppable. There was an inordinate, but somewhat understandable, lack of faith in Libertas and an overestimation of the communist movement. Then, after more than a decade of peace from the end of the Korean conflict into the early 1960s, the protracted and expensive use of force was again extended in the case of Vietnam, albeit with a flawed strategy. The length and financial cost of this conflict made the Korean conflict look mild by comparison. The Vietnam War became a lightening rod for international political criticism about the entire concept of Libertas being superior to Anti-Libertas. By the 1970s, in large measure, the peoples and the governments of Libertas-based nations had lost the will to continue the struggle against communism. They also had long since lost concern about other macro forms of Anti-Libertas.

This atmosphere did not change until the Thatcher-Reagan

movement led a renewed effort to call the bluff of the communists that set in motion the downfall of the Soviet Union. The hallmark of the Thatcher-Reagan foreign policy initiative was a new confidence in the power of Libertas and a more realistic appreciation of the inherent deficiencies of a communist system. This outlook was vindicated once the resultant Soviet defense spending—and the continued cost of their aggression in Afghanistan and elsewhere—caused the virtual bankrupting of the already weakened Soviet Union.

A transformation was also proceeding within China, but it was almost exclusively an economic liberalization. The Chinese leadership under Deng Xiaoping recognized the impracticality of communist economics long before the fall of the Soviet Union and began a steady process of conversion toward more free enterprise. This conversion is not nearly complete, nor has it yet led to substantial political liberalization, but it has sparked incredible economic growth and a revitalization of more economic and social liberty.

However, other than the external catalyst of strong posturing by the West, the advance of Libertas in the former Soviet bloc was internal, as it is certainly true with China as well. The progress was not caused by a forceful occupation from Libertas powers. The limited use of the proactive extension of Libertas during the Cold War, such as in Korea and Vietnam, was always aimed at periphery countries and was never realistically contemplated for the dominant powers of the USSR and China.

As much as the United States, along with other Libertas powers, had consistently maintained eloquent rhetoric concerning the spread of Libertas as far back as Theodore Roosevelt and Woodrow Wilson, the majority of the actions were decidedly isolationist or self-interested. Libertas was never aggressively pursued as a cause in and of itself. It was an afterthought; installed in vanquished postwar-nations in a defensive strategy against further threats from those previous enemies.

The fall of the Berlin Wall was the symbolic crescendo of the

victory of theoretical Libertas and the disintegration of communist theory. The new Thatcher-Reagan spirit of the 1980s and
the post-Soviet enthusiasm of the 1990s included a more overt
advocacy for the advance of Libertas in other Anti-Libertas nations. And there was much to cheer about. The period from the
late 1970s until the turn of the century included dramatic progress for Libertas elsewhere in the world. This incredible advance
of Libertas is often credited to the decline of communism, as if
it were the Anti-Domino Theory. There is no doubt the decline
of communism throughout the world did have a far-reaching
impact. However, the emphasis of the negative — the impracticality of communism — obscures the more comprehensive truth
that Libertas was a more successful method of human interaction than all forms of Anti-Libertas. This transformation from
the 1970s until today represents a remarkable story that must
not be ignored. It is an important turning point in history.

Where Has the Advance of Libertas Occurred During the Past Quarter of a Century?

In total, there was significant improvement of Libertas in over
60 countries during those years. The advance of Libertas occurred across the globe and across a multitude of cultures. This
most recent wave of Libertas improvement was dramatically
broader than anything in previous history, although it has not
received the media attention it has deserved.

Latin America

In Latin America, the large populations in Mexico, Brazil, and
Argentina made improvement, as did some of the less popu-
lous countries of Belize, Bolivia, Dominican Republic, and
Uruguay. The most spectacular Latin American advancement
was in Chile, El Salvador, Panama, and Peru, all of which had
previously come very close to either totalitarianism or anarchy.
Improvement of economic freedom was also found in Costa

215

Rica, which was the Latin American country with already the longest tradition of political freedom. There are still some countries in the region resisting improvement—notably Colombia and Haiti—but only Venezuela experienced a serious deterioration of freedom and only Cuba holds on to a complete philosophy of Anti-Libertas. The current condition of Libertas in Latin America could not have been anticipated by observers from a quarter of a century ago. It is the second most substantial advancement of any region, surpassed only by the miracle of Eastern Europe.

Eastern Europe

In Eastern Europe, the fall of the Iron Curtain brought new hope to all the countries that had been under the dominance of the Soviet Union or actually within it. Not all of the nations in the region have made a stellar transition to Libertas—notably Russia and the Ukraine—but there has been widespread progress in Bulgaria, Croatia, the Czech Republic, Hungary, Latvia, Lithuania, Poland, the Slovak Republic, and Slovenia. Finally, the new crowning jewel of the region is Estonia, which has recently achieved some of the highest Libertas ratings in the world.

Asia

The recent progress in Asia was built upon the previous successes in Japan, Hong Kong, and Singapore. There was great advancement next in South Korea and Taiwan, then in Thailand and the Philippines. Even Indonesia began making progress, although it has regressed of late. All of these advancements may eventually pale in comparison to those of India and China because of the enormous size of those two countries. India had a relatively strong tradition of political and civic freedom, but had many illiberal economic practices until the late 1990s, when they made important improvements. As previously mentioned, China had a strong tradition of no political or civic freedom,

216

but it has embarked on a long road of economic liberalization since the early 1980s.

Iberia

Spain and Portugal had a long record of fascist dictatorship from the 1930s into the 1970s. These illiberal conditions were reversed in the mid 1970s as both countries transitioned to liberal democracies and, today, remain two of the top 30 nations in freedom.

Sub-Saharan Africa

Many casual observers are of the opinion that no progress has been made in Africa and it is undeniably a regional laggard in the transition to Libertas. However, despite the incredibly negative starting point, there are examples of Libertas gaining footholds in sub-Saharan Africa. Most notably are the solid advancements that can be observed in Botswana, Ghana, and South Africa, as well as economic liberalization — without political liberalization — in five other nations.

Middle East and North Africa

In some respects, the region of North Africa and the Middle East (MENA) is even more intractable than sub-Saharan Africa. In this region, only Israel has made strong gains in Libertas through internal efforts. A few others, such as the United Arab Emirates and Qatar, have made economic liberalization a priority, but there are no shining examples as can be found in other regions. It is possible that long occupations in Afghanistan and Iraq will create the conditions for Libertas to take hold. This external catalyst may even provide the momentum for the expansion of Libertas elsewhere in the region. However, these experiments will probably take considerable time. In the long run, it will ultimately be the responsibility of the people in this region to strive for their own Libertas.

Traditional Libertas Nations

It is heartening for humanity to focus on the successes of the recently converted nations struggling to build Libertas in their countries, but there was a simultaneous reawakening of the forces of Libertas within the traditional powers during this timeframe from the late 1970s until the turn of the millennium. This reawakening was substantial and it proves the resilience of Libertas for the long run.

From the Progressive Era in the late nineteenth century through the 1970s, virtually all Libertas-based nations experimented with very illiberal economic practices, some more than others. Many of these nations had become increasingly sluggish economically by 1980. They still maintained high levels of political and civic freedom, but their economic freedom had often sunk to dangerously low levels. Two such countries — New Zealand and Ireland — made sweeping changes that dramatically revitalized their economies. Twelve other such countries made solid improvements that led them back to high levels of economic freedom and strong growth rates; these included Australia, Austria, Canada, Denmark, Finland, Iceland, Italy, the Netherlands, Sweden, Switzerland, the United Kingdom, and the United States.

Overall

The substantial advancement of Libertas during the past 25 years has included progress in every region. This recent march of Libertas has included progress within diverse cultures and, importantly, even among some of the most impoverished and undeveloped countries. The dramatic progress of Libertas during this time period did not occur via the forceful intervention of Libertas powers.[4] The progress made by these new or

---

4. This is with the exception of a small number of cases such as those of Panama, Afghanistan, and Iraq.

renewed advocates of Libertas was internally driven. It was widely welcomed by the traditional Libertas powers and it was encouraged through the continued liberalization of world trade policies, but it was still an internal phenomenon. These internal advancements included some nations that had little experience with Libertas and some that were relatively undeveloped at the start.

This evidence leads to a reasonable conclusion that the majority of Libertas building in the future still will occur through internal efforts. There is historical justification for optimism in this regard. The Libertas-based world is anxious to assist the Anti-Libertas nations in ways other than force and the Anti-Libertas nations have ample examples to follow. The growth of Libertas geographically has been astounding and there is now a virtual magnetic attraction to the forces of Libertas. It is clearly the only way out of poverty and misery for the remaining Impoverished World.

Will Achieving the Conditions of Libertas Be Easy for the Most Intractably Impoverished Nations?

The optimism about the advance of Libertas must be tempered by a variation of the Law of Diminishing Returns. Libertas has advanced so broadly around the world in the past thirty years that the only remaining Anti-Libertas countries are the most intractable. The vast majority of these are in two regions, that of sub-Saharan Africa and MENA (Middle East & North Africa), while three (North Korea, Myanmar, and Cuba) are in other regions. If these remaining Anti-Libertas cases were easily solved, they would have joined the recent wave of liberalization around the world.

The majority of the remaining cases represent conditions of brutal dictatorships. Dictators of this nature have historically proven to be incredibly resistant to liberalization from within. The people of these nations either must rise up to depose the dictator or bide their time until the dictator dies. The death of

219

these dictators in the future through natural death or rebellion will provide an opportunity to institute liberal changes. The people and the representative leaders of the people must be prepared to fight for Libertas at that time. This will require an understanding of the full aspects of Libertas and an appreciation for the path to modernity.

There have been apparent attempts to liberalize in the past by semi-benevolent dictators and newly victorious opposition leaders who often looked to the Prosperous World for examples to follow. These attempts were not always successful. Some of these semi-benevolent dictators or newly victorious opposition leaders sent a number of their best and brightest young people to be educated in prosperous, Libertas-based countries. They had ample opportunity to utilize the vast accumulated knowledge of the Libertas-based world, including the latest scientific inventions and managerial techniques to improve their desperate circumstances. Yet, in the unsuccessful cases, the opportunity was squandered because they failed to grasp or to utilize the one overriding truth of the modern age: lasting and significant human advancement will not be achieved until the spontaneous order of Libertas is in place.

The spontaneous order of Libertas is not something that can be easily *willed* by a dictator, a legislature, or tribal elders. The sustainable prosperity of Libertas cannot be transferred via loans, grants, or the transference of historical accumulation. The success of Libertas requires a political structure of constitutions and laws that succeed at protecting the citizens from coercion (crime and war). It requires an economic structure that supports free enterprise and free trade. It requires a social structure that supports freedom of association, freedom of religion, freedom of thought, freedom of speech, and a wide range of personal freedoms.

Yet even if a benevolent dictator or an intelligent legislature establishes a formal structure of Libertas rules, there might still be more informal cultural hindrances to Libertas. For example, family traditions may still severely restrict personal freedom (arranged marriages, primogeniture) or very rigid behavior restrictions may permeate the society through deep educational or religious training. In particular, although slavery has long since been minimized in the world, many cultures still treat one-half of their citizens (women) as virtual slaves. Some of these nations still have vestiges of formal slavery.

Such cultures will probably have difficulty in converting to Libertas in the near term, but the blueprint for success is readily available. The nations that remain mired in poverty and coercion must begin building the formal structures of Libertas and encouraging other informal cultural changes if they desire to join the rest of the world in overcoming the *Four Ds* of disease, destruction, destitution, and death.

NINETEEN

The Expansion Challenge

"For all great wars are now civil wars. They are not battles against an alien foe but internecine struggles within one closely related, intricately interdependent community. Modern war tears apart huge populations which have become dependent upon one another for the maintenance of their standard of life – in some degree, for the maintenance of life itself...That is why pacifism has so recently ceased to be an other-worldly aspiration and has become the working doctrine of practical men. For it was in the nineteenth century that the self-sufficiency of nations, of local communities, and of individuals, gave way to a deep and intricate interdependence. Men found themselves living in a Great Society."[1]

—Walter Lippmann, 1937

Is Positive Governmental Structure Still Important?

The limitation of governmental intrusion is of crucial concern for all nations. However, the remaining Anti-Libertas nations must simultaneously recognize the tremendous importance of government in establishing the conditions conducive for Libertas. Many countries have struggled and unnecessarily delayed their progress by not laying the proper groundwork that government must provide in emerging societies. For these countries, anarchy is a bigger threat than excessive government intervention.

This point has been courageously researched and described by the award-winning economist Hernando de Soto in convinc-

---

1. Lippmann, Walter. *The Good Society*. New Brunswick: Transaction Publishers, 2005. 161.

ing detail. He has studied emerging economies in Latin America and discovered the *lack* of government to be a huge problem. A large percentage of the population in these cases has been essentially shut out of the formal economy because of the inadequate establishment of property rights and a lack of access to an impartial court system.[2]

The use of government in emerging societies is important. Exactness of property ownership and fairness of conflict resolution are essential for individuals to build equity for their future and to secure the benefits of their labor. This is especially true in societies where hierarchical, paternalistic, and intolerant societies have consistently stymied individual power for centuries. The structure of impartial and fair governmental administration of Libertas can overcome generations of illiberal conditions much faster and more completely than most observers acknowledge today.

This is where the Prosperous World can provide the most help for nations attempting to emerge from the tyranny of Anti-Libertas. We can offer to provide clear guidance. We can help individuals in those nations understand the fundamental concept of Libertas as the absence of coercion, as the unleashing of individual initiative. It is imperative not to focus too keenly on pure democracy and majoritarian rule because such structures, standing alone, are likely to perpetuate the previous illiberal conditions of minorities. It is crucial to stress the concept of limited government that concentrates almost exclusively and relentlessly on protecting citizens from coercion.

There are limits to how much the Prosperous World should and can help the Impoverished World. It is understandable that the people in the Prosperous World are reluctant to expend lives to forcibly overthrow brutal dictators. Additionally, it has proven to be counterproductive to merely give financial aid without any understanding of how that aid may be used

2. De Soto, Hernando. *The Mystery of Capital*. New York: Basic Books, 2000.

to strengthen illiberal leadership elites. However, there is no excuse for ignoring the pleas for help from individuals trapped in Anti-Libertas destitution and brutality. The most important action is to stop perpetuating the ridiculous idea that "they are not ready for Libertas." That argument is analogous to the argument once made that the slaves on southern plantations should not be freed because they were not "ready" to think for themselves.

The individuals in these societies, regardless of how far behind the modern curve, are human beings. The only proven method to modernity and prosperity is to institute the structure of Libertas. This path, like life itself, is difficult. It requires careful thought, hard work, discipline, and sacrifice. The role of the outside world, at the very least, is to provide a clear understanding of the history of Libertas. By doing so, the new nations can avoid some of past mistakes and concentrate on the conditions most likely to achieve positive results in the places that need positive results the most.

Are the Nations Recently Freed from Anti-Libertas at an Insurmountable Disadvantage?

As counter-intuitive as it seems, some of the best opportunities to gain greater prosperity and progress through extensive Libertas are possessed by the countries previously devoid of Libertas. These include the countries behind the old Iron/Bamboo Curtain and the countries in what was previously known as the Third World. Such countries can more easily *wipe the slate clean* and institute more pure structures of Libertas than can the traditional beacons of Libertas. The reason for this is relative motivation and experience. Countries that have previously enjoyed the most Libertas, with resultant prosperity and peace, have two strikes against them. First, they are already prosperous and have less societal motivation to continue the enrichment process. Second, their success tends to trick their democratically elected elites into believing that such success was the result of elite decision-making, as opposed to the hard work and ingenuity of individuals. It also tricks these elites into believing that more extensive elite decision-making will result in greater relative success, when in fact the result will be the opposite.

This is not to say that all of the impoverished countries and societies will choose Libertas and prosper quickly. Many of these countries will remain mired in human misery for the short-term. This is not because of the selfishness of the Libertas-based nations, but because of the lack of triumph of individuals in impoverished countries to successfully fight for the transformation to more liberal structures. However, it is likely some of these countries will take advantage of the opportunity to wipe the slate clean, establish more pure structures of Libertas, and make progress toward prosperity with incredible speed. Although we should not expect overnight success, it is conceivable that some of these newcomers will succeed even faster than older success stories, such as Germany and Japan after WW II, the Asian Tigers in the latter half of the twentieth century, and the resurging South American countries in the 1990s.

Will the Transition Toward More Free Trade Continue?

Such a positive transformation from previous international outcasts usually engenders a parochial concern among the already prosperous countries and often causes increased suspicion of free trade and a desire to institute restrictive trade policies. Yet a preponderance of evidence proves that free trade secures the fastest and best progression for humankind, not only for the fast-growing new economies, but also for the more mature economies.

There are certainly disruptions associated with free trade, but these are the same disruptions associated throughout any network of free enterprise. Libertas is based upon individual freedom. With that freedom there is an increase of human flexibility, along with responsibility. Humans interact in ways that cannot always be anticipated. Some of them succeed and some fail, but most of those who fail have further opportunities to try again. We specialize, we learn new skills, and we try to maximize our own interests within the larger interaction of supply and demand.

Free trade is merely the extension of free enterprise beyond borders. The result of free trade is that an ever-increasing number of humans are participating more fully in overall human interaction around the world. The freedoms that once were negotiated among municipalities or provinces are now expanding to most of the nations of the world. As this occurs, the aggregate amount of human brainpower being used and shared is growing. The positive-sum effect is growing. The increased flexibility and the increased specialization are benefiting the entire world, although it often temporarily disrupts the conditions of some. Isolated attempts at unilateral trade restrictions are either rejected or they backfire. As Milton Friedman has so expertly explained, countries that attempt unilateral restrictions usually end up benefiting their trading partners by inefficiently subsidizing a domestic industry, which results in effectively subsidizing the consumers of the other nations.

The result of bilateral or multilateral free trade does not result in dividing up the same size product among a larger group of people (negative-sum), nor does it entail dividing up a slightly larger product among a slightly larger group (zero-sum). The result of free trade is the creation of a much larger total product divided by more people, equaling much more per person (positive-sum). Free trade creates a positive-sum product; just the same as other aspects of Libertas. And free trade is what ensures that nation-state hegemony is no longer relevant. The continued advancement of Libertas, the progress of mankind, and the emergence of the *common individual* depend on the new hegemony of the individual that is fostered by free trade and all of the components of Libertas.

Is Ethnocentrism Destined to Be Supplanted by Multiculturalism?

The history of Libertas over the past five hundred years has included a steady progression of multiculturalism and a steady decline of ethnocentrism. This is to be expected from a method of human interaction based essentially on tolerance. The traditional Libertas-based nations from Western Europe and North America have long traditions of multicultural inclusion and tolerance, with the notable and regrettable exceptions of pre-modern cultures, which will be discussed momentarily. The newer adherents of Libertas from East Asia to Eastern Europe to South America and far beyond are now living in an era of unprecedented peace and exchange among most nations. This is an era of global travel, migration, business integration, and cultural exchange. And it is voluntary multiculturalism that is not restricted to the elites of these societies.

However, there is a clear line where serious friction still exists. It is the line where the modern world — now mostly based on Libertas — meets the pre-modern or less-modern world, which is always based on Anti-Libertas. This danger zone is nothing new. The history of war and widespread violence during the past five hundred years has often featured the unequal clash between the modern and the pre-modern cultures. The military rivalry between modern powers has recently been eliminated by the spread of Libertas throughout the modern world. However, the friction between the modern and pre-modern cultures remains.

Humans have never developed good mechanisms for the peaceful coexistence of modern powers in contact with pre-modern societies. Even Libertas-based stalwarts have most of their darkest history included in this type of struggle. The United States, in particular, is still scarred by the detestable outcome of the primary contact of the country with pre-modern culture, that being Native Americans (annihilated) and Africans (enslaved). Similar struggles have occurred throughout recorded history, with the inevitable result that the most developed and more modern culture ends up dominating the conflict, usually brutally, and often through the near total annihilation of the less modern culture.

The difference in recent years is twofold. First, there is dramatically more sensitivity today for protecting human life. Second, as modern cultures have become progressively more prosperous and more modern, the conflict has expanded beyond merely the conflict with pre-modern or aboriginal societies and now includes societies that were considered modern about six hundred years ago. This is the essence of the conflict between much of the Islamic Middle East and the rest of the world. Some pre-modern societies are mostly inwardly dangerous, such as those of sub-Saharan Africa. Unfortunately, the Islamic MENA cases represent intractable Anti-Libertas conditions and external danger.

What Are the Direct Challenges to Libertas in the Near Term?

There are still challenges to the growing spontaneous order of Libertas, despite the historical evidence of substantial advancement of the masses over the past five hundred years. These challenges can be overcome. The track record of our species and the steady history of the growth of Libertas lead one to conclude that future success is overwhelmingly probable. Yet, in the short-run, the problems should engender the care and concern of all humans. The foremost challenge is also the least recognized and was the primary subject throughout Part Three of this book. That was the conflict of how to maintain Libertas in the face of the public confusion about the role of *chance*, the inherent deficiency of democracy, and the superiority complex of elite decision-makers. However, the secondary challenge, to be discussed now, is the most dangerous in the near term.

This is the challenge facing us from the international Islamic terrorist cabal mostly centered in the Middle East and North Africa (MENA). This cabal represents a disparate group of clerics and their adherents attempting to resist the progress of the masses. They believe in the superiority of their elite interpretation of religion that calls for extreme intolerance, enslavement, and violence. This resistance is generally couched as pro-Islam, but the root cause of the movement is an anti-modernization sentiment and a jealousy at being so far behind the remainder of the masses in the Prosperous World. The United States takes much of the brunt of this anger because it is the current leading power within the Libertas structure, but the anger is genuinely anti-modernization, anti-Libertas, and anti-human.

Another reason the United States takes the brunt is directly related to the American foreign policy strategy (and similar strategies by other Libertas powers) in the Middle East during the second half of the twentieth century. This strategy — just as was the case with the Cold War strategy — was based on practicality rather than philosophy. The primary foreign policy strategy in the region was dominated by a practical goal of keeping the oil flowing in a politically volatile region. The philosophical strategy of encouraging Libertas was often ignored, sometimes even subverted. Anti-Libertas despots in the region were supported under this foreign policy as long as they promoted the free flow of oil to the world markets. This foreign policy did not create the newer forms of illiberal violence in MENA, but neither did it help prevent those formations.

In retrospect, this previous foreign policy appears to have been both philosophically inconsistent and practically unproductive. Yet this is only now recognizable because of the hindsight available to us after witnessing the horrendous rise of Islamic terrorism as manifested in the events of September 11, the Madrid train bombings, the Bali nightclub explosion, the London transportation bombings, and similar acts. The rise of Islamic terrorism was not *caused* by the Prosperous World or the West. There was a historic role played by the Libertas powers in the MENA region over the past couple of centuries, some positive and some negative, but the societies that have given rise to Islamic terrorism are largely of their own creation.

This includes the fact that the citizens of these nations allowed themselves to be dominated by small elite groups of people who maintain a philosophy that is completely Anti-Libertas in nature.

This is yet another example of an *elite* group—ruling dictators, royal families, religious clerics, and their fanatical recruits—attempting to make decisions for the masses, to the detriment of those same masses. The masses in the Islamic nations could improve their lot in life dramatically within one generation if they embraced peace and Libertas. This fact makes the Islamic terrorist movement yet another bankrupt philosophy that uses indiscriminate violence to resist the progress to peace and prosperity for their supposed constituents, in favor of regression to the certainty of destruction and destitution.

The moral and practical deficiencies of the Islamic terrorist movement are destined to cause the ultimate failure of their goal. However, the intensity of their hatred of all non-believers or *infidels* creates a great deal of short-term danger for the civilized world. Their hatred toward humanity has been manifested in a new culture of aggressive and indiscriminate violence that has been directed toward a wide variety of targets. The leaders of the civilized world must marshal the will and the forces to defeat this enemy of humanity. Any delay, indecision, or lack of solidarity in this effort will merely extend the danger and expand the damage caused by the terrorists over time.

The defeat of this cabal is inevitable. It will occur either from within, with the people rising up to reject the fanaticism, or it will occur from without, with the military forces of Libertas physically overwhelming them. The most probable scenario is a combination of the two. However, there is no evidence whatsoever to suggest this latest Anti-Libertas movement will wither away without continued and steady confrontation from the champions of Libertas. There is always likely to be stark disagreements among Libertas powers as it concerns how best to proceed in the confrontation with this newest wave of Anti-Libertas, just as there were disagreements in the past, but there should be no disagreement that Islamic terrorism must be confronted.

However the confrontation proceeds, the outcome will once again be the triumph of Libertas. The progress of Libertas will continue, even in the remotest corners of the world, because the adaptive nature of humans will always gravitate towards the type of human interaction that is most successful. This outcome could be predicted by observing the historic progress of Libertas.

PART SIX
Epoch of the Common Individual

TWENTY

The Illusion of Hegemony

"Within a world of free trade and democracy there are no incentives for war and conquest."[1]

—Lugwig von Mises, 1944

Can the United States Help or Is It a Hegemonic Power to be Feared?

The United States clearly had a rare adaptive advantage in the late 1700s. The advantage of time and place, along with the special individuals contributing to the founding process, created the Libertas necessary for the United States to grow. It took merely a century to reach parity with the leading powers of the world. It took only another century to morph into a new world hegemonic power unique in human history.

The uniqueness of the hegemonic power of the United States is manifested in many ways. Most obviously, this is a hegemonic power of unprecedented economic and military proportion, with an unparalleled gap between the primary power and potential rivals. This overwhelming power frightens many casual observers around the world and often results in vitriolic resentment. However, the other uniqueness associated with the hegemony of the United States, once properly recognized, should relieve such concern. The much less obvious uniqueness is that this hegemonic power is not really American-centric, although it appears that way on the surface. This is a novel and com-

---

1. Mises, Ludwig von. *Omnipotent Government.* Grove City: Libertarian Press, 1985. 3.

235

plex concept, but crucial in understanding the past and future of Libertas.

The first evidence of this point is the fact that the United States has taken great pains to ensure that it does not conquer and amass territory. The United States has rarely exhibited imperialistic tendencies and such tendencies have virtually disappeared in the past quarter of a century. The most common tendency is actually anti-imperialist or isolationist. There are exceptions, of course, but the exceptions do not disprove the rule.[2]

Even in the modern role as *world policeman*, the United States is extremely cautious not to get bogged down in any action that might remind the country of the experience in Vietnam. The Gulf War in 1991 is an obvious example of this tendency. The anti-imperialist tendency caused the allied forces to exit too quickly in the Gulf War. They only remained longer in the later cases of Afghanistan and Iraq because of the desire to establish a framework of Libertas in the region. This unusual desire to *nation-build* would not have occurred had it not been for the extraordinary terrorist attacks of September 11, 2001 and the increasing threat to global Libertas by Islamic terrorism. After September 11, the strategy appears to have changed. The more recent foreign policy strategy (the Bush Doctrine) has incorporated the expansion of Libertas as an integral component of an aggressive security plan. Whether that strategy continues to be more than rhetorical and whether it continues to be supported by the voters in the United States and elsewhere is still an unanswerable question.

The second evidence of the new hegemony not being American-centric is the fact that the hegemonic power is significantly diffused. This is the case first within the traditional Anglo coalition (United Kingdom, Canada, Australia, and New Zealand)

---

2. The most egregious exceptions included the Spanish-American War and the Panama Canal. Afterwards, virtually all exceptions were directly related to two questionable foreign policy strategies: The Domino Theory and the pre-September 11th Middle East Strategy of "damn the issue of Libertas, just keep the oil flowing."

and second within the larger component of the Prosperous World that adheres to the general concept of the Libertas-based approach, even if more or less so than that of the United States. Although many of these nations may vehemently disagree over the intervention in Iraq, they are all still closely bonded together economically and philosophically. The global economy is intricately integrated and it is a force that even the United States cannot ignore.

Some observers may theoretically accept these arguments about the illusion of United States hegemony, but still believe there must be hidden desires for world domination within the motives of the nation. Yet, just as with our previous discussions concerning other group-interests, there is no real group-motivation in the United States. The motivation of the country is merely the sum of its parts. There may be some individuals in the United States desirous of world domination, some may even temporarily be in high levels of the government, but the majority of citizens are deeply opposed to aggressive governmental involvement in foreign countries for anything other than temporary defensive or humanitarian purposes.

The primary evidence about the hegemonic power not being America-centric, however, is that this modern stage of human adaptation is not really centered around the concept of nation-state at all. It is instead moving toward a new hegemony of individual power. This is the Age of Libertas and that means the Age of the Individual in the political, business, and social realms. The world is becoming increasingly more connected and more individualized. The Internet allows for communication that is both massive and customized at the same time. The inhabitants of the world are increasingly sharing books, movies, foods, newspapers, clothes, automobiles, technology, ideas, and many other aspects of life. Despite the surface appearance of homogenization, the effect is actually an increase of diversity. More people are exposed to more cultural aspects from all over the world, instead of being relegated to the singular cultural influences into which they were born.

It is at this point that some observers raise their complaints about the supposed domination by American or western culture. They have it wrong. This is the establishment of world culture, highly complex and individualized, with unique variances as diverse as the number of people on earth. It might appear to be dominated by the United States but that is only because the major movie and music studios are based in the United States. These just happen to be the most visible components of culture, but they do not comprise culture overall.

Is the United States Destined to Remain the Recognized Leader of Libertas?

The final point here is to admit that the United States and most western European democracies are continually sliding away from the ideals of Libertas in many ways, at least in relative terms. Additionally, the special adaptive advantage the United States once enjoyed is no longer relevant and the country is saddled with two unusual historical burdens. The first is the burden of becoming the *de facto* world policeman. The second is the racial tension created by the legacy of slavery, segregation, and failed social policies. Both of these burdens are hindering current progress toward more Libertas and prosperity within the United States. Additionally, the former is seriously straining the relationship between the United States and other Libertas powers.

These conditions are not conducive for the continued improvement of Libertas in America. The United States no longer ranks in the top five nations in economic or socio-political freedom. The very strong Libertas tradition in the United States will probably preclude any dramatic fall in relation to other Libertas nations, but a slow slipping away has been occurring and is likely to continue indefinitely. Other nations with lesser traditions are likely to be more aggressive in faithfully creating the conditions of Libertas in the future. This is because there is still a lingering "conflict of visions" and the winning side of that conflict is easier to recognize in a country such as Estonia than it is in the United States. This issue of "visions" is where we next turn our attention.

TWENTY-ONE

The Maintenance Conundrum

"To this approaching ruin, there appears to be but one possible barrier, a disillusionment of men's minds in the possibility of advancing progress by the coercive violence of legislation, and a juster appreciation of the truth that the forces which make for civilization and justice are inherent in a free society, and are the direct antithesis of the empirical regimentation of an artificial state."[1]

—Thomas MacKay, 1895

Is There Still a "Conflict of Visions"?

The fundamental political and philosophical conflict of today boils down to a conflict between those who favor coercion planned by elite decision-makers against those who favor substantial Libertas by the people and for the people. This is the difference between Islamic extremists and the remainder of the world. It is also the difference between democratic interventionists who believe government is the solution to every problem and those who believe individual initiative and responsibility are the only sure way to achieving the greatest good for the greatest number.

This is the conflict so brilliantly described by Thomas Sowell in his *A Conflict of Visions*,[2] which he accurately claimed to represent the fundamental, underlying cause of most political differences over the past few hundred years. That assessment is

---

1. Mackay, Thomas. "Empiricism in Politics." *Herbert Spencer and the Limits of the State.* Ed. Michael Taylor. Bristol: Thoemmes Press, 1996. 55.

2. Sowell, Thomas. *A Conflict of Visions.* New York: Basic Books, 2002.

particularly poignant. Although the argument and related disagreements continue at high volume in the political discourse of today, the primary battle in this argument has been won.

The victory has gone to the point of view represented, in Sowell's words, as the *constrained* vision. This is the vision acknowledging the limitation of the human mind, the limitation of human ability to specifically construct the details of social outcome, to right every wrong, to play God. The battle is over because more and more people around the world are opting for Libertas. The battle is over because more and more examples exist that prove the fundamental ineffectiveness of the *unconstrained* vision. The battle is over because more and more people around the world are opting for the better life and the limited vagaries of chance that exist in the prosperous Libertas-based countries. They are rejecting the pandering promises of elite decision-makers that proclaim the ability to solve every problem through elaborate bureaucratic intervention and coercion.

Once people appreciate that life is uncertain and constantly changing and, therefore, perfection and certainty are impossible, then they acknowledge diversity of thought, they are tolerant of the opinion of others, and they are peaceful. This is true because they know that the *means* of our society are structural and cooperative, while the *ends* are individualized and personal. On the contrary, those who still imagine they have found certainty and perfection in a particular *visionary end* or goal, are always likely to abandon any restraint of *means* for the achievement of that certain and perfect goal, only to subsequently find that perfection was not realized and those *means* brought unnecessary misery to many.

This particular realization is gaining ever-greater acceptance among people around the world. Some people do not always recognize it directly through conceptual discussion, but they do so indirectly through the common sense realization that we can achieve so much more through cooperation and tolerance than we can through coercion and the belief in perfection. This is a fundamental change in the method of human interaction that can be called the *triumph of the common individual*. The conflict of visions represented the leading intellectual debate from before the Enlightenment to the end of the millennium. The result of the debate is an increasing realization of the wisdom of the constrained vision.

One could argue that the seventeenth, eighteenth, and nineteenth centuries represented the infancy of widespread *human cooperation*, which was manifested in limited testing of comprehensive forms of Libertas in isolated geographic locations. In this same vein, the twentieth century represented the adolescence, which included intense struggles between strong and comprehensive forms of both Libertas and Anti-Libertas. Our species has now reached maturity. Generations of intellectuals in the twentieth century were understandably influenced by the world wars and catastrophes of that century to arrive at two false conclusions. One was that the conditions of human life were deteriorating and the other was that *individuals* could not be trusted. It is becoming increasing obvious to the casual observer that the world wars and communist totalitarianism were anomalies in our human history; not representative of a trend, but actually the opposite of the larger trend. The broader trend is the *emergence of the common individual* and the realization that expansive human participation in life through the structure of Libertas is the ultimate cause of the discernable improvement of human well-being.

This includes the common individual deciding against certain quick-fix, centralized solutions currently promulgated by altruistic elites. Conservative doomsayers are no less wrong about the future than are their interventionist anti-Libertas adversaries. Conservative doomsayers believe that western democracies are destined to degenerate into total socialistic coercion as the majority of voters slowly vote away the private property, free enterprise, and minority rights that are hallmarks of Libertas. However, it should be noted that such recent regression has occurred mostly through the determined effort of a political and social elite of altruistic, but misguided leaders.

This elite has included the greater part of those with the most influence, that being the media, academia, and the communication arts (books, television, movies, etc.).

Although the masses must be held ultimately responsible for enabling this political and social elite to flourish, there are signs everywhere that the masses are continuing to become better informed, making rational adaptive decisions, and appreciating the superiority of Libertas to the alternatives. These signs are numerous and they are intricately connected to many of the observations discussed throughout this book. The increasing complexity of life is requiring individuals to utilize more information and make more careful decisions for themselves. This, in turn, facilitates more demand for narrowcast information distribution channels, which in turn gives more people more information, and the cycle continues.

Perhaps the most telling example comes from the changes in the television and radio news media in the United States. Not long ago, the American public had very little exposure to politics and current events via television and radio, with the exception of the thirty-minute window each evening on network television and the occasional five-minute radio news brief. Then there came the advent of one 24-hour television news channel and one widely successful talk radio show. Now there are numerous 24-hour news channels and a multitude of talk radio shows and, if that were not enough, people continue the conversation about news stories and current events on the Internet in the blogosphere. This can be called the *news diffusion* phenomenon.

The universe of individuals making use of these new outlets continues to expand at a rapid rate. As more individuals have access to more general information and more details about policy decisions, they are more prepared to participate directly in the process, especially voting *with their feet*. The result of this participation is a reversion to a common sense, down-to-earth movement and a dramatic reduction of the need for elites. This includes not only a reduction in the need for an elite, but an eventual revulsion toward elites who presume to speak on behalf of groups based on theoretical ideology instead of practical positions. The common sense approach of the common individual includes a requirement for hard results and clear evidence as opposed to flowery theory and abrasive rhetoric.

Will Libertas Be Embraced and Appreciated by the Masses?

The *news diffusion* phenomenon described above is just one part of the overall phenomenon of Libertas. Both the sub-phenomenon of news diffusion in the United States and the overall phenomenon of Libertas globally are attracting new adherents at a surprising rate. Most of these new adherents do not even consciously recognize the phenomenon and many adherents are coming from unexpected sections of society. Just as the nations previously devoid of Libertas have the greatest opportunity to transform their future for dramatic improvement, so too do the least prosperous individuals within the Libertas-based nations have the similar opportunity.

The migration away from some aspects of Libertas in most western democracies during the twentieth century was caused mostly by socio-political elites attempting to fix the problems of life on behalf of the populace. The altruistic motive of those elites belies their fundamental contempt for the intelligence, the fortitude, and the ability of the *common individual*. It also belies the fundamental belief of these altruistic elites in their own superiority and their own desire for centralized decision-making.

The rejection of these elites and the rejection of the Anti-Libertas nanny-state theories will continue indefinitely, not because people do not care about the less fortunate, but because they *do* care and it is common sense to go with what works. The continued success and advancement of Libertas is contingent on the majority of the masses rejecting the patronization of the altruistic elite for the alternative of succeeding on their own and for their own satisfaction. This includes rejecting the politicians that insist on big government solutions to every problem, rejecting the continued expansion of governments, and rejecting the ever-increasing rise of the nanny-state. This rejection is not a rejection of altruistic motives. It is rather a realization that Libertas — with an emphasis on the individual and on individual decision-making — is a certain road to near universal prosperity and happiness (the greatest good for the greatest number). While Anti-Libertas — with an emphasis on centralized decision-making by elites — is a certain "road to serfdom." The rejection of the altruistic elite by the majority of the masses may appear to be unlikely, especially since those elites promise such easy solutions for some large portions of the population. This has resulted in the near electoral domination of some sections of the citizenry in most western democracies. However, there are continual signs of even the staunchest voting blocks coming to the realization that the promises have not been fulfilled and cannot be fulfilled. The empty promises are giving way to a back-to-the-basics renewal of the power of individuals and the realization of the impotence of centralized decision-making.

Perhaps the best example of this phenomenon of a traditional and staunch constituency abandoning the centralized elite involves education in the inner city in the United States. The altruistic elites have steadfastly supported centrally administered government school systems, despite the abysmal record of such schools. The elite argument for this support generally has centered on the needs of the poor, especially in the inner cities, despite the fact that the evidence shows those were the people most harmed by the ineffectiveness of the elite solutions. Now, across the country, more people within the core constituency of the inner city are becoming advocates of a free market educational competition based upon voucher systems that give these fragile young people a much greater chance of success in life than the previous elitist system. This is just one sign among many of the fundamental change of attitude; a change that is not as much representative of any political victory as much as

246

a victory of common sense, reality, and greater individual responsibility in life.

TWENTY-TWO

Emergence of the Common Individual

"We are all Marxists now." [1]
"We are all Keynesians now." [2]

We are all Hayekians now.

—R L Hogan, 2006

Has Libertas Created a New Age of Historical Development?

The evidence shows a continual expansion of Libertas in the world. It has not yet triumphed in every nation, but the historical evidence leads to the overwhelming probability that it will evolve to become the social framework in every corner of the globe. The current evolution of Libertas has led to exceptional multiculturalism and ethnic tolerance. Libertas has led to unprecedented human prosperity and well-being. Libertas has led to the decline of the nation-state and the emergence of the *common individual* as the deciding force in the world.

The triumph of Libertas signals the advent of common individuals thinking for themselves, governing for themselves, and, most importantly, pursuing the greatest good for the greatest number one person at a time. This is the triumph of cooperation over coercion as the primary structural component of human interaction. This represents the success of humans *taming*

---

1. This is an informal comment attributed to Sir William Harcourt, British Chancellor of the Exchequer, in 1888.

2. This is an informal comment attributed to Richard Nixon, President of the United States, in 1971.

themselves. This change is so fundamental that it constitutes a new epoch of the human species.

> **The Three Epochs of Humankind**
>
> - **Primitive Pre-History**
>   **(prior to 3500 BC)**
> - **Coercive Geographical Civilizations**
>   **(3500 B.C. — 2000 AD)**
> - **Cooperative Global Civiliation**
>   **(2000 AD and thereafter)**

Our Libertas-based prosperity evolved as an unplanned, spontaneous order. It was facilitated by some necessary structural conditions—the conditions necessary to substantially restrict coercion—but those conditions then allowed individuals the freedom to be creative, energetic, and flexible. The result has proven to be magnificent, but it was not planned by a centralized authority, nor specifically designed. Such an achievement could not be planned. The minds of any elite group are not capable of such an achievement.

This was the primary point throughout the work of Friedrich Hayek and was aptly expressed in *Law, Legislation, and Liberty Volume I* when he said:

> It is because it was not dependent on organization but grew up as a spontaneous order that the structure of modern society has attained that degree of complexity which it possesses and which far exceeds any that could have been achieved by deliberate organization. In fact, of course, the rules which made the growth of this complex order possible were initially not designed in expectation of that result; but those people who happened to adopt suitable rules developed a complex civilization which then often spread to others. To maintain that we must deliberately plan modern society because it has

become so complex is therefore paradoxical, and the result of a
complete misunderstanding of the circumstances. The fact is,
rather, that we can preserve an order of such complexity not
by the method of directing the members, but only indirectly
by enforcing and improving the rules conducive to the forma-
tion of a spontaneous order.[3]

This prosperity of the *spontaneous order* is a product of the people, multitudes of individuals, not directed from centralized
governments. We have created, without design, a new epoch
of the common individual. The prior historical epoch concentrated on and relied upon the elites of society. The elites had
almost exclusive access to education, political power, and economic capital. Only the elites had leisure time for reasoned
thought, while the masses toiled for daily survival. Although
the elites sometimes exploited the masses, more recently the
elites became the defender of the masses, promulgating socio-
political structures ostensibly designed to protect and help the
masses. This approach assumed that common individuals were
not capable of thinking or succeeding on their own.

Why Has the "Common Individual" Emerged?

How can individuals successfully resist the substantial power
of the elites and why has the common individual emerged? The
answer to both questions is the same. Individuals and society
are adapting according to their instinct to thrive. This includes
a trial-and-error process until better results emerge. The wilting
of the remnants of the New Deal and the crashing of the programs of the Great Society are now providing ample examples
of errors to avoid. More and more of us now see that individuals can best make adaptive decisions closest to themselves. Society is nothing but the sum of its parts; therefore, what is the

---

3. Hayek, Friedrich A. *Law, Legislation and Liberty Volume 1*. Chicago: The University
of Chicago Press, 1973. 50.

best adaptive strategy for individuals also becomes the *de facto* best strategy for society.

Many a pundit has remarked that our political leaders today are not as good as in the past. It is true. They do not need to be as good as in the past because, as each year goes by, the masses of individuals have less and less need for elite decision-making on their behalf. The mental capability of humans, as individuals, has not changed appreciably over the past five hundred years. However, the capability of the masses as a whole has changed substantially over that period of time. This is because more and more of the populace have experienced the freedom, the education, the access, the structure, and the Libertas to think for themselves, to act in their self-interest, to succeed, to enjoy the fruits of their labor, and to ignore the remaining elite that constantly denigrate the Common Individual. By and large, the best and most capable leaders in our societies today no longer participate in government, because they know they can get so much more accomplished, both selfishly and altruistically, outside the auspices of government.

This triumph of the Common Individual is our universal history. Humans have always been adapting, but now we have reached a new plateau in our progressive advancement. It represents the great expansion of the utilization of our primary evolutionary advantage: our brains. It took millions of years for humans with advanced brains to evolve, but our civilized history includes only the past 5,500 years. Our brains have not evolved significantly in that shorter period of time and it may take millions of more years to see noticeable biological changes. What has changed is the *utilization* of those brains.

This new plateau of human development is not a "civilization." It represents a species-wide fundamental change in human behavior. The last such plateau was reached several thousands of years ago when humans made the transition from hunter-gatherers to agriculturists. The metamorphosis to agriculture and civilizations was the beginning of a long and arduous journey of humans learning how best to live with one

252

another, how to tame themselves. The initial 5,000 years of civilization involved the struggle of humans to build a better life, but mostly through the use of coercion by elites and the subjugation of the majority of people. This necessarily limited the amount of brainpower—the primary human advantage—utilized. The last 500 years of civilization has involved more and more societies recognizing the inherent advantage of cooperation (Libertas) and the ever-widening use of brainpower.

This started by the extension of Libertas to most males in a small corner of Europe. It later expanded into many more geographic areas. The practice of slavery and indentured servitude was mostly abolished. Women were eventually included into the process. During the past 500 years there has been a substantial increase in the utilization of human brainpower by the inclusion of so many more humans in the process of societal guidance through the advent of widespread Libertas.

This is our universal history. Our species started with a very long period of evolution at the mercy of the forces of biology. We then began domesticating the resources of the Earth largely at the mercy of geography. Finally, within the past 500 years, we have begun taking much greater control of our destiny by vastly expanding the utilization of our mental resources. This has been achieved through the use of an intricate structure of human cooperation—based on Libertas—resulting in an explosion of human betterment. This latest phase of our universal history has now gained speed and is rapidly coming to dominate all human societies because the undeniable success of Libertas is now self-evident.

Does the Victory of Libertas Signal the "End of History"?

The victory of Libertas over the large-scale, non-democratic elites of Anti-Libertas, such as fascism and communism, has been characterized as "the end of history." This was meant to suggest only that the big historic struggles among competing societal structures might be over. This appears to be true. However, it does not mean that actual history or the adaptation of humans is over. In many respects, history is becoming more interesting, although more complex and very different from previous centuries or millennia. History has shifted from an emphasis on the *macro* to an emphasis on the *micro*.

The past macro focus included an emphasis on civilizations, nations, governmental institutions, mega-corporations, international governing bodies, large-scale unions, broadcast media, inflexible assembly lines, etc. The new micro emphasis centers squarely on individuals, but includes small businesses, home-based businesses, independent contract labor, narrowcast media, mass customization, globalization, the Internet, etc. This is a new epoch in human history. It represents the emergence of the Common Individual.

This may seem to be a paradoxical conclusion. How can individuals remain important and continue progressing when the most hegemonic, centralized governmental power in history, the United States, is at its apex? The answer is, as previously noted, that despite the missteps of misguided and well-intentioned interventionists everywhere, governments (and broad organizations in general) are becoming increasingly irrelevant.

The Internet is the best analogy to describe the power of individuals and a fine example of the phenomenon of individual emergence. The Internet is not centrally managed or controlled by government and yet it has more power and influence than if it were centrally managed and controlled by government. The more people participate, the stronger the Internet becomes and the more resources are available to individuals, thus the stronger they become in aggregate. It is a wonderful example of a positive-sum effect. The phenomenon of the Internet is very similar to the overall phenomenon of Libertas. With the geographic expansion and the positive-sum aspects of Libertas, more individuals are participating in the creation of better lives, which consequently helps many others they never see or know.

It is easy to see what caused the Internet exuberance of the late 1990s. The emergence of the microchip, software, fiber optics, and satellite technology has helped to create an environment of remarkable impact on the growth of human participation. In some respects it is similar to that which the Gutenberg movable type printing press helped to create over five hundred years ago. The difference is that although the Gutenberg printing press greatly expanded the availability of diverse knowledge and discussion, it was still a *broadcast* medium with the power to decide content residing at the control of the owners of presses. The Internet is allowing the participants to control the content.

The power of new technologies is adding to the speed in which Libertas is spreading around the world. The Internet and satellite television are allowing people (especially young people) around the world to experience more freedom than in previous generations. This early-life experience raises new levels of expectations for Libertas to ever-broader audiences. The impact of the technology is forcing more illiberal autocrats to reform. This process has become a virtuous cycle in a manner that is irreversible. The excitement and the optimism are contagious.

Can Common People Resist the Decay of Democracy?

The advance of Libertas to date has caused an incredible number of everyday people within democracies to reject centralized, elite decision-making in general. They have increased the amount of self-planning in their lives. This occurs far beyond traditional political activity within the many other aspects of life. More than anything else, they vote *with their feet.* They move to a different neighborhood, they buy a different product, they change schools, they change careers, they emigrate to another country, they go to work for a competitor, they shop elsewhere, they start their own business from their basement, they switch churches, they write their own reviews on the Internet, they begin their own discussion groups, they conduct their own research, etc. This is not the old world where big governments, big businesses, and big religious denominations were the primary influencers and where those elite decision makers shackled the perimeters of most individuals. Common people everywhere are making these life changes more frequently than in the past.

As Libertas evolves and the methods of human interaction change, there are inevitable adjustment periods. Not everyone adjusts at the same rate and there are adjustment pains, but the long-term result is the growth of the individual. As individuals adapt, they are essentially performing a sort of calisthenics of their brain. More people are participating in the full process of human interaction and more people are participating at expanded levels. This adaptation includes understanding the limitations of governmental, centralized decision-making. Libertas will win the smaller battle within democracies just as it won the larger battle against monarchy, fascism, and communism.

Libertas will win the struggle because of the emergence of the common people. This emergence includes not only the political power of the people, but also the evolution of a popular appreciation of Libertas. This event has been long anticipated. Thomas Mackay predicted it much more than a century ago. He claimed that the approaching ruin being brought by collectivism could only be stopped by an understanding on the part of most people that Libertas was better than any elite management of society.

TWENTY-THREE

The Future of Libertas

"Freedom means that in some measure we entrust our fate to forces which we do not control; and this seems intolerable to those constructivists who believe that man can master his fate – as if civilization and reason itself were of his making."[1]

—Friedrich Hayek, 1976

Is the Ascendancy of the Common Individual Inevitable?

The relative pace of progression among the nations of the Prosperous World is contingent upon their ability to resist the trap of centralized decision-making, except as necessary to maintain order and peace. Now that the big fight against non-democratic elites is over, the struggle is mostly internal, it is against our own lack of self-discipline, and it is against our own tendency to self-destruct with good intentions. The major western democracies, including the United States, continually moved away from certain components of Libertas during much of the twentieth century, not from the cause of outside force, but from the cause of internal good intentions.

Thankfully, despite the frequent missteps caused by unintended consequences and despite the tendency of democratic elites to attempt to solve every societal problem through elite decision-making, the positive progressive adaptation of mankind continues relentlessly because our humanistic adaptive nature compels it. Adaptation attempts that do not succeed are

---

1. Hayek, Friedrich A. *Law, Legislation and Liberty Volume 2*. Chicago: The University of Chicago Press, 1976. 30.

eventually discarded and adaptation continues. If some prosperous nations abandon Libertas too much, they will be forced to correct their direction or they will be supplanted by other nations with superior structures of Libertas. Their citizens might change the leadership by vote or they might choose to emigrate elsewhere. Many elite leaders, in both democracies and non-democracies, are beginning to enhance components of Libertas in order to attract capital investments, jobs, and prosperity. They follow this trend, even if they personally despise Libertas, because they know that the enterprise of the world will otherwise pass by them.

This was a major theme of the Thomas Friedman's bestseller *The Lexus and the Olive Tree*.[2] He described the global phenomenon of the influence of Libertas that is essentially forcing governments everywhere to adhere to the major components of Libertas or be left behind in the dustbin of history. Many readers of that book, perhaps even the author himself, may be dismayed or disturbed by this phenomenon, but the power and influence of the phenomenon are quite clear. It is a force that has no leader, no visible political organization, no true beginning or end. This is what makes it a universal history and this is what makes it unstoppable.

Not all individuals adapt positively, nor do all societies, but taken in aggregate and on average, individuals and humankind are generally adapting toward a more productive society. The force of individual common sense by the common individual is already beginning to turn the tide against the elites who have squandered resources on unsuccessful schemes of good intentions. This internal battle of good intentions will not be won or lost through elites. It will be won or lost through common people. It is unrealistic to expect politicians *not* to pander to the public, so it is imperative for the public to reject the pandering. This is not as unlikely as might be expected and the phenomenon goes far beyond politics.

---

2. Friedman, Thomas. *The Lexus and the Olive Tree*. First Anchor Books ed. New York: Anchor Books, 2000.

Are We the "Last Man"?

Philosophers still question whether the progress of Libertas has an underlying flaw involving human character and happiness. Is the emergence of this new common individual a sign of the *last man* as described by Nietzsche and discussed by Fukuyama; a "man without chest," lacking the necessary recognition stated by Hegel to be so crucial to the satisfaction of humans? The answer is: certainly not. The model of Libertas has not prevented individual achievers from continuing to be "men with chests," although the migration to widespread peace has largely reduced the traditional role of military service in providing such achievement. The model of Libertas has actually expanded the opportunity for virtually every man and woman to be blessed with the satisfaction of achievement, whether large or small by comparison.

Contrary to the concern of Nietzsche, the emergence of the common individual has positioned our species for an exponential growth of morality and personal satisfaction. No longer can the responsibilities of morality and behavior be blamed on the elite, the king, the pope, the dictator, the legislature, the titans of industry, the Ivy League, the United Nations, etc. Now, the responsibility rests squarely on the shoulders of ordinary people.

This responsibility facilitates the personal discipline necessary to build up personal morality and then to enjoy the satisfaction of that personal accomplishment. This life is not easy. It is a complex and confusing world and people have to work hard to adapt and thrive. A centralized elite group will not necessarily direct us in our activities. We must develop our own internal fortitude and spirituality. Yet this test, this exercise, will provide ample motivation for continual improvement and the results will provide for ample human satisfaction.

Our global society is in the very early stages, the beginning of this new epoch. And yet the spontaneous order created through Libertas has already resulted in a spectacular increase in prosperity, peace, security, health, and the welfare of humankind. Some acolyte followers of Nietzsche still cling to the deep pessimism of no human progress, but by doing so, they ignore the history unfolding before us. In the mid-twentieth century, after two devastating world wars and the emerging nuclear showdown, such deep pessimism was both fashionable and understandable. Today, the horrible calamities of the first half of the twentieth century are beginning to appear as aberrations, not trends. Now, after the withering of autocratic regimes in Asia, southern Europe, and Latin America and the collapse of global communism, there is no excuse for such abject pessimism. The remnants of such pessimism are sad and revolting, but more importantly, counter-productive to the advancement of the greatest good for the greatest number and, therefore, basically immoral.

What Is the Most Probable Future Outcome for Mankind?

The forces of Libertas around the world have ample reason to fear the Islamic terrorist threat in the short run and they should marshal considerable effort to protect Libertas from this threat. However, in the long run, the force of human progress will crush these resistors to Libertas, just as it will eventually crush virtually all resistance to Libertas. We can no more return to widespread Anti-Libertas coercion than could our forefathers return to being hunter-gathers once agriculture had spread across the globe. This phenomenon of the growth of Libertas constitutes both a universal history and the making of a very bright future.

This bright future is based on the fact that each day, all around the world, more and more individuals are participating in more and more Libertas. Even in the western democracies where government interference increases, the private aspects of Libertas are thankfully growing faster than the forces of Anti-Libertas and the people look upon the unnecessary waste of good intentions as a nuisance more than a society-threatening problem. In the other parts of the world, the worst Anti-Libertas governments are falling or adapting and billions of people are gaining ever-increasing exposure to Libertas.

These developments are not only good for the individuals by their own efforts, but these developments are also good because of the cumulative effects and residual benefits created by the positive-sum effect. As individuals obtain the opportunities that come with Libertas, the vast majority of them advance their lot in life very quickly. A small percentage of them become super-achievers that invent and create ideas and physical objects that benefit the entire society. As these new or expanded participants gain access to more Libertas, larger numbers of people improve their condition, larger numbers of people become super-achievers, and all future generations get the luxury of utilizing the additional accumulation.

The inherent adaptive nature of humans compels the inevitable extension of Libertas. There is no reason to expect anything other than the continued expansion of Libertas on average. Therefore, there is every reason to expect continued human progress with no foreseeable end. This is brightness indeed!

TWENTY-FOUR

Conclusion

"The possibility of men living together in peace and to their mutual advantage without having to agree on common concrete aims, and bound only by abstract rules of conduct, was perhaps the greatest discovery mankind ever made."[1]

— Friedrich Hayek, 1976

We discussed the *goal of our species* much earlier in this work. After admitting there can be no true goal of *humankind*, other than the sum of billions of individual goals, reasonable minds can agree that we should want to wish everyone well. The question then arises as to how to best achieve that goal.

Our species did not exactly concern itself with such consequential and universal matters for most of recorded history. For the first five millennia of civilized history, human interaction was often dominated by the use of force and coercion, resulting in uneven and negligible advancement in the well-being of most people. There were isolated highlights, but little sustainable progress, and most humans lived in the shadow of disease, destruction, destitution, and death. Then, during roughly the last few hundred years — representing only about one-tenth of civilized history and one one-hundredth of the lifespan of our species — a critical mass of the components of Libertas developed that fundamentally shifted human interaction to mostly voluntary cooperation and included the limitation of coercion. This critical mass of Libertas started small and isolated, but began

---

1. Hayek, Friedrich A. *Law, Legislation and Liberty Volume 2*. Chicago: The University of Chicago Press, 1976. 136.

spreading and improving. Despite occasional setbacks, it has now spread to become the predominant form of human interaction in the world.

Wherever Libertas has spread, unprecedented prosperity and progress have followed. The shadow of human existence has now largely become health, peace, prosperity, and life. The benefits of the rule of law, social freedom, limited government, private property, free enterprise, free trade, and democracy have all been discussed at some length over time, but usually as separate disciplines. It was the coming together of all these separate aspects that created full Libertas and has caused a fundamental change in human history.

It was claimed during the Enlightenment and thereafter that humans had been endowed by their creator with certain inalienable or natural rights, including the rights of life, liberty, and the pursuit of happiness. This is obviously false. These are not natural rights. They were not the predominant practice of humans for most of history. Our species had to tame itself and come to the realization that these rights constituted the best method of interaction. These rights were not natural; they had to be imposed onto what had previously been a culture of coercion.

The new culture of Libertas is still evolving and still requires serious thought and discussion. The discussion of this topic receives precious little attention in our modern world. Most serious discussion today seems concentrated on specific problem solving, rather than on the structural issues that are pivotal to the success of Libertas. The discussion of full Libertas (in its entirety) has been somewhat out of favor with the generation of baby boomers. In the previous generation, Milton Friedman, Friedrich Hayek, and Ludwig von Mises spent virtually their entire careers discussing the topic, first as economists, and then expanding into the political and social aspects. Their work has heavily influenced my own and I am most grateful for their scholarship. I have attempted to augment the study of Libertas by analyzing the place of Libertas over the span of all human history, as well as noting how the spread of Libertas has enabled the emergence of the common individual.

The theory of universal history put forth in this book can be summed up succinctly in the following quote by John Zane in his profound work *The Story of Law*, written in 1927:

> *Man began as an animal, responding merely to his surroundings, and the fact that he so began has led the Behaviorists to assert that such he has always remained. Their favorite thesis is that the individual man today is just what society has made him. This is true in a measure, but since man became civilized, the exact converse is shown to be true by the history of law. Society now is what the individual man is making it. Somewhere in the development, by gradual and imperceptible degrees, the animal man passed from the stage of the brute wholly obedient to its circumstances and surroundings, to that of a being who, by his own purposeful mentality, could so alter the impact of his surroundings upon himself, that he could rise above the external world of the senses into the realm of the inner life of the spirit and could make it true that human society will become what the individual shall make it.*[2]

The optimism shared here with you is not based in wishful thinking. Instead, it is based in historical experience as outlined throughout the book. The advance of our species is, in fact, the advance of individuals based upon the fruits produced by individuals, including the greatest fruit of all. That "great fruit" is the implementation of abstract social structure that restricts coercion and encourages individual initiative. This tremendous event, this growth of Libertas, represents our universal history.

Nobel laureate Frederick Hayek spent the majority of his career explaining why Libertas is the most advantageous method of human interaction. The following are Hayek's own words

2. Zane, John Maxcy. *The Story of Law*. Indianapolis: Liberty Fund, 1998. 12-13.

with some of his primary points about Libertas and the peaceful, prosperous spontaneous order created by Libertas:

> *The Great Society arose through the discovery that men can live together in peace and mutually benefiting each other without agreeing on the particular aims which they severally pursue. The discovery that by substituting abstract rules of conduct for obligatory concrete ends made it possible to extend the order of peace beyond the small groups pursuing the same ends, because it enabled each individual to gain from the skill and knowledge of others whom he need not even know and whose aims could be wholly different from his own...That we assist in the realization of other people's aims without sharing them or even knowing them, and solely in order to achieve our own aims, is the source of strength of the Great Society...If we wish everyone to be well off, we shall get closest to our goal, not by commanding by law that this should be achieved, or giving everybody a legal claim to what we think he ought to have, but by providing inducements for all to do as much as they can that will benefit others.*[3]

He said: "...not by commanding by law..., but by providing inducements..." This is precisely the point. The nuisance of interventionist policies is more than merely a nuisance. It is a danger. This has nothing to do with the irritation people feel from high taxation and the waste of their tax dollars. It has everything to do with the fact that the intervention is doing more harm than good for the very people that it is intended to help. Worst of all, the careful attention that could be used to improve the structural conditions of Libertas and therefore dramatically improve the opportunity to those people who most need help, are being diverted into projects of good intention that lead to

---

3. Hayek, Friedrich A. *Law, Legislation and Liberty Volume 2*. Chicago: The University of Chicago Press, 1976. 106-110.

bad results.

Fortunately, through the experience of history, people have the opportunity to learn from mistakes and make adaptive choices. History can be fascinating and entertaining, but more importantly, it can be useful. If we understand why humans have progressed, then we can utilize that information for establishing a better world in the future. It is not really a question of "if," but a question of "when," because the adaptive nature of humans is obvious. This adaptive nature virtually ensures the continued success of Libertas because it has proven to be the most successful method of human interaction.

However, no course of human interaction is certain. There is no doubt that the world is complex far beyond my ability to understand everything. Uncertainty is the only thing that is certain. Yet I am a great believer in predictive probability based upon historical evidence. After reviewing the evidence, it appears that the forces of Libertas are virtually unstoppable. This viewpoint is not based upon illogical assumptions or emotions. The clear facts of the history lead to this assessment. The conclusion is *self-evident*.

R. L. Hogan
2006

Bibliography

Adair, Douglass. *Fame and the Founding Fathers*. Indianapolis: Liberty Fund, 1998.

Adams, Henry. *The Education of Henry Adams*. Paperback ed. Oxford: Oxford University Press, 1999.

Arendt, Hannah. *Lectures on Kant's Political Philosophy*. Paperback ed. Chicago: The University of Chicago Press, 1992.

Ashton, T. S. *The Industrial Revolution*. 1997 ed. Oxford: Oxford University Press, 1997.

Bacon, Francis. *The Major Works*. Oxford: Oxford University Press, 1996.

Bagehot, Walter. *Physics and Politics*. Paperback ed. Chicago: Ivan R. Dee, 1999.

Bainton, Roland H. *The Reformation of the Sixteenth Century*. Boston: Beacon Press, 1985.

Bastiat, Frederic. *The Law*. Second ed. Irvington-on-Hudson: Foundation for Economic Education, 1998.

Benedictow, Ole J. *The Black Death*. First ed. Woodbridge: The Boydell Press, 2004.

Berlin, Isaiah. *The Crooked Timber of Humanity*. Princeton Paperback ed. Princeton: Princeton University Press, 1997.

Berlin, Isaiah. *Liberty*. Oxford: Oxford University Press, 2002.

Berlin, Isaiah. *The Proper Study of Mankind*. First paperback ed. New York: Farrar, Straus and Giroux, 2000.

Boccaccio, Giovanni. *The Decameron*. Second ed. London: Penquin Books, 2003.

Boortz, Neal, and John Linder. *The Fair Tax Book*. First ed. New York: Regan Books, 2005.

Brinton, Crane. *A Decade of Revolution*. First paperback ed. New York: Harper & Row, 1963.

Buchanan, James M., and Gordon Tullock. *The Calculus of Consent*. Indianapolis: Liberty Fund, 1999.

269

Callahan, Gene. *Economics for Real People*. 2nd ed. Auburn: Ludwig von Mises Institute, 2004.

Colbourn, Trevor. *The Lamp of Experience*. Indianapolis: Liberty Fund, 1998.

Collingwood, R. G. *The Idea of History*. Revised ed. Oxford: Oxford University Press, 1994.

Comte, Auguste. *Introduction to Positive Philosophy*. Indianapolis: Hackett Publishing Company, 1988.

Conze, Edward. *Buddhism: Its Essence and Development*. First Harper Torchbook ed. New York: Harper & Row, 1959.

Copleston, F. C. *Medieval Philosophy*. First Harper Torchbook ed. New York: Harper & Row, 1961.

Creel, H. G. *Confucius and the Chinese Way*. First Harper Torchbook ed. New York: Harper & Row, 1960.

Darwin, Charles. *The Origin of Species*. New York: Gramercy Books, 1979.

Davies, Norman. *Europe: A History*. First HarperPerennial ed. New York: HarperPerennial, 1998.

Descartes, Rene. *Discourse on Method and Meditations*. Indianapolis: The Liberal Arts Press, 1960.

De Soto, Hernando. *The Mystery of Capital*. New York: Basic Books, 2000.

Diamond, Jared. *Guns, Germs, and Steel*. Paperback ed. New York: W. W. Norton & Company, 1999.

D'Souza, Dinesh. *The Virtue of Prosperity*. New York: The Free Press, 2000.

Durant, Will. *The Story of Philosophy*. First Pocket Books ed. New York: Pocket Books, 1953.

Easterly, William. *The Elusive Quest for Growth*. Cambridge: The MIT Press, 2001.

Eberstein, Alan. *The Mind of Friedrich Hayek*. New York: Palgrave Macmillan, 2003.

Feulner, Jr., Edwin J. *Intellectual Pilgrims*. Washington: Edwin J. Feulner, Jr., 1999.

Fogel, Robert William. *The Escape from Hunger and Premature Death, 1700-2100*. Paperback ed. Cambridge: Cambridge University Press, 2004.

Bibliography

Friedman, Milton, and Rose Friedman. *Free to Choose*. New York: Harcourt Brace Jovanovich, 1979.

Friedman, Milton. *Capitalism and Freedom*. Fortieth Anniversary ed. Chicago: The University of Chicago Press, 2002.

Friedman, Thomas. *The Lexus and the Olive Tree*. First Anchor Books ed. New York: Anchor Books, 2000.

Fukuyama, Francis. *The End of History and the Last Man*. New York: The Free Press, 1992.

Fukuyama, Francis. *State-Building*. Ithaca: Cornell University Press, 2004.

Fung, Yu-Lan. *A Short History of Chinese Philosophy*. First Free Press Paperback ed. New York: The Free Press, 1966.

Gibbon, Edward. *The Decline and Fall of the Roman Empire*. Paperback ed. New York: The Modern Library, 2003.

Gilder, George. *Wealth & Poverty*. San Francisco: ICS Press, 1993.

Gilder, George. *Microcosm*. New York: Simon & Schuster, 1989.

Gilderhus, Mark T. *History and Historians*. Fifth ed. Upper Saddle River: Prentice Hall, 2003.

Gimpel, Jean. *The Medieval Machine*. Paperback ed. New York: Barnes & Noble Books, 2003.

Gordon, David. *The Philosophical Origins of Austrian Economics*. Auburn: Ludwig von Mises Institute, 1996.

Gwartney, James, and Robert Lawson. *Economic Freedom of the World 2004 Annual Report*. Vancouver: The Fraser Institute, 2004.

Hartwell, R. M. *A History of the Mont Pelerin Society*. Indianapolis: Liberty Fund, 1995.

Hayek, Friedrich A. *The Constitution of Liberty*. Paperback ed. Chicago: The University of Chicago Press, 1978.

Hayek, Friedrich A. *Law, Legislation and Liberty Volume 1*. Chicago: The University of Chicago Press, 1973.

Hayek, Friedrich A. *Law, Legislation and Liberty Volume 2*. Chicago: The University of Chicago Press, 1976.

Hayek, Friedrich A. *Law, Legislation and Liberty Volume 3*. Phoenix ed. Chicago: The University of Chicago Press, 1979.

Hayek, F. A. *The Road to Serfdom*. Fiftieth Anniversary ed. Chicago: The University of Chicago Press, 1994.

Hegel, Georg Wilhelm Friedrich. *The Philosophy of History*. New York: Dover Publications, 1956.

Hegel, Georg Wilhelm Friedrich. *Reason in History*. First ed. Indianapolis: Bobbs-Merrill Education Publishing, 1953.

Heilbroner, Robert L. *An Inquiry Into The Human Prospect*. First ed. New York: W. W. Norton & Company, 1974.

Herder, Johann Gottfried. *Another Philosophy of History and Selected Political Writings*. Indianapolis: Hackett Publishing Company, 2004.

Hobbes, Thomas. *Leviathan*. London: Penquin Books, 1968.

Hogue, Arthur R. *Origins of the Common Law*. Indianapolis: Liberty Fund, 1985.

Howard, Philip K. *The Death of Common Sense*. New York: Random House, 1994.

Huizinga, Johan. *The Waning of the Middle Ages*. Mineola: Dover Publications, 1999.

Hume, David. *Essays: Moral, Political, and Literary*. Revised ed. Indianapolis: Liberty Fund, 1985.

Hume, David. *David Hume Selected Essays*. New York: Oxford University Press, 1993.

Hume, David. *An Inquiry Concerning Human Understanding*. Indianapolis: Bobbs-Merrill Education Publishing, 1955.

Hutt, W.H. *The Keynesian Episode*. Indianapolis: Liberty Fund, 1979.

Iggers, Georg G. *Historiography in the Twentieth Century*. Middletown: Wesleyan University Press, 1997.

Jardine, Lisa. *Worldly Goods : A New History of the Renaissance*. New York: W. W. Norton & Company, 1996.

Jasay, Anthony de. *Justice and Its Surroundings*. Indianapolis: Liberty Fund, 2002.

Jones, Eric. *The European Miracle*. Third. Cambridge: Cambridge University Press, 2003.

Bibliography

Kant, Immanuel. *Basic Writings of Kant*. Ed. Allen W. Wood. New York: The Modern Library, 2001.

Kant, Immanuel. *On History*. Upper Saddle River: Prentice Hall, 2001.

Kant, Immanuel. *Prolegomena to Any Future Metaphysics*. Cambridge: Cambridge University Press, 1996.

Kierkegaard, Soren. *Papers and Journals: A Selection*. London: Penquin Books, 1996.

Kohn, Georg Childs. *Dictionary of Wars*. Revised ed. New York: Checkmark Books, 1999.

Landes, David. *The Unbound Prometheus*. Cambridge: Cambridge University Press, 1969.

Landes, David S. *The Wealth and Poverty of Nations*. New York: W. W. Norton & Company, 1998.

Lindsey, Brink. *Against the Dead Hand*. New York: John Wiley & Sons, 2002.

Lippmann, Walter. *The Good Society*. New Brunswick: Transaction Publishers, 2005.

Locke, John. *The Second Treatise on Civil Government*. Amherst: Prometheus Books, 1986.

Madison, James. "Number 51 Checks and Balances." *The Federalist*. Ed. . New York: MetroBooks, 1961.

Magnet, Myron. *The Dream and the Nightname*. First paperback ed. San Francisco: Encounter Books, 2000.

Maitland, Frederic William. *A Historical Sketch of Liberty and Equality*. Indianapolis: Liberty Fund, 2000.

Mann, Charles C. *1491*. 1st ed. New York: Alfred A. Knopf, 2005.

McNeill, William H. *The Pursuit of Power*. Chicago: The University of Chicago Press, 1982.

Mill, John Stuart. *On Liberty*. New York: The Liberal Arts Press, 1956.

Mill, John Stuart. *Utilitarianism*. Indianapolis: Hackett Publishing Company, 1979.

Mises, Ludwig von. *Bureaucracy*. Cedar Falls: Center for Futures Education, 1983.

Mises, Ludwig von. *Human Action*. Scholar's ed. Auburn: The Ludwig von Mises Institute, 1998.

Mises, Ludwig von. *Omnipotent Government*. Grove City: Libertarian Press, 1985.

Mises, Ludwig von. *Socialism*. Indianapolis: Liberty Fund, 1981.

Mises, Ludwig von. *Selected Writings of Ludwig von Mises*. Indianapolis: Liberty Fund, 2002.

Mises, Ludwig von. *Theory and History*. Auburn: The Ludwig von Mises Institute, 1985.

Mises, Ludwig von. *The Theory of Money and Credit*. Indianapolis: Liberty Fund, 1980.

Mitchell, B. R. *European Historical Statistics 1750-1970*. Abridged ed. New York: Columbia University Press, 1975.

Montesquieu, Charles de Secondat. *The Spirit of Laws*. Amherst: Prometheus Books, 2002.

Moore, Stephen, and Julian L. Simon. *It's Getting Better All the Time*. Washington: Cato Institute, 2000.

Murray, Charles. *In Our Hands*. Washington, D.C.: The AIE Press, 2006.

Murray, Charles. *Losing Ground*. Tenth Anniversary ed. New York: Basic Books, 1994.

Nash, Ronald H. *The Meaning of History*. Nashville: Broadman & Holman Publishers, 1998.

Nietzsche, Friedrich. *Basic Writings of Nietzsche*. New York: The Modern Library, 2000.

Nietzsche, Friedrich. *The Portable Nietzsche*. New York: Penguin Books, 1976.

Nietzsche, Friedrich. *Thus Spake Zarathustra*. Unabridged ed. Mineola: Dover Publications, 1999.

Nisbet, Robert. *The Present Age : Progress and Anarchy in Modern America*. Indianapolis: Liberty Fund, 1988.

Nisbet, Robert. *The Quest for Community*. San Francisco: ICS Press, 1990.

Olasky, Marvin. *The Tragedy of American Compassion*. Washington: Regnery Publishing, 1992.

Oppenheimer, Stephen. *The Real Eve*. Paperback ed. New York: Carroll & Graf, 2003.

Bibliography

Pagden, Anthony. *Peoples and Empires*. New York: The Modern Library, 2001.

Paine, Thomas. *Representative Selections*. Revised ed. New York: Hill and Wang, 1961.

Passmore, John. *The Perfectibility of Man*. Third ed. Indianapolis: Liberty Fund, 2000.

Paterson, Isabel. *The God of the Machine*. New Brunswick: Transaction Publishers, 2005.

Patterson, Orlando. *Freedom Volume I: Freedom in the Making of Western Culture*. New York: Basic Books, 1991.

Peck, M. Scott. *The Road Less Traveled*. 25th Aniversary ed. New York: Simon & Schuster, 2002.

Pinker, Steven. *The Blank Slate*. New York: Viking, 2002.

Pomeranz, Kenneth. *The Great Divergence*. Princeton: Princeton University Press, 2000.

Powell, Jim. *The Triumph of Liberty*. New York: The Free Press, 2000.

Rand, Ayn. *Capitalism: The Unknown Idea*. New York: Signet, 1967.

Roberts, J. M. *The New History of the World*. Fourth revised ed. Oxford: Oxford University Press, 2002.

Rothbard, Murray N. *America's Great Depression*. Fifth ed. Auburn: Ludwig von Mises Institute, 2000.

Rousseau, Jean-Jacques. *The First and Second Discourses*. New York: St Martin's Press, 1964.

Rousseau, Jean-Jacques. *The Social Contract*. London: Penquin Books, 1968.

Schelling, Thomas C. *Choice and Consequence*. Cambridge: Harvard University Press, 1984.

Seldon, Arthur. *Government Failure and Over-Government*. Indianapolis: Liberty Fund, 2005.

Sen, Amartya. *Development as Freedom*. First Anchor Books ed. New York: Anchor Books, 1999.

Smith, Adam. *The Essential Adam Smith*. Ed. Robert Heilbroner. New York: W. W. Norton & Company, 1986.

Smith, Adam. *An Inquiry Into the Nature and Causes of The Wealth of Nations.* 1994 Modern Library ed. New York: The Modern Library, 1994.

Smith, Adam. *The Theory of Moral Sentiments.* Liberty Fund ed. Indianapolis: Liberty Fund, 1982.

Spengler, Oswald. *The Decline of the West.* Abridged ed. New York: Oxford University Press, 1991.

Solzhenitsyn, Alexander. *One Day in the Life of Ivan Denisovich.* New York: Bantam Books, 1963.

Sowell, Thomas. *Black Rednecks and White Liberals.* First ed. San Francisco: Encounter Books, 2005.

Sowell, Thomas. *A Conflict of Visions.* New York: Basic Books, 2002.

Sowell, Thomas. *Ethnic America.* New York: Basic Books, 1981.

Sowell, Thomas. *The Vision of the Anointed.* New York: Basic Books, 1995.

Steele, Shelby. *The Content of Our Character.* New York: HarperPerennial, 1990.

Steele, Shelby. *A Dream Deferred.* New York: HarperPerennial, 1994.

Strogatz, Steven. *Sync : The Emerging Science of Spontaneous Order.* New York: Hyperion, 2003.

Sumner, William Graham. *Social Darwinism.* Englewood Cliffs: Prentice Hall, 1963.

Tocqueville, Alexis de. *Democracy in America.* New York: Mentor, 1984.

Toynbee, Arnold J. *A Study of History* (Abridgement of Volumes I-VI). Abridged ed. New York: Oxford University Press, 1987.

Vile, M. J. C. *Constitutionalism and the Separation of Powers.* Second ed. Indianapolis: Liberty Fund, 1998.

Voltaire, Francois-Marie Arouet. *Philosophical Dictionary.* London: Penguin Books, 1972.

Voltaire, Francois-Marie Arouet. *The Portable Voltaire.* New York: Penguin Books, 1977.

Von Laue, Theodore H. *The World Revolution of Westernization.* New York: Oxford University Press, 1987.

Bibliography

Wanniski, Jude. *The Way the World Works*. Fourth ed. Washington: Regnery Publishing, 1998.

Welch, Holmes. *Taoism: The Parting of the Way*. Revised ed. Boston: Beacon Press, 1966.

Wells, Spencer. *The Journey of Man*. Paperback ed. New York: Random House, 2003.

Wilson, Edward O. *On Human Nature*. Cambridge: Harvard University Press, 1978.

Wood, Gordon S. *The Radicalism of the American Revolution*. New York: Vintage Books, 1991.

Wright, Robert. *Nonzero: The Logic of Human Destiny*. First ed. New York: Pantheon Books, 2000.

Yergin, Daniel. *The Commanding Heights*. New York: Simon & Schuster, 1998.

Zane, John Maxcy. *The Story of Law*. Indianapolis: Liberty Fund, 1998.

15 Great Austrian Economists. Ed. Randall G. Holcombe. Auburn: Ludwig von Mises Institute, 1999.

The Anti-Federalist Papers and the Constitutional Convention Debates. Ed. Ralph Ketcham. New York: Signet, 1986.

The Black Death: A Chronicle of the Plague. Ed. Johannes Nohl. New York: Ballantine Books, 1960.

The Conservative Mind from Burke to Eliot. Ed. Russell Kirk. Washington: Regnery Publishing, 1986.

Freedom in the World 2004. New York: Freedom House, 2004.

From the Cannon's Mouth. Ed. Milo M. Quaife. Detroit: Wayne State University Press, 1959.

Herbert Spencer and the Limits of the State. Ed. Michael Taylor. Bristol: Thoemmes Press, 1996.

Ideas of History : Volume One Speculative Approaches to History. Ed. Ronald Nash. New York: E. P. Dutton & Co, 1969.

The Libertarian Reader. Ed. David Boaz. New York: The Free Press, 1997.

Military History. Ed. Robert Cowley, and Geoffrey Parker. Boston: Houghton Mifflin Company, 1996.

The Portable Enlightenment Reader. Ed. Isaac Kramnick. New York: Penguin Books, 1995.

The Pursuit of Certainty : David Hume, Jeremy Bentham, John Stuart Mill, Beatrice Webb. Ed. Shirley Robin Letwin. Indianapolis: Liberty Fund, 1998.

Toward Liberty. Ed. David Boaz. Washington: Cato Institute, 2002.

Index

Index

M

MacKay, Thomas, 241, 256
Madison, James, 47, 136, 191-193, 198, 206
Madrid, 230
Magna Carta, 85, 120, 123, 153
Magnet, Myron, 181
majoritarianism, 42, 137-138, 224
Major Yongneup Swamp, 98
manorial system, 152-153
Maryland, 143
Marx, Karl, 20, 30, 88, 249
Maya, 26, 60, 83
Menand, Louis, 118
Menger, Carl, 201
Mesopotamia, 26, 31
Messina, 7-8, 10-11
Metternich, Prince Klemens, 99
Mexico, 215
Middle Ages, 29, 49, 60, 62, 120
Middle East and North Africa (MENA), 45
Mill, John Stuart, 151
Minor Yongneup Swamp, 98
Minoa, 26, 31
Mises, Ludwig von, 97, 177, 201-202, 235, 264
monarchy, 60-61, 67, 85, 117, 120-121, 125, 146, 165, 207, 256
Mongolia, 99
Montesquieu, Charles de Secondat, 72, 149
Mont Pelerin Society, 197, 198-204
Mount Etna, 8
multiculturalism, 228, 249
Murray, Charles, 181
Myanmar, 133, 219

N

Native Americans, 143, 211, 228
negative-sum, 80, 227
Napoleon, 49, 125, 126
Netherlands (Holland), 63, 65, 68, 93, 151, 218
New Deal, 251
Newton, Isaac, 48, 82
New World, 52, 63
New Zealand, 65, 93, 211-212, 218, 236

Nietzsche, Friedrich, 30, 239, 260
Nixon, Richard, 99, 249
Norman Conquest, 49, 126
Norway, 93

O

Olasky, Marvin, 181

P

Paine, Thomas, 2
Panama, 215, 218, 236
Patterson, Isabel, 131
Peace of Westphalia, 122-123
Peck, Scott, 110
Pericles, 47
Persia, 26, 60
Peru, 215
Philippines, 216
Phoenicia, 26
Piazza, Michael de, 9
Poland, 63, 151, 216
population, 54-55, 66-67, 78, 91
Portugal, 63, 68, 151, 217
positive-sum, 80-82, 106, 159, 227, 254, 261
prehistory, 22-24, 31, 32
Priestley, Joseph, 205
Principals of Economics (Carl Menger), 201
printing press, (Gutenberg), 82, 84-85, 255
Progressive Era, 34, 156, 218
Prussia, 63, 151
Public Choice, 173
Punic War, 7

Q

Qatar, 217

R

race, 26, 238
Reagan, Ronald, 213-215
realpolitik, 99
Reformation, 69, 85, 122
Reign of Terror, 125
Renaissance, 35, 85, 122
Revolutionary Period, 20, 49, 53, 121, 168

Index